DATE DUE

GAYLORD

PRINTED IN U.S.A.

D1225223

WOODROW WILSON

AND A REVOLUTIONARY

WORLD, 1913–1921

WOODROW WILSON

AND A REVOLUTIONARY

WORLD, 1913–1921

EDITED BY ARTHUR S. LINK

THE UNIVERSITY OF NORTH CAROLINA PRESS

CHAPEL HILL

Library of Congress Cataloging in Publication Data

Main entry under title:

Woodrow Wilson and a revolutionary world, 1913–1921

   (Supplementary volumes to The papers of Woodrow Wilson)
   "Papers . . . originally presented at an international symposium
at Princeton University from October 10 through October 12,
1979"—Introd.
   Includes index.
   Contents: Woodrow Wilson and the Mexican Revolution /
Lloyd C. Gardner—Woodrow Wilson and the Russian Revolution /
Betty Miller Unterberger—Woodrow Wilson and the rebirth of
Poland / Kay Lundgreen-Nielsen—Woodrow Wilson—war aims,
peace strategy, and the European left / Inga Floto—[etc.]
   1. United States—Foreign relations—1913–1921—Congresses.
2. World War, 1914–1918—United States—Congresses. 3. Wilson,
Woodrow, 1856–1924—Congresses. I. Link, Arthur Stanley.
II. Series
E768.w66   973.91'3'0924   82-2565
ISBN 0-8078-1529-2   AACR2

CONTENTS

132635

INTRODUCTION

The papers printed in this volume were originally presented at an international symposium at Princeton University from October 10 through October 12, 1979, which I arranged and the Woodrow Wilson Foundation sponsored. Commentaries were also read by Andrew J. Lindsay of the University of Oxford, Kendrick A. Clements of the University of South Carolina, John W. Long of Rider College, Wilton B. Fowler of the University of Washington, Piotr S. Wandycz of Yale University, Marian Drozdowski of the University of Warsaw, Jacek R. Wedrowski of the Institute for the Study of Advanced Capitalist Economies, Warsaw, Klaus Schwabe of the Historical Institute, Aachen, John E. Reinertson of the Department of State, George W. Egerton, University of British Columbia, Lawrence E. Gelfand of the University of Iowa, André Kaspi of the University of Paris (the Sorbonne), Edward H. Buehrig of Indiana University, and Inis L. Claude, Jr., of the University of Virginia. In addition, most of the persons who are currently doing research and writing on the general theme of the conference, "Woodrow Wilson and a Revolutionary World," were also present and participated in lively discussions.

Wilson was the first President of the United States since Washington, Jefferson, and Madison to face a world torn by revolutions and world war. The papers in this volume make it clear that Wilson was the pivot of foreign policy in the twentieth century. For the United States, he laid down the guidelines for its foreign policy since 1921: antiimperialism, anticolonialism, self-determination, and the search for peace, world order, and some form of collective security. For the world, he set forth the agenda of international problems and goals that are still as important now as they were in his own day. The papers in this book, as I have said, not only illuminate these statements; they also give evidence of the enormous complexities, ambiguities, and difficulties that beset Wilson in his quest for a new liberal world order. Finally, they remind us that the effort to implement Wilson's ideals must still go on if humankind is to survive.

I express my sincere gratitude to the authors for their patience with me while we worked together to prepare the final versions of their papers; to the Woodrow Wilson Foundation, for financing the symposium and the publication of this book; to Dr. Pendleton Herring, President of the Woodrow Wilson Foundation, for his support of and participation in the symposium; to all the participants in the symposium, for making it a memorable affair; to Margaret D. Link, William A. Link, and Susannah Hopkins Jones, for indispensable editorial help; and finally, to Lewis Bateman of The University of North Carolina Press, for helping to see the manuscript through to publication.

Princeton, New Jersey   Arthur S. Link
July 27, 1981

WOODROW WILSON

AND A REVOLUTIONARY

WORLD, 1913-1921

Chapter One

WOODROW WILSON AND THE

MEXICAN REVOLUTION

LLOYD C. GARDNER

Mexico was quiet for thirty-four years. During that era, 1876–1910, Porfirio Díaz ruled, mixing favor and force in whatever proportions necessary to maintain his power. He was also lucky. The sweeping economic changes wrought in Mexico during his dictatorship and the underlying divisions within Mexican society actually delayed the formation of an effective opposition and diverted potential revolutionary causes into local struggles. Even after the revolution of 1910 began, no organized political party led it. Before its force was spent a decade later, perhaps a million Mexicans—one of every eight—had died.[1]

The revolution began when Francisco Ignacio Madero, a liberal landowner from Coahuila, published a manifesto which demanded free and orderly elections. But Madero also proclaimed himself Provisional President of Mexico and designated November 20, 1910, as the day on which Mexicans should rise up in arms against the regime. At first Díaz resisted. When several local leaders rallied to Madero's banner, the old man heeded the advice of his inner circle and left Mexico. He left behind a final dark prophecy: "Madero has unleashed a tiger, let us see if he can control him."[2]

To the outside world, the Mexican Revolution of 1910 was indeed a tiger let loose to rampage across the country and to kill foreigners and destroy their property. The antiforeign element of the revolution held together diverse groups within the country, and gave it a needed focus. But a better image of the revolution is that of a volcanic explosion which released century-old feelings that Mexicans were the sub-

jects of numerous injustices on account of their position in the industrial world-system. "It moved by fits and starts," Eric Wolf writes of
the revolution, "and in numerous directions at once; it carried with it
the bastions of power and the straw-covered huts of the peasantry
alike. When it was finished, it had profoundly altered the characteristics of Mexican society."[3]

The Mexican Revolution, to put the issue in its broadest context,
represented the first serious challenge to the international order established by the industrial nations after the middle of the nineteenth
century. Mexico had repulsed an effort by France to reestablish formal empire in Latin America, but during the Díaz era the country
accepted its position—for the time being—under metropolitan hege-
mony. Díaz had attempted to preserve Mexican "independence" by
balancing off rivalries among the expanding powers. His understanding of the structural weaknesses of the world-system did not preserve
his regime, but the great-power influence in Mexico did provide revolutionary leaders after him with somewhat greater room for maneuver. Great Britain and the United States were the most determined
rivals in Mexico, but Germany also played a large role. Indeed, it was
the fear of German-Mexican connections that both stimulated and re-
strained Anglo-American diplomacy in response to the revolution.

In February 1913, General Victoriano Huerta overthrew Madero.
This military *coup d'état* set off the most violent phase of the Mexican
Revolution and occurred, as fate would have it, just as Woodrow
Wilson was about to assume office as President of the United States.
Wilson was a Democrat and a reformer. As such, he was deeply suspicious of the power of the "special interests" at home and of "Dollar
Diplomacy" abroad. Mexico was the first crisis that he faced; he was
still struggling with the implications of the revolution when he left
office eight years later. But what he learned in those years of turmoil,
beginning with the Mexican Revolution, proved to be fundamental to
his effort to formulate a "new diplomacy" to meet the challenges of
his—and now our—Age of Revolution.[4]

At the end of the Díaz era, an American diplomat with long experience summed up the situation as matters stood on the eve of the revolution: "The American Embassy in Mexico City was really a workshop.
The demands for advice were constant, beginning at 9 o'clock in the
morning and extending very frequently if not generally until 1 or 2
o'clock at night. During the troubled period—which describes pretty

nearly the entire period of my service in Mexico—we did in the embassy 33 per cent of the correspondence of the Department of State here in Washington."[5] Although Europe and China were always more exciting, the work of the Department of State was concentrated on matters much closer to home. Americans had gone into Mexico in increasing numbers and thought of themselves as pioneers responding to the same urge as those who had gone west into the territories. American capital had likewise penetrated Mexico. By 1910, American firms enjoyed the largest share of the estimated $1.5 billion invested in Mexico. Foreign capital extended into almost all areas of commerce and industry; for example, it controlled 97 percent of mining and more than 90 percent of the petroleum industry.[6]

Railroads, which made the great North American domestic market possible, also came to Mexico. But in that country they had not brought economic independence. Indeed, they had quite the opposite effect. With the advent of the railroads, much of the land of northern Mexico had come under the control of firms in the United States, and they served better as pipelines from the Mexican interior to American markets than they did as a stimulus to Mexico's economic development.[7]

Americans competed with Mexicans at all levels except the lowest. In northern Mexico, for example, most Mexican miners were forced to sell their ores to the American Smelting and Refining Company. A significant exception was the Madero family, which had been able to maintain an independent smelter at Monterrey. These would-be entrepreneurs came to realize that foreign control of raw materials and processing checked their ambitions to enter heavy industry, while light industry remained stunted because of the small domestic demand, which in turn was a product of the ancient *hacienda* landowning system.[8]

To make matters worse, Americans entrenched themselves at the top of the *hacienda* system. Prominent among these American heirs of the old Spanish colonial system was the publisher William Randolph Hearst, whose newspapers later sounded the alarm and demanded that President Wilson intervene in Mexico. Between 1900 and 1911, the total number of United States citizens living in Mexico rose to well over 50,000, and more than 10,000 resided in Mexico City.[9] Along the Avenida San Francisco, the principal commercial street of the Mexican capital, the businesses were almost wholly foreign-owned. The foreigners lived apart, in "the most interesting and best improved part of Mexico City."[10]

Compared with Spanish rule, observed the wife of an American diplomat who witnessed the beginning of the revolution, a century of independence had left Mexico with very little. "We, of the north, have used it only as a quarry, leaving no monument to God nor testaments to man in place of the treasure that we have piled on departing ships or trains."[11] So it also seemed to Mexico's ruling elite in the last years of the Díaz reign. This group, known as the *Científicos*, had already begun to disparage Díaz for his inability to improve Mexico's status in the eyes of the rest of the world.

Divisions within the elite thus surfaced before Madero ever raised his cry of protest, and the nationalistic drive to control Mexico's natural resources began a full decade before the Constitution of 1917. Díaz was confronted with a draft of a new mining law, for example, by a supposedly docile Mexican Congress which contained an article prohibiting "foreign corporate bodies" from henceforth acquiring mining properties within Mexican territory. What the drafters had in mind was a law designed, not to shut off the inflow of foreign capital, but to force non-Mexican investors to forego their special status as concessionaires and to obey the same laws as those which governed Mexican citizens and their property.[12]

Consul-General B. H. Ridgely reported to Washington his deep concern over the trend in Mexican policy. "It is certain," he asserted, "that this plan, if promulgated, will operate to the serious disadvantage of American enterprises already existing in Mexico and it is equally certain that it will prevent American capital in the future from seeking investment here."[13] When Venustiano Carranza promulgated the Constitution of 1917, with its restrictions on the operation of capitalistic enterprises, the reaction in Washington was very much the same. So far as Americans with property interests in Mexico were concerned, the letter of the law was less important than the spirit then emanating out of Mexico and—as the Bolshevik Revolution seemed to demonstrate—also spreading around the world.

In this earlier instance, Díaz was still able to squelch the advocates of restrictions. But their arguments set the agenda for the revolution. Díaz believed that Mexico could not do without the goodwill of the capitalistic powers if it was to become a modern state, as the term was then understood. His critics charged that the attempt had produced paltry returns thus far and would continue to deprive the country of any chance to achieve equality. Mexico was regarded as "backwards" by the industrial world. It could not overcome this stigma until the nation took full control of its own resources and thus its destiny.

How much time was left, even then, for a peaceful transformation presided over by moderates who wished to open up opportunities for a bourgeois and nationalistic triumph? The Mexican countryside was riven by disputes between the *haciendas* and Indian communities, disputes with roots all the way back to colonial times. In recent years, the development of commercial agriculture and the growth of a working class in the mines and oilfields had aggravated these conflicts. The surge of agrarian and labor protest had not yet found a focus or effective leadership, but the *Partido Liberal Mexicano* (PLM) espoused revolutionary socialism on a European Marxist model. What was especially significant was that the sentiments of disaffected intellectuals who read Kropotkin, Bakunin, and Marx began to have a broad impact, even in the South, where the leader of Indian protest movements, Emiliano Zapata, had begun a revolt during the Díaz period.[14]

Díaz was not unaware of the possibility for revolution. In 1906, he received a report that minced no words:

> Make no mistake about it: the present movement is not isolated, nor is it confined to the working class. On the contrary, it is very widespread, and in it are participating, directly, individuals from all social classes: from the wealthy, in a small proportion; from the bourgeoisie, in a larger proportion; from the lower classes in a growing quantity, urged along by the other two. . . .
>
> The accumulated experience of history teaches us that, when no one looks after the people, the people take care of themselves; and when the people take care of themselves, it is no river that runs along in its riverbed, but a deluge that inundates.[15]

Francisco Madero did not enjoy an opportunity to read this report, but he acted to control events and to look after the people before the deluge inundated his class. Unfortunately, he was not equal to the task.

It was hardly surprising that foreign governments had come to believe that Díaz represented the natural order in Mexico. Anyone who tampered with that order did so at his own peril and put at risk the work of nearly four decades. Madero thought that he could modernize Mexican politics without bringing on disaster or alienating the leaders of the world industrial order. He marched on Mexico City, and the old man departed. Nothing else would go so well.

Perhaps it was beyond the capacity of anyone who came from Madero's background, or who was schooled in the tenets of nineteenth-century liberal thought at European and American universities, to take charge of a twentieth-century revolution in a nonindustrial country. However, Madero was no innocent. His family clan had a real vested interest in opposition to Díaz, as did other would-be Mexican entrepreneurs. The Maderos were not only large landholders; they also owned the biggest Mexican smelting operation and were deeply involved in growing cotton for Mexico's new mills. Calculation and cunning were not absent from Madero's personality. Even so, he was terribly miscast in the role that he only half wished to play in the first place.

Madero could not appease the reactionary forces which surrounded him in Mexico City, nor could he reach out with an effective program to command the loyalty of the scattered revolutionary armies assembling in the hills and valleys of the countryside. During his short tenure as an elected President, five major revolts occurred. Besieged by these warring elements of his own people, Madero could not gain the approval of the American Ambassador, Henry Lane Wilson, who dined each evening with upper-class Mexicans or supra-class foreigners. Along with them, Ambassador Wilson considered Madero a threat, not simply because he had overturned the *ancien régime*, but also because he was an incompetent doomed to bring with his failure "Indian rule in Mexico."[16]

"Upon one occasion he said to me," Wilson later testified about an encounter with Madero in the presidential palace, "'George Washington is sitting right there beside you, listening to every word that you say.'"[17] How could anyone regard such a mystic with anything but contempt? Wilson did not hide his lack of sympathy for Madero at any time—not in testimony before the United States Congress, or earlier, when Wilson's lack of sympathy for Madero contributed to an atmosphere in Mexico rife with conspiracies and reeking of betrayal. Wilson played, and thought that it was his duty to play, a direct role in the outcome of the last revolt against Madero in February 1913, from which emerged a potential heir to claim the Díaz legacy—General Victoriano Huerta.

In this final struggle, Madero faced a combined force which included Felix Díaz, a nephew of the old dictator, and other lesser figures with a variety of personal and political ambitions. Madero had been obliged to grant General Huerta more and more authority to combat these dissidents. Rumors of shadowy negotiations in the quiet corners of the city had it that Huerta had reached an agreement with the men whose hirelings were drawn up before the presidential palace. Whatever truth there was in those stories, Huerta was in negotiation with Ambassador Wilson, whose behavior was increasingly that of a pro-consul in the outskirts of empire. The Ambassador had taken it upon himself to inform members of the Mexican Congress that they need not fear the landing of American troops from the ships that President William Howard Taft had sent to Mexican waters when the disturbances began—that is, "if the President resigns and order is restored."[18]

It was a most remarkable performance, even for an Ambassador used to operating without detailed instructions, and it did not end there. After Huerta succeeded in ousting Madero, Ambassador Wilson hurriedly summoned the diplomatic corps to the American Embassy to urge them not to wait for orders from home before offering recognition to the General, since "it was essential to give the new government immediate support."[19] Wilson knew they had much to lose, because he personally had presided at a meeting between Huerta and Felix Díaz at which the conspirators decided that the General should become Provisional President, and, somewhat less certainly, that they would support Díaz for the office of President when things calmed down.

This "Compact of the Embassy" drew congratulations from many quarters in Mexico City, but it also made Ambassador Wilson personally responsible for Huerta's behavior. He could not, after all, claim the credit for saving Mexico from anarchy (or worse), without shouldering the blame if something went wrong. The subsequent murder of Madero and his Vice-President under circumstances that pointed to Huerta immediately cast a dark shadow across what Ambassador Wilson believed had been an altogether successful example of crisis management. The Ambassador assured Sir Francis Stronge, British Minister in Mexico, that he accepted Huerta's explanation that the two had met their death in a cross fire during an escape attempt. He and the German Minister, Wilson went on, had warned the General against such a danger. But what was over was over. He was now urging Washington all the more to support Huerta as the only man who could pacify the country. Stronge listened to this account without comment. However, on the next day he reported to London that there was no doubt that Huerta's men had ordered and carried out the murders and that the new regime had justified them as the first important step "to facilitate pacification of the country."[20]

This discrepancy did not unduly upset Stronge. However, in the United States, press speculations about the exact nature of the Ambassador's role in the gruesome outcome of Madero's presidency posed a more serious issue. Was this an example of the conduct of "Dollar Diplomacy"?[21] Moreover, Woodrow Wilson had successfully campaigned only months before against the "special interests" which he said dominated the Republican party and the nation and had promised that he would bring them under popular control. Now, what would he *actually* do?

Despite Ambassador Wilson's assurances, indeed pleas, that Huerta would quickly restore Mexico to a healthy state in the international community, the outgoing Republican administration hesitated to extend recognition. Secretary of State Philander C. Knox had many things on his mind. No doubt he was sensitive to criticism of Ambassador Wilson's dubious behavior. No doubt, also, Knox was reluctant to hand over a faulty, or incomplete, brief to his successor. He was much too good a lawyer to allow that to happen. One has the impression, however, that Knox already knew that a simple palace *coup* would not end the Mexican Revolution. He wanted Huerta to commit himself to settle a range of issues, from relatively minor territorial disputes, to the much larger questions of Mexico's foreign debt and proposed plans for American aid in stabilizing the economy.[22]

"[I]t is left to you," Knox cautioned Henry Lane Wilson, "to deal with this whole matter of keeping Mexican opinion, both official and unofficial, in a salutary equilibrium between a dangerous and exaggerated apprehension and a proper degree of wholesome fear."[23] It was necessary to make it clear to Huerta—and to others who might have "revolutionary" inclinations—that no Mexican government could survive without Washington's approval and that the United States expected to supervise affairs in Mexico before things really got out of hand. This admonition may be said to have begun the period of "watchful waiting" in the American response to the Mexican Revolution.

The argument arose, and was brought up again later, that, if Taft had only recognized the Huerta regime, Mexican-American relations would never have deteriorated to the dangerous impasse that followed President Wilson's refusal to deal with Huerta. Wilson could have avoided becoming embroiled in Mexican politics. The General would have obtained the necessary foreign aid to stabilize his regime, the rebel cause would have withered away, and, who knows, Huerta might have done very well, not only for himself, but for Mexico as well?[24]

According to this analysis, Wilson's idealism and moral imperialism were not only mistakes, but were also important causes of the lengthening and deepening of the revolution. As Robert Lansing, then Counselor of the State Department, put it in 1914, what was going on—at least while Huerta was in power—was little more than a "conflict between military oligarchies," in which the Mexican people had no real stake. One had to be suspicious, however, because those who advanced the argument asserted also that the alternative to Huerta was anarchy.[25]

It was natural to downplay the internal causes of the Mexican Revolution at the height of the imperial era before the First World War. Thus Lansing also held that America's rivals were eager to take advantage of Washington's errors in dealing with the Mexican situation. The nature of that challenge, he asserted in a memorandum on the Monroe Doctrine, was now determined by the drive for investment in railways, mines, cotton cultivation, and a myriad other enterprises. "With the present industrial activity," he wrote, "the scramble for markets, and the incessant search for new opportunities to produce wealth, commercial expansion and success are closely interwoven with political domination over the territory which is being exploited."[26]

When his initial arguments for diplomatic recognition failed, Ambassador Henry Lane Wilson had turned to exactly this appeal. Unless the new administration acted soon, Huerta would seek help from Europe. The consequences for Americans and their future expectations from Mexican holdings would be ruinous. In Mexico, then, Woodrow Wilson confronted a test involving a whole series of questions. With some of these he was almost totally unfamiliar. He had considered others for many years, ever since he first began to ponder the relationship between revolution and democracy.

Wilson was nine years old when the Civil War ended, and he

experienced the results of America's "Second Revolution" all around
him in the South of the era of Reconstruction. By 1889, when he
wrote a review of James Bryce's *The American Commonwealth*, the
turmoil of these years had passed. Why should democracy be natural
to some countries, he asked, and impossible for others? "Why has it
been cordial and a tonic to little Switzerland and to big America, while
it has been as yet only a quick intoxicant or a slow poison to France or
Spain, a mere maddening draught to the South American States?"
And why, the young political scientist went on, had England developed democratic institutions by slow and steady stages, "while so
many other states have panted toward democracy by constant revolution?"[27] What is striking, of course, is that Wilson seems to have
forgotten the American Civil War, and that for him (and for others of
his time), the French Revolution offered the great lesson of errant
democracy. In an unpublished essay written during the summer after
his graduation from Princeton, Wilson had probed into the legacy
that France had bequeathed to the modern world. The history of
France since 1789, he wrote, had produced "little more than a record
of the alternation of centralizing democracy with centralized monarchy, or imperialism—in all cases a virtual despotism."[28]

Throughout his life, Wilson feared the desperate swings of revolution and reaction. They prevented the growth of democracy even in
lands far removed from France and the rest of revolution-prone
Europe. Wilson's fleeting sympathy with socialism in the 1880s gave
way to an ambiguous conservatism in the next decade before he
eventually attained national prominence as a reform Governor of
New Jersey and then Democratic candidate in 1912 for the presidency. To a degree, Wilson's views of American expansion, like those
of many contemporaries, rested on the notion that, unlike European
imperialists, Americans were expanding the area of freedom. Indeed,
expansion was part of America's mission to the world, and, not incidentally, the remedy for the revolution-reaction syndrome. He spoke
of America's preparation for a world role with deep conviction. "Our
interests must march forward, altruists though we are: other nations
must see to it that they stand off, and do not seek to stay us."[29]

But Wilson could also sound like Albert J. Beveridge at the height
of his rhetorical efforts. Empire had been a gift of Providence, he
declared at the conclusion of a popular history of the United States. It
was a gift which brought America close to the Far East, the greatest of
all potential markets, and which all the world coveted—"the market

for which statesmen as well as merchants must plan and play their game of competition, the market to which diplomacy, and if need be power, must make an open way." And again in 1907 (although he was simply describing things as they were): "Since trade ignores national boundaries and the manufacturer insists on having the world as a market, the flag of his nation must follow him, and the doors of the nations which are closed against him must be battered down. Concessions obtained by financiers must be safeguarded by ministers of state, even if the sovereignty of unwilling nations be outraged in the process."[30]

Wilson looked often to famous British thinkers in the formulation of his thoughts on contemporary politics. He thought Edmund Burke the master of them all, but he admired Richard Cobden and believed him to be "much nearer to the measure of my powers."[31] Here was the source of both strains of the future President's justification of American expansion. John H. Hobson, author of the era's most famous study of imperialism, also admired Richard Cobden, and for reasons that help us to understand Woodrow Wilson. Hobson wrote a biography of Richard Cobden which defended the free-trader against critics, who, in a later time scorned his views and demanded greater state intervention to correct social injustice and curb imperialistic warmongering. Hobson's defense was simple: in Cobden's day, state intervention could only serve special interests.[32]

The problem to wrestle with now, Hobson concluded in *Imperialism*, was how to unlock the grip which these special interests held on national policy. Cobden might have failed, but he was not wrong. "The chief economic source of Imperialism," Hobson contended,

has been found in the inequality of industrial opportunities by which a favored class accumulates superfluous elements of income which, in their search for profitable investments, press ever farther afield: the influence on State policy of these investors and their financial managers secures a national alliance of other vested interests which are threatened by movements of social reform: the adoption of Imperialism thus serves the double purpose of securing private material benefits for favored classes of investors and traders at the public cost, while sustaining the general cause of conservatism by diverting public energy and interest from domestic agitation to external employment.[33]

Wilson could not have given a better description of what he criticized as Republican "Dollar Diplomacy." By upbringing a southern
Democrat, suspicious of tariffs and the banking power—the ancient
sources of northern "imperialism" in his homeland—Wilson was
naturally sympathetic to such views. He no doubt approved as well of
Hobson's insistence that imperialism was as much a question of conscience and moral choice as it was of markets and raw materials. With
Cobden, Wilson began with the belief that free trade and imperialism
were antithetical; but, with Hobson, he later maintained that, for the
present and future, the problem was far more complex. Mexico accelerated his and the nation's learning process.

Wilson's essentially Hobsonian view of imperialism—that it was an
"adopted" policy pushed forward by a "favored class"—blended well
with his long-held attitudes about revolution and democracy. In private notes for a college lecture, he had set out to describe the ambiguous reputation of democratic political institutions. "Their eccentric
influence in France, their disastrous and revolutionary operation in
South America, their power to intoxicate and powerlessness to reform . . . have generally been deemed to offset every triumph or
success they can boast."[34]

Wilson was already coming close to the thesis that the failure of
democracy, and the prevalence of revolutions in an area of European
influence such as Latin America, were closely related. Just as France
swung wildly between despotic centralized democracy and imperialism, so the Latin American states imitated that behavior as they strove
to throw off the power of foreign interests through revolution. Often,
moreover, these "revolutions" were mere deceptions which one set of
interests fostered and which European (or American) capitalists supported in order to improve their own position. In either case, a new
code of international behavior would have to accompany the reedu-
cation of such states.

After his inauguration, Wilson's first pronouncement on Latin
America condemned those "who seek to seize the power of government to advance their own personal interests or ambition." He
desired to promote the most cordial understanding and cooperation, continued the statement, "between the peoples and leaders of
America. . . . As friends, therefore, we shall prefer those who . . . protect private rights, and respect the restraints of constitutional provision."[35] Depending to an extent upon who the reader was, this

statement was either a freeze on change or the beginning of an effort to take the constitutions of Latin American states seriously. The statement, while general in nature, had obvious implications for Mexican-American relations, where Huerta had apparently interrupted what was taken to be encouraging progress toward political modernization. Huerta's *coup* was also a likely instance in which European imperialism would intrude, or be invited in, to take advantage of the latest revolution-reaction cycle.

The British Ambassador in Washington, Sir Cecil Spring Rice, foresaw trouble ahead in Anglo-American relations if Mexico became an "issue" in national politics. The crusade against privilege and power had already eulogized Madero as a martyred progressive. Spring Rice was alarmed at Secretary of State William Jennings Bryan's statement that a "fair and free election . . . will put everything to rights in Mexico." Those who voted for Woodrow Wilson, Spring Rice reported to London, looked upon Mexico as an extension of American political struggles. "It is singular how the majority of Americans are rather pleased than otherwise at the losses of rich Americans in Mexico."[36]

Given the public atmosphere, it was perhaps difficult for those who wanted to impress Woodrow Wilson with the opposite view to gain access to him directly, especially not after he had received Madero's widow at the White House. Such interested persons talked with Colonel Edward M. House, however, and he gave the President their views. A plan which Delbert Haff submitted, and which various companies with holdings in Mexico endorsed, called for recognition of Huerta, provided that he guarantee to hold an early election. Haff's plan also proposed that both the government and the rebels suspend hostilities and bind themselves to accept the results of the election. Wilson and House had spoken privately about Mexico on several occasions. As early as April 1, 1913, they had discussed the opinion held by Edward N. Brown, the American head of the Mexican National Railways, who insisted that, if the present administration did not succeed, the Mexican situation would lead to one of two results: American intervention or disintegration.[37]

House agreed with Brown that Ambassador Henry Lane Wilson should not be recalled until it was clear whether Huerta intended to honor the Compact of the Embassy, that is, until Felix Díaz had been elected President of Mexico. And, observed the President's friend, if recognition was granted prematurely, General Huerta would be able to borrow money "to maintain the fight against Díaz, and it was a question whether this was a good thing."[38]

Wilson may have hoped that the issue would be resolved so simply, but he already had good reason to doubt the outcome. Thus Wilson continued to wait for some sure sign of the direction of events in Mexico. "I have to pause and remind myself," he told the cabinet on one occasion late in May 1913, "that I am President of the United States and not of a small group of Americans with vested interests in Mexico."[39] Wilson was even more concerned, naturally, about European and British "vested interests," and the possibility that they would attempt to take matters into their own hands. Henry Lane Wilson had kept up a steady stream of telegrams and dispatches on that subject, but the more he insisted, the more convinced Washington became that Huerta was the *European* "candidate" to replace the departed old dictator. "The British minister informed me a few days ago that he thought it entirely fair to make use of the opportunity growing out of the present embarrassed relations with the United States to push British enterprises in every direction."[40] Such language suggested special pleading, but, worse for the Ambassador's cause, American consuls in various outlying districts did not confirm Henry Lane Wilson's ever-confident assurances that Huerta would soon triumph over his new foes. "If any of our consuls," the Ambassador began a complaining telegram to Bryan, "have inadvertently been sympathizing with local activities against the Federal Government for supposedly good motives they should, in my opinion, be instructed to avoid such complications and to work for submission to the Federal authorities, by which alone peace can be restored."[41]

Many of the consuls did, in fact, sympathize with Huerta, but their reports cast still more doubt on Henry Lane Wilson's credibility. Governor Venustiano Carranza of Coahuila had declared that his state would not accept Huerta's authority. Emiliano Zapata, the agrarian leader in Morelos, joined forces with Carranza in a loosely fashioned "Constitutionalist" alliance whose only basis was to drive out the usurper. Neither had been happy with Madero's vague promises, but his death produced the sacred cause that triggered the real explosion in Mexican politics.[42]

Colonel House was more inclined than President Wilson to try one of the various schemes proposed by American property holders, but even he had pointed out that recognition might give Huerta an opportunity to seek a way to avoid his "obligations" under the Compact of the Embassy. If Wilson had recognized Huerta's government, it might or might not have put an end to the fighting. Was it not likely, in the event that the fighting did continue, that, at some point after recognition, pressure would mount for intervention on Huerta's behalf? A civil war loomed, and proponents of recognition certainly risked putting the United States on the side, not of legitimacy and progress, but of treachery and reaction. Lines were being drawn, not along old diplomatic practice, but for a new age. Politics and diplomacy were already intertwined in ways that the First World War would soon demonstrate; Mexico was a foretaste of an era in which nothing happened that was not a "world event."

Every discussion of Mexico was now tinged with this realization and its implications for domestic politics. Thus in the House of Commons, Josiah Wedgwood rose to ask a question about the British government's position on the "Constitutionalists." "May I ask the hon. Gentleman," he began, addressing himself to the government's spokesman, "why he speaks of General Carranza's forces as 'rebels'? Are they not fighting for freedom?" The Under Secretary of State for Foreign Affairs would not grant the point. "I think the word 'rebels' describes them in the absence of their being conquerors."[43]

The sands were fast running out on the age of old diplomacy, as every member of the House of Commons would soon have reason to know. President Wilson, meanwhile, believed rightly that the men who had served their time under the sway of that practice, and with those assumptions, could not inform him properly about Mexico. Hence the parade of special agents which Wilson sent to be his eyes and ears, and then to bear his messages to various leaders of the anti-Huerta forces. One of these, William Bayard Hale, summed up their findings in a few words. Mexico was undergoing a struggle "between surviving medievalism . . . and modern civilization."[44]

British recognition of Huerta indicated to Wilson and Bryan on which side that government would cast its lot. American leaders may have believed that the Foreign Secretary, Sir Edward Grey, had acted at the behest of one group of special interests, or even for one or two oil barons, but the evidence suggests that several general considerations motivated Grey. Primary among these were trade and stability. On March 12, 1913, Grey informed Sir Francis Stronge that Hamar

Greenwood, M.P., had called at the Foreign Office on behalf of British and Canadian firms. Greenwood urged His Majesty's Government to extend diplomatic recognition to Huerta's new regime. "He said that people did not realize the great influence of Great Britain in Mexico and that whatever action you took would be followed by the representatives of the other powers." Greenwood was satisfied to learn that His Majesty's Government was disposed to act as soon as an announcement of formal accession was made. The M.P. left the Foreign Office greatly relieved.[45]

Diplomatic recognition in this era (as in others, for that matter) was never a simple question of taking cognizance of a *de facto* situation and acting accordingly, and most especially not in instances involving the great powers and countries far down the scale of the order that they dominated. Greenwood understood this fact, as did Grey, who made decisions daily, even hourly, on how much leverage to apply in each situation to keep things moving smoothly.

Unfortunately for British policy, the man Grey chose to carry it out, Sir Lionel Carden, suffered from a poor reputation among American policymakers in general and lacked subtlety in timing or language. An interview he gave reporters, which appeared in the *New York World*, a newspaper which enjoyed special favor in Washington during the Wilson years, sealed the matter. Woodrow Wilson knew nothing about Mexico, Carden allegedly began. "I see no reason why Huerta should be displaced by another man whose abilities are yet to be tried. . . . Safety in Mexico can be secured only by punitive and remedial methods and a strong man."[46]

President Wilson ended speculation about whether the United States would accept a British lead by recalling Henry Lane Wilson. In his place went John Lind, former Governor of Minnesota, who carried no letter of accreditation, and who made it plain that his mission concerned only the terms for Huerta's prompt withdrawal from office. If the General would agree to hold elections, and not stand as a candidate, the Special Agent told Federico Gamboa, Mexican Foreign Minister, the American government would then assure bankers that it would "view with pleasure" an immediate loan to Mexico. A refusal would not, he emphasized, be tolerated under any circumstances. The United States would act. It would, "First, use the financial boycott. Second, recognize the rebels. Third, intervene."[47]

When Huerta refused, and the Mexican press denounced the bribe offer, Lind began to carry out the threat. He was careful to assure

Americans in Mexico that President Wilson had no intention of stir-
ring up a hornet's nest, and his mention of Felix Díaz as a possible
candidate for the presidency surely reinforced the point.[48] It would
be hard to imagine a replacement for Huerta less likely to disturb the
social and economic order—or less likely to be acceptable to the men
in arms against the regime. Apparently, therefore, Wilson still thought
the Compact of the Embassy, if fulfilled, could get Mexico back on the
right track.

Wilson's famous Mobile Address of late October 1913, nevertheless,
put the Mexican question into a "reform" context that went far beyond the specifics of the Lind mission. "We have seen material interests threaten constitutional freedom in the United States," he told this
audience of North and South American businessmen. "Therefore we
will now know how to sympathize with those in the rest of America
who have to contend with such powers, not only within their borders
but from outside their borders also."[49] He had discarded a sentence in
the final draft of the speech that made the point in even sharper
language. "As in Cuba," he had originally planned to say, "the United
States was willing to lend its assistance in the securing of independence from a foreign political power, so in Mexico this nation is willing to assist in maintaining Mexico's independence of foreign financial power."[50]

It was still not clear exactly which "reform" context Wilson had in
mind. Without the sentence he left out, the speech read much like a
domestic rallying call for progressives to join in opposing trusts; with
the sentence left in, the main objective appeared to be the elimination
of "foreign" (i.e., non-American) interests. Colonel House, who favored dividing up the world's work among the industrial powers, saw
the difficulty. Lind's loan offer, he noted, came very close to the proposals that he had been hearing from private financiers who wanted
to bring law and order to Mexico by economic intervention. Yet the
idea of sending someone down to Mexico to be "practically the direct-
ing force" appealed to House: "If this country could send a representative into Mexico like Lord Cromer was sent to Egypt and remain
until the country was reconstructed, it might be a way out."[51]

The British wondered whether Wilson had anything so concrete in
mind. Perhaps he simply did not know what he was doing. After the
Mobile Address, it became imperative to find out if the President was
naive, bent on driving out all interests except purified American capitalists, or just playing for time. Grey sent Sir William Tyrrell to Wash-

ington to seek the answer—if there was one. Tyrrell came away from
several conversations with Wilson with assurances that, once Huerta
was out of the way, the administration would exert every influence
that it could to insure that a future Mexican government would create
a situation "under which all contracts and businesses and concessions
will be safer than they were." Every instance where a usurper such as
Huerta had succeeded in overthrowing valid constitutional governments, Wilson asserted, "put the lives and fortunes of citizens and
foreigners alike in constant jeopardy."[52]

Wilson pointed out, for example, that the "Constitutionalist" commander at Tuxpam had assured him that he was governing "on a
constitutional basis, his attitude being to guarantee interests of foreign and domestic oil corporations existing in regions which he oc-
cupies, fulfilling in this manner the demands of civilization and not
being governed by caprice or vengeance."[53] Tyrrell was impressed.
But, he wondered, did the President understand that, in order to
fulfill his promises, he would have to proclaim a *de facto* protectorate
over the Central American countries as well as Mexico? If Wilson did
not, Tyrrell reported to London, others in Washington did, and they
actively sought "to achieve that object."[54]

House had been talking about Lord Cromer and Egypt, after all,
and Tyrrell no doubt heard other expressions along those lines. And,
in fact, over the next several years, American policy verged on the
Cromer solution. Wilson intervened twice with military force, but
in each instance he rejected advice to take the opportunity to order a
full-scale occupation such as the one that was carried out in Haiti.
Robert Lansing later offered two reasons for the administration's
reluctance to run such a risk: first, German intrigues and fear of
playing into Berlin's hands; and, second, military unpreparedness.
The War Department had advised that it would take nearly 500,000
troops to do the job, and only 35,000 were available before 1917.
"[S]o I refrained in spite of the intense desire that I had to make the
Mexicans pay full measure for their misdeeds."[55]

According to Lansing, the United States did not because it dared
not. The development of Wilson's thought on the Mexican Revolution followed different paths, however, as "watchful waiting" gave
way to a more active attempt to influence the outcome of the struggle
between Huerta and the "Constitutionalists."

At first, Wilson's policy toward events in Mexico seemed aimed at
getting General Huerta to abide by the promises that he had made to

Felix Díaz. As it became clear that he could not cement the widening fissures, the President began to reexamine the entire situation. Ironically, Huerta's durability was probably a key factor in this process, for it gave him time to study the roots of the conflict and forced the "Constitutionalists" to begin to formulate a program. Despite various efforts to deprive Huerta of outside support, and despite a surreptitious policy of supplying his opponents with arms, Huerta's elimination had not been accomplished by the end of 1913. Nor did that seem likely unless something dramatic happened to bolster the fortunes of his opponents.[56]

Instead, the outlook was for a long civil war. In late January 1914, the State Department was actively negotiating with Carranza's representative in Washington, Luis Cabrera, and was attempting to win assurances that the First Chief would not accept support from "foreign" sources or from the "special interests." Cabrera answered a series of queries put to him with a general statement of policy: "The civil policy of the Constitutionalists will be to accomplish the needed— and it may be radical—reforms by constitutional and legal methods, respecting at all times the rights of property, the upholding of just and equitable concessions, the observance of contract rights, and opposing confiscation and anarchy."[57]

Cabrera's further assurances that there was no distrust of the United States in Mexico and that the "Constitutionalists" would approve American aid in case of famine may have given Wilson a much too optimistic expectation that he could deal with the revolutionary leaders as if he was negotiating with progressives from the other party to secure the passage of difficult legislation. Colonel House was more cautious about an alliance with the "Constitutionalists"; in early March, he urged Wilson not to intervene until he had first secured the cooperation of Great Britain, France, Germany, and Spain.[58] In any event, the President seized upon a minor incident in mid-April 1914 to land forces at Veracruz. The episode sparked fears of war and left Wilson exposed to criticism from all sides.[59]

Carranza pretended to be outraged at this unwanted interference. Beyond pique at this blatant display of "Yankee" arrogance, the First Chief clearly felt that he could not appear to be beholden to President Wilson and still maintain control of an increasingly volatile situation. He could accept arms or money, but not when the price included the unsought use of force against Mexicans. Only Mexicans could shoot at Mexicans and maintain the purity of the cause. Carranza knew also that Wilson had sent special emissaries to his rivals within the anti-Huerta movement. Were the landings an attempt, then, to deprive him of leadership?

Wilson may have misjudged the depths of anti-Americanism before he plunged ahead with the landing at Veracruz. Perhaps not. In any event he believed that other considerations overrode that danger. What were these? The answer is complicated, even if it begins with the obvious point that an insult to the flag in this era often triggered serious "consequences." Wilson may even have enjoyed the thought that he might use an imperialistic ploy against the imperialists. However that may be, in April 1914, Wilson's long-standing belief that the Latin American revolutionary penchant had its origins in the European revolution-reaction cycle came to a head.

Latin America was, in this sense, a mirror-image of Europe—although a distorted one. European imperialism produced the injustices that led to revolution; Latin American revolution produced intervention and imperialism. Wilson certainly had reason to be concerned that some combination of imperialistic forces might preempt what he was coming to think of as a personal mission. In February, in a meeting with Thomas B. Hohler, a British diplomat en route to Mexico City, Wilson reviewed the reasons why he thought that the trouble in Mexico was not a simple political problem. "So long as the present system under which whole provinces were owned by one man continued to exist," Wilson insisted, "so long there would be perpetual trouble in the political world."[60]

To Hohler's amazement, the President then extolled the virtues of Pancho Villa. The "sword of the revolution," Wilson called him, a man who knew his limitations and who could be counted on, when the time came, to give way to someone who could manage the political affairs of Mexico. Wilson was also confident that whoever emerged would listen to "capable and disinterested advice." Hohler's reaction to all this brought on a rapid-fire exchange. Villa was an abhorrent creature, began the diplomat, a murderer. Wilson interrupted. The man he killed had been sent by Huerta to bribe him, said the President, to induce him to desert the "Constitutionalists." If Mr. Hohler had been presented with such an offer, would he not kick him out? "Yes," came the reply, "but hardly into the next world." Wilson persisted. Suppose these events occurred at sea?[61]

When Villa "executed" a British citizen, William Benton, under clouded circumstances, this fencing took on more serious aspects.

Spring Rice came to the State Department with a warning that the incident would arouse deep feelings across the Atlantic. The implication was that the United States somehow shared responsibility for Villa's reckless behavior and brutality. Bryan was more than ready to do battle. "We are giving them [the 'Constitutionalists'] arms as you are giving Huerta arms. . . . We are friends with them, as you are friends with Huerta. We are no more responsible than you are for all the crimes Huerta has committed."[62]

A few weeks later, the State Department received reports from Berlin that Germany would consider drastic action if any of its nationals were harmed. From Mexico came reports of large arms shipments heading toward the country from both Europe and Japan. Information reached Washington that the British legation in Mexico City expected Huerta to win.[63] Spring Rice's new warning, delivered at the State Department on April 8, 1914, sounded especially ominous in this context. If Huerta withdrew from the oil fields at Tuxpam, the Ambassador told one of Bryan's aides, the situation would become very dangerous. "[P]ublic opinion in England," he said, "would take a very serious view of [the] menace to such immense British interests within eighteen miles of British ships, and . . . it was impossible to predict what action would be taken."[64]

As it happened, Spring Rice exceeded his instructions with this statement; but the administration took it to heart. What weight it had in the decision to land forces a few days later at Veracruz it is impossible to say, but Wilson had ample reason to believe that he was forestalling "outside" intervention in support of Huerta. The *New York Times* picked up on the point. If nothing had been done after the insult to the flag, read its editorial, "our European friends" would have been justified in believing that the United States could not look out for anybody's interests in Mexico.[65]

House was pleased, because he thought that the moment for the Cromer solution had arrived. "We should treat Mexico very much as we have Cuba," he wrote in his diary, "and for the same reasons." In London, Ambassador Walter Hines Page gave Sir Edward Grey his prediction. "[T]he real authority for a time after Huerta," he confided, "would have to be General [Leonard] Wood."[66] Both thought a Mexican protectorate had become inevitable. Both were wrong, for Wilson was not inclined to seek an American counterpart to Cromer in Egypt.

Whether events would have led Wilson in that direction if the ABC

powers—Argentina, Brazil, and Chile—had not offered to mediate
the crisis cannot be determined from historical evidence. The mediation accomplished only one thing, but probably saved Wilson from a
hard decision. It permitted Huerta to make an unforced withdrawal
and to follow Porfirio Díaz into exile. On June 15, 1914, Wilson received the young journalist, John Reed, at the White House. Wilson
was very favorably disposed toward Reed and had cited his articles on
the agrarian causes of the revolution in private correspondence with
Ambassador Page. To talk about Mexico, said the President, he had to
go back to his statement in March 1913, which had condemned revolutions. Revolutions did not get started in Latin America without
some outside sign of approval, "and the financial interests who back
such outbreaks for their own purpose know that perfectly well." A
proper interpretation of that statement, therefore, would not be that
the administration opposed necessary change, but that it did not support either directly or indirectly the looting of Central and South
America.[67]

Wilson followed that candid statement with a curious justification
and rather complicated version of his decision to occupy Veracruz.
He said that his actions had been designed to prevent General Huerta
from reuniting the country behind an anti-American crusade. Still
more curious, Wilson told Reed that certain concessions, while originally illegal, had acquired legitimacy with the passage of time. Lord
Cowdray's oil holdings—practically the British navy's whole supply—
came under such a heading, and would have to be insisted upon, right
or wrong.[68]

Wilson did not permit Reed to publish the interview, perhaps because it was too candid. It is interesting in this regard that, five days
after the discussion with Reed, Secretary Bryan dispatched a warning
to the "Constitutionalist" commander, Candído Aguilar, which complained that he was not protecting the oil fields. Moreover, Aguilar
demanded payment of special taxes of doubtful legality. If this behavior did not stop, Bryan informed the American consul in Tampico,
an "energetic protest" to Carranza would follow.[69]

In other words, Wilson found that he was having considerable difficulty in distinguishing between the infamous "special interests" and
the legitimate expansion of capitalistic enterprise. On the Fourth of
July, to make matters more complicated, Wilson delivered a stinging
indictment of "Dollar Diplomacy" in a speech which continues to

rank, not only at the top of his various statements on governmental responsibility in foreign policy, but also with the best of other Presidents as well. If American enterprise exploited the masses in other countries not strong enough to resist, he asserted, it ought to be checked, not encouraged. "I am willing to get anything for an American that money and enterprise can obtain, except the suppression of the rights of other men. I will not help any man buy a power which he ought not to exercise over his fellow beings." A great deal had been said about the loss of property and lives in Mexico, he went on, and these ought to be accounted for "sometime." "But back of it all is the struggle of a people to come into its own, and, while we look upon the incidents in the foreground, let us not forget the great tragic reality in the background which towers above the whole picture."[70]

To gauge the impact of this speech, or to weigh it against the various diplomatic representations that the administration would make over the next several years which warned Carranza not to go too far, is an impossible exercise. One thing is certain. Neither Wilson nor Carranza could argue that there was anything in the speech to discourage radical change. In November 1914, Wilson gave reporters an "off-the-record" statement on Mexico that continued in the vein of the speech on the Fourth of July. The landing at Veracruz had been necessary to maintain the nation's dignity, he began, but also to accomplish a "vital thing." "We got Huerta. That was the end of Huerta. That was what I had in mind. It could not be done without taking Veracruz. It could not be done without some decisive step to show the Mexican people that he was all bluff."

Wilson's listeners could have been forgiven the thought that the American President was also claiming the leadership of the Mexican "Constitutionalist" cause:

> The very important thing—the thing I have got at heart now—is to leave those people free to settle their own concerns, under the principle that it's nobody else's business . . .
>
> And the reason that the troops did not withdraw immediately after he was got rid of was that things were hanging at such an uneven balance that nobody had taken charge; that is, nobody was ready to take charge of things at Mexico City. I have said all along that I have reason to feel confident, as I do feel confident, that nothing will go seriously wrong with Mexico City, so far as the interests we are surely responsible for are concerned.[71]

Other nations did have a right to expect Washington to use its good offices with the new government. "Any representations we make to Mexico, she will naturally feel are the most important that could be made to her. I think that is all." The reporters did not have a chance to explore that glancing reference, but it was well known that, despite public optimism, Mexican-American relations were not progressing smoothly. Bryan had even gone so far as to threaten to withhold diplomatic recognition, "as we withheld it from General Huerta," in an effort to induce the desired assurances from the First Chief that he would cease persecuting the church or violating the property rights of foreigners, and that he would issue a general amnesty.[72]

Affronted, Carranza replied that, while the lives and property of foreigners would be protected, all these issues would be decided "according to the best interests of justice and our national interests." This brought a sharper response, in turn, from Bryan. Excesses of any kind, even toward his own people, might make it morally impossible to recognize Carranza. The First Chief should be aware, said Bryan, that if he could not obtain American approval, he could not obtain loans, and his government "must speedily break down." The war in Europe had put him in a weaker position in this regard than Huerta had been in, Bryan ended, and Carranza had to understand that the United States could not recede from its demands "without deep and perhaps fatal consequences to the cause of the present revolution."[73]

At one point, House and Wilson had agreed that Villa was "the only man of force in sight." Carranza was not equal to the situation and would have to be told that "he will not be recognized unless he maintains himself as he should, and nonrecognition means failure."[74] It would be difficult to maintain that these hectoring communications from Bryan or private musings about Villa's suitability, as compared to Carranza, were consistent with what Wilson told reporters in November: "The thing I have got at heart now—is to leave these people free to settle their own concerns, under the principle that it's nobody else's business."

Yet Wilson had turned down a proposal from his Secretary of War that implied a march on Mexico City from the coast in order to prevent Carranza from achieving power. "There are in my judgment no conceivable circumstances," Wilson wrote Lindley M. Garrison, "which would make it right for us to direct by force or threat of force the internal processes of what is a profound revolution, a revolution as profound as that which occurred in France. All the world has been shocked ever since the time of the revolution in France that Europe should have undertaken to nullify what has been done there, no matter what the excesses then committed."[75]

When put alongside Wilson's statements and writings about the French Revolution in his youth, this letter to Garrison suggests that Wilson had reached a turning point in his interpretation of both events, and that he had gone beyond even the views that he had expressed to John Reed. A sharp turn in the Mexican Revolution was also taking place, as Carranza found it necessary to solicit the support of the radical wing of the "Constitutionalist" movement in order to assure himself a victory over Villa and Zapata. Headed by Álvaro Obregón, this group signed a pact by which it agreed to furnish "red" battalions to Carranza, provided Carranza carried out true social reforms. The First Chief was not Obregón's prisoner, however, and what finally developed was a successful transformation of a peasant rebellion under a loose alliance of local leaders into a centralized bourgeois revolution.[76]

Carranza exploited a number of men and events to attain this end—and he made excellent use of Mexican nationalism. On January 7, 1915, Carranza issued an executive decree which prohibited the development of oil lands without the express permission of his government. From then until the promulgation of the Constitution of 1917, the central issue in Mexican-American relations was whether Mexico had a legal right to impose regulations that it thought appropriate on the oil industry and other foreign property, even if they contravened the terms of the original concessions. Carranza walked a high wire on this issue, threatening all sorts of prohibitions but never tilting things too far. Indeed, oil production continued to rise throughout the entire period, as did American investments. In 1917, Americans had a $15,000,000 stake in Mexican oil; in that same year, those fields produced more than 55,000,000 barrels of crude. In 1918, the figure reached 65,000,000 barrels—the third highest in the world.[77]

Much of the time, moreover, Carranza did not even control the oil-producing areas. General Manuel Pelaez, an adventurer who claimed loyalty to Pancho Villa, successfully withstood the central government's attempts to take possession of the fields throughout the Carranza era. Pelaez extracted his own "taxes" from the companies, paid over as protection money. This money also kept away Carranza's sol-

diers and shielded the producers from the laws and regulations which
Mexico City sought to impose.[78] Secretary of State Robert Lansing
gave his blessing to the arrangement; he asked only that the companies not claim official backing for paying ransom.[79]

Carranza complained, with justification, that American officials
chided his government for its inability to restore order throughout
Mexico but at the same time provided clandestine aid to those who
resisted. Besides Pelaez, there were flirtations with Pancho Villa.
These came to an end, however, when Wilson put a last minute veto
on Robert Lansing's efforts to organize intervention under the guise
of mediation. The idea was to have Latin American nations join the
United States in a call for a conference of the "rival factions," which
would be instructed to establish a provisional government that could
be recognized and given financial support.[80]

Originally, Lansing had intended to exclude Carranza. However, in
a seeming about-face, the President told Lansing that the conference
could not begin with a "clean sheet of paper to write on." What had
begun as a scheme to get rid of the First Chief thus became an effort
to persuade his rivals to accept his leadership. Carranza had bolstered
his own case, however, or, rather, Obregón had, with a military victory
over Pancho Villa at the battle of Celaya. Even so, Wilson's second
thoughts about the Lansing plan contained these sentences: "The first
and most important step in settling affairs of Mexico is not to call
general elections. It seems to me necessary that a provisional government essentially revolutionary in character should take action to institute reforms by decree before the full forms of the constitution are
resumed."[81]

Wilson's acceptance of the idea that revolutionary change must
precede elections might be dated much earlier than August 1915. But
now he was ready to implement his belief and to recognize that his
previous assumptions about revolution and democratic institutions
were inadequate guides for a successful policy.[82] On October 19,
1915, the United States extended *de facto* recognition to Carranza and
attempted to draw a distinction between it and *de jure* recognition.
The purpose of the distinction was not entirely clear, except to hint
perhaps that Carranza did not yet qualify for other forms of American support.

But it was Villa who felt himself the principally injured party. In-
furiated by the American decision to recognize the First Chief, Villa

issued a revolutionary manifesto of his own and then rode across the border to attack Columbus, New Mexico.[83] This perverse act of revenge against his former "friends" had origins in Woodrow Wilson's early attempts to sound out Huerta's opponents. After all, it had occurred to many observers that the President seemed willing, even determined, to go on and on, sorting through the claimants until he found one to his liking. In any event, within a week of the raid on Columbus, General John J. Pershing led a troop of soldiers into Mexico in search of Villa.

Once again there was talk of war. Wilson feared that the "extremist consequences" might follow, he wrote House. "But INTERVENTION (that is the rearrangement and control of Mexico's domestic affairs by the U.S.) there shall not be either now or at any other time if I can prevent it."[84] House wished him not to close the door entirely; he suggested that a weak policy would have an adverse impact on the President's keen desire to take the lead in the "European situation." "Heaven knows," he responded, "you have done all that a man could do to help the people there, and the fact that they are not able to follow your kindly lead, is no fault of yours."[85]

The Pershing expedition did not, however, bring on a true war crisis. Actually, it all worked out well for Carranza. Villa was kept busy slipping the noose, while the First Chief went ahead with plans for a new constitution and diverted the attention of radicals to the Yankee intruders. His conservative opponents, those inside Mexico and those who plotted in exile colonies abroad, were likewise kept off stride, for they could not seem to be antipatriotic. Carranza thus controlled the social question by keeping it linked to nationalism. Wilson also gained from the Pershing expedition and diverted the mounting pressure behind the American interventionist movement into channels that he fully controlled. The American troops never caught Villa.

The fuss over the Pershing expedition had not died down completely by February 1917, when Carranza promulgated the new Mexican constitution. It caused a storm of protest from the oil companies, British and American, that neither government could ignore. The complaints centered on Article xxvii, which vested all subsoil mineral rights in the nation. This provision gave the oil men a very bad case of the jitters—so bad, indeed, that they were prepared to do just about anything to prevent Carranza from implementing Article xxvii with restrictive legislation. Lansing fired off the first salvo in an

extended diplomatic war that would not really end for twenty-five
years. He admonished Carranza that Article xxvii "was fraught with
possible grave consequences affecting the commercial and political
relations of Mexico with other nations." The United States could not
acquiesce in any direct or indirect confiscation of foreign-owned
properties.[86]

British diplomats were even more distressed. Every industry in
Mexico was endangered. "Carranza will one day no doubt accomplish
his own ruin but [the] process may be slow owing to [the] lack of
organization and knowledge of his opponents, unless outside influences come into operation."[87] As matters developed, the British were
prepared to bring those "influences" into operation if Wilson could be
persuaded to cooperate. But in the meantime, as German-American
relations approached the final breaking point, the administration decided to send an ambassador, Henry P. Fletcher, to Mexico, the first
since Henry Lane Wilson had been recalled. Sensational revelations
of German meddling contained in the Zimmermann Note (made
available to the United States by British Intelligence), and the subsequent American declaration of war, certainly justified a serious effort
to keep differences over the constitution from escalating yet again to
a crisis point. But Fletcher's mission soon stirred up criticism from the
oil companies.

Fletcher was no "softie"; he had learned his trade as a "Dollar
Diplomat." But his recommendations for trade concessions to Carranza did not strike the oil men as the best way to proceed. "It is
immaterial to us who is President of Mexico," Harold Walker of the
Huasteca Petroleum Company wrote to Fletcher, "so long as what we
bought and the industry we created remains ours, and so long as our
American employees, friends and associates in Mexico, receive the
protection which a civilized government is expected and required to
accord them." Walker continued: "I cannot forget your words the first
time I had the honor of meeting you, 'The sole point with those
people is to make them live up to their international obligations.' You
said the whole thing there. That is the solution of the Mexican problem. That solved it from 1878 to 1911. It is our hope that such attitude will solve it for another thirty years."[88]

If Walker had his way, it really would not matter who was President
of Mexico. But Carranza had no intention of playing a cardboard
Díaz just to suit the oil companies. In February 1918, he issued a

decree requiring them to register as Mexican entities and to pay rents and royalties to the central government. The companies complained that the proposed taxes were overly burdensome, but their real concern was the principle. Mexico had taken the first step to strip them of diplomatic protection—the first step, it was argued, toward confiscation. It was not only a question of what Mexico would do next, moreover, but also of what other countries would do—in Colombia, for example, where expectations for a huge oil strike ran high—or some other country, and then another.[89]

When Carranza launched a military offensive against Pelaez, Lord Reading, the new British Ambassador in Washington, approached Wilson with an appeal that might lay the groundwork for a coordinated effort to rid the Allies of this Mexican menace. Reading presented what he called "definite information" that the attack on Pelaez had been ordered in Berlin. Wilson dismissed the plea with a reminder that rumors of Carranza's intention to disrupt oil production had been rife in the past. As for German intrigue, the present situation arose from a more simple origin, the desire to substitute "Constitutionalist" forces for those of Pelaez, "and thus to obtain whatever benefits in money or otherwise were available."[90]

Wilson did permit Lansing to send a sharp note on April 2, 1918, that directly accused the Mexican government of aiming at confiscation and warned of action "to protect the property of . . . [American] citizens in Mexico divested or injuriously affected by the decree."[91] When Ambassador Fletcher then notified Washington that he was no longer sure whether the Mexican question could be prevented "from distracting our attention and efforts from the Great War," the Wilson administration backed off from even a limited threat. On June 7, indeed, the President told a group of Mexican newspaper editors: "We had no right to interfere with or to dictate to Mexico."[92] And in the future, he concluded, nations dealing with Mexico would have to stay within "bounds of honor and fair dealing and justice, because so soon as you can admit your capital and the capital of the world to the free use of the resources of Mexico, it will be one of the most wonderfully rich and prosperous countries in the world."[93]

Neither Carranza nor the British Foreign Office was sure which voice represented the foreign policy of the United States—the one which spoke of action to protect the property of American citizens, or the one which declared that it had no right to dictate or interfere.

Carranza insisted upon releasing the American warning of April 2 to the press in order to point out the contradiction, yet he also indicated an interest in a private loan from American bankers to finance his "Constitutionalist" revolution. Here was a strange turnabout! Carranza had always claimed that the United States Government had prevented loan negotiations in order to bring pressure on him to yield to its demands. With the February decree, however, he himself had made the oil question the focus of the revolution, yet he was now seeking aid from financiers whose interests were sure to be linked with those of the oil companies. To be sure, the bankers had not always approved of the oil companies' proposals to prevent implementation of Article xxvii, but they were still unlikely to sympathize with a "radical" reform program. It did not strike them that it was good business to provide capital to be wasted in civil war or on unwise "social legislation."[94]

Carranza's motives were never easy to fathom. Since he now lacked a Pershing expedition on which to focus nationalistic sentiment and lacked the radical vision of Mexico's future held by the left wing of the "Constitutionalist" movement, Carranza may have seized on the oil question as a diversion. In that case, his willingness to negotiate with American bankers could be interpreted as a signal to watch what he did, not what he said. On the other hand, the explanation may be that the First Chief wanted to keep his opponents, domestic and foreign, off balance. In all likelihood, he was seeking genuine reform along lines proposed as early as the debate of 1910 over a new mining law, that is, a minimum program of control of Mexico's natural resources and updated social legislation.

Reports of growing foreign interest in the progress of a movement linked to Robles Domínquez may also have influenced Carranza to seek an accommodation with Washington and Wall Street. However that may be, British diplomats were certainly urging the Domínquez alternative in the summer of 1918. They were under the impression also that American bankers were interested in his movement, which envisioned a simultaneous uprising in several cities, along with a counteroffensive from Pelaez. Two British diplomats, Cunard Cummins and Thomas B. Hohler, met with Assistant Secretary of State Gordon Auchincloss in an effort to convince him that "merely a nod of approval and laxity in permitting ammunition to enter that country" would be enough to encourage the Mexicans themselves to "depose Carranza and establish a Government comprised of educated and respectable people who would be well disposed towards the Allies."[95]

Auchincloss attempted to sidetrack the conversation. He replied that the American government naturally had no objection to Mexicans settling their own affairs. But no matter what tack Cummins and Hohler took, Auchincloss would not agree to give "a nod of approval" or anything else. Pressed for a definite reply, the Assistant Secretary stated that Wilson's public statements prohibited any change in American policy. "These declarations, as the world knows, have included respect of the weaker nations by the more powerful, and noninterference in the internal affairs of other nations." How could the American government, having made these statements, encourage intrigue or any movement designed to overthrow an established and recognized government in Mexico?

Cummins then delivered a parting shot:

> My regret was accentuated by the fact that if the situation were wisely handled not only could we destroy the hopes of Germany through the instrumentality of Mexico but once and for all dispose of the Mexican question and all its dangers. The difficulties of solving the Mexican situation had been greatly exaggerated. Not only could an intelligent and honest government, well disposed towards us, be established in that country within two months, but by the same measures revolution could be stamped out for all time.

How much of this remarkable conversation was repeated to President Wilson is impossible to say. But he did approve loan negotiations between a committee of bankers and Carranza's representatives. These continued for some months and ended with a tentative agreement in early 1919. The bankers had sought to give the impression that their offer, as they advised the State Department, represented the "culmination of everything that has been hitherto tried," and was the "only possible alternative to a very much more drastic procedure with regard to Mexico than has heretofore been contemplated."[96]

The heart of the proposal was to be a treaty, in effect a charter, which guaranteed "a satisfactory basis for the operation of business enterprises in Mexico by the nationals of other countries."[97] The key issue, it thus appeared, was not whether Mexico could impose taxes and regulations, but whether the United States Government would maintain the essentials of the metropolitan relationship with the rest of the world. This relationship required the protection of the "diplomatic" status of foreign enterprise operating in the nonmetropolitan areas. What the bankers wished, in other words, was to sustain something approaching the extraterritorial rights that the great powers had forced upon China at the height of the imperial era. The bankers had been contemplating some such plan to contain Mexican nationalism since the time of Madero.

"The problem is substantially the same as that of China," Paul M. Warburg had written to the State Department in early 1913. "Only the fullest security, only a larger group and only a large loan can bring about a solution; only substantial funds will bring about a strong government, but, just as in China, a weak Government would not dare to enter upon a negotiation which, by pledging the customs house revenues, might hurt the Nation's pride."[98] A treaty signed by two sovereign powers might be a way to avoid damage to Mexico's pride and yet secure all the necessary guarantees.

But Mexico gave the bankers no reply in 1919. Finally, in early May, a reminder was sent to Ambassador Cabrera in Washington. The answer was not what the bankers wanted to hear. Cabrera stated "frankly" that, since all the nations had their financial situation pending, "I consider it would be worthwhile to wait for some time before we can make an arrangement for our debts, at least until we know the general rules that the principal countries will adopt for that purpose."[99] In other words, Mexico would consider only terms similar to those offered to Great Britain and France when they arranged to pay their war debts to the United States.

Once the bankers' offer was rejected, what was left? Wilson had refused to countenance a full-scale invasion in 1914 and again in 1916. He had turned down Lord Reading's oblique offer, and nothing came of the more direct appeal in the Auchincloss conversation. Yet Wilson had sanctioned the financial negotiations. Robert Lansing, for one, was not prepared to let the Mexican question drag on indefinitely, especially once the war had ended. Hence he made a final attempt to nudge Wilson into the Cromer solution at the end of 1919 and into the first days of the new year.

Lansing had been looking into various "uncivilized" acts since midsummer in search of a good case, but the precipitating event was the arrest of an American consular agent in Puebla, William O. Jenkins. The Secretary of State denounced Carranza's "studied impertinence" and reminded Cabrera of American accomplishments in the recent war. Lansing repeated this conversation to an aide and added that he thought "a war might be a good remedy for the local internal situation."[100]

Preoccupied with Bolshevism and the apparent evidence of its influence behind strikes and political unrest at home, Lansing was not the first, and certainly not the last, to propose to meet both difficulties with drastic action. But another factor probably weighed more heavily as he prepared a brief for the punishment of Mexican wrongdoings. Since 1914, the United States had warned Carranza to expect dire consequences if he failed to accept American guidance and ignored normal standards of international behavior. And nothing happened. Here was the United States, triumphant victor in the Great War, unable to work its will with little Mexico.

On December 19, 1919, Lansing warned Wilson that, if Carranza gained his point—that is, if he succeeded in forcing the oil companies to recognize his new petroleum codes before they were permitted to drill and pump oil—American prestige would certainly suffer. The oil industry and oil users generally would suffer, but the worst of it was the implied concession on the all-important point of the relationship between the foreign companies and the host government.[101]

Two weeks later, on January 3, 1920, Lansing sent Wilson a revised version of a memorandum by Fletcher. Boiled down to one sentence, it suggested that Carranza be given not more than five weeks to provide adequate assurances that he would take new measures to protect American lives and property, agree to a mixed commission to adjudicate claims arising out of the revolution, and—most important—permit the Hague Tribunal to decide whether Article XXVII could apply to pre-1917 concessions.

Should Carranza refuse this ultimatum, the American Ambassador would ask for his passports and leave the nation's interests under the protection of some other embassy. Lansing admitted in his covering letter that it was fair to say that many people believed that intervention had to follow as a matter of course. However, intervention was not a necessary consequence. The shock value of breaking off that way might straighten Carranza out—*OR* it was

possible that severance of relations would have the effect finally of
eliminating President Carranza as the head of the Mexican Government by the action of the Mexicans themselves, as the election of
his successor will take place next June; although Carranza has a
year to serve as President. Finally, should relations be severed now
we will be in a position to renew diplomatic relations with a new
President upon an entirely just basis and upon such conditions and
assurances as may be deemed advisable. I understand that candi-
dates for the Presidency are in practically all instances convinced
that the Carranza attitude toward the United States has been
disastrous for Mexico and many patriotic Mexican people believe
that the novel provisions of the new Constitution are a great
obstacle to economic progress to Mexico and her credit abroad, and
that the new Constitution will be amended.[102]

Lansing closed with an odd twist. He had reason, he said, to believe
that the oil companies would not greet the plan "with cordial approval." It was too clever. This attempt to force Wilson's hand most
likely led to Lansing's dismissal and the appointment of Bainbridge
Colby at the head of the State Department.[103] It would be wrong, of
course, to suggest that the Mexican situation caused the split between
Lansing and Wilson. The President had never trusted Lansing's judgment on big issues, and the feeling was more than reciprocated. Always jealous of his prerogatives, Wilson found the Secretary's
attempts to invade this territory by summoning cabinet meetings during his illness intolerable.

But it is difficult to see how Wilson could have refused Lansing's
advice, especially in view of his illness and limited physical capacities,
without dismissing the Secretary of State. All that Lansing needed was
that "nod of approval" which British diplomats had wanted. By dismissing Lansing, Wilson may well have reasoned that the option (or
question) of intervention could not be raised again, no matter what
course his illness took. All of the foregoing is speculative but not
inconsistent with what is known about Wilson's refusal to go beyond
diplomatic protests and limited military actions. And neither time
when he used the latter did he aim to overthrow Carranza.

As it happened, Carranza did accomplish his own downfall and
death in an unsuccessful effort to impose a handpicked successor.
Wilson did not oppose the State Department's insistence that the new

men in power "meet our requirements." These no longer included a requirement that Mexico submit Article xxvii to the Hague Tribunal, but they did insist upon a treaty or protocol guaranteeing that it would not be applied retroactively. Prerecognition discussions with Mexican emissaries continued sporadically through the summer and fall of 1920. No progress resulted.[104]

Norman Davis was in charge of the American side in these talks. "I stated," he reported to the White House after one of these conversations, "that if a concession were illegal, it would seem to me that the illegality should be established through the orderly process of court decisions and then if there were a denial of justice it could be taken up through diplomatic channels."[105] There was not much give in that position; nor could there be if the issue was to be treated as one of principle.

Neither, then, could Carranza's successor, Álvaro Obregón, assent to a position which, in effect, negated the revolution. Obregón was no longer the staunchly radical leader of the "red" battalions; and he believed that a settlement of the Yankee "question" was a prerequisite to redirecting the revolution toward pressing domestic problems. But he would not yield on Article xxvii. Obregón may also have bristled at a none-too-subtle display put on for him when he visited Washington before he assumed power in Mexico. According to Auckland Geddes, the third British Ambassador in Washington in the Wilson years, Obregón "had been shown everything in the naval, military and aviation Departments, and . . . thoroughly understood [the] power of [the] United States."[106]

In light of what was happening in Washington, the dismissal of Lansing looms larger, perhaps, than Wilson himself may have thought at the time. Weary of the Mexican problem, and still wary of the advice that he received, Wilson sent George Creel to Mexico City on a mission to break the impasse. Had he listened to Creel or to Henry Morgenthau, the impasse might indeed have been broken. Wilson nominated Morgenthau to succeed Fletcher, but the Senate had not yet confirmed his nomination. Morgenthau believed that the only way to proceed was to drop all conditions and to recognize the new government. Peace prevailed in Mexico, Morgenthau insisted, but the only way that Obregón could obtain the necessary strength to maintain a government that dealt fairly with others was by American recognition. His need for economic aid would also be "a great guaran-

tee for their good behavior." Mexicans were in a mood to be conciliatory because they feared the prospect of a Republican victory in
November "and the danger of General Wood being put in charge of
military affairs."[107]

Republican Senators Henry Cabot Lodge and Albert Fall blocked
Morgenthau's nomination. Fall had held hearings on Mexico in an
effort to build momentum for breaking off recognition and possibly
even for intervention.[108] Fall's star witness had been Henry Lane
Wilson, who raised the specter of a "new empire of the Montezumas
set up in the palace of Chapultepec." Although Carranza himself was
a white man, the former Ambassador had testified, " 'Mexico for the
Mexicans' under the rule of democratic institutions means Mexico for
the Indians, because if the majority rules the Indian will rule in
Mexico."[109]

The committee's counsel suggested to Wilson that the slogan that
he had repeated really meant "the property of the foreigner for the
natives." Yes, Wilson replied, and "Indian rule in Mexico . . . means
the rule of a population 80 percent of which is unable to read or
write." American property had been unsafe under Carranza. How
much more unsafe would it be if nothing was done to stop the
insidious progress of this revolution?

When Creel returned from Mexico, Wilson asked Bainbridge Colby
to look into the results of his mission and the recommendations of
Henry Morgenthau. Both were swallowed up as a result. Creel had
too much experience in government to accept Colby's explanation
that the promises given him in Mexico City had been superseded by
Obregón's statements on another occasion. Creel charged that the oil
companies had got to Colby. The charge was denied, of course, and
Colby went to great lengths to justify the Department's unwillingness
to proceed with recognition.[110]

Auckland Geddes was an interested observer of the intraadminis-
tration struggle to formulate a Mexican policy during these last
months of the Wilson administration. Geddes's reports did not suggest that the oil companies had captured Colby, but a variety of
private interests had indeed succeeded in keeping the question of
recognition open until it was seen whether the Obregón regime was
likely to be stable. Representatives of the oil companies, Geddes
added, were in fact meeting with State Department people to work
out an acceptable formula that would lead to recognition. The im-

passe that mattered now was not the one between Mexico and the United States, but one between two schools of thought within the United States. Wilson's only requirement was that Article xxvii not be made retroactive. Creel had obtained such a pledge. But there was another school of thought. "This school wishes to extract unspecified guarantees from Obregón of such a nature that a considerable section of [the] Mexican people will be thrown into violent opposition— probably into armed revolt. Their idea then appears to be either to support or to replace Obregón as his malleability and circumstances of the moment make more desirable."[111]

Wilson had refused to recognize Huerta; now he acquiesced in the State Department's determination not to recognize Obregón. Was that the only difference wrought in eight years of "watchful waiting"? Wilson's decision to permit the Republicans to decide the issue clouds a final answer. Taft had turned the problem over to him in 1913, but Woodrow Wilson's motives were different. It is doubtful, to begin with, that recognition would have had more than symbolic impor- tance, given the political atmosphere during his last year in office and the Senate's refusal to confirm his nomination of an ambassador to Mexico. Second, it is worth considering that, had Wilson insisted any- way, over the heads of the State Department and other determined opponents, the results for Mexico could have been worse. By not acting, Wilson left the Republicans free to debate their own policies without being put on the spot to reverse another Wilson policy.

One conclusion that emerges from a study of Wilson and the Mexi- can Revolution is that the President had to confront the policy-making apparatus, his closest advisers, and his own assumptions as much as he did Huerta and Carranza. As Wilson's understanding of the revo- lution changed, so did his assumptions. What he saw happening in the rest of the world deeply influenced his view of Mexico. The pro- mulgation of the Constitution of 1917, America's entrance into the war, and the Bolshevik Revolution all occurred within the space of a few months. Wilson refuted the interventionist accusation that Ger- many was behind Carranza's attempts to "take-over" the oil fields. But he could not deny that war and revolution blended into a challenge that was etched with stark clarity following the Bolshevik Revolution.

Bolshevik assertions that modern imperialism was not a choice that governments made from a range of options, but an inevitable circum- stance of late capitalism, did not convince Wilson. Yet the areas of certainty in his thought were growing smaller. The Bolsheviks would have to be opposed, but he was far less sure that capitalism could be reformed than he had been when he first confronted the foreign-policy responsibilities of the presidency.[112] As was reflected in his policy toward the Mexican Revolution, this uncertainty helps to explain Wilson's willingness to approve diplomatic protests and admonitions, and his unwillingness to intervene; his hope that Carranza would be able to legislate social change; and his realization that elections and democratic "political processes" had to follow revolutionary self-determination.

Wilson had a closer look at revolution and war than any of his predecessors in the office. He began as an expansionist, full of nineteenth-century liberal assumptions. He ended in a different mood. Corporate capitalism and the governmental bureaucracy had not yet evolved, in 1913, into the complementary (even symbiotic) forces they would become later in the century. The First World War provided the most sustained and powerful stimulus to that tendency up until that time, but so also did the persistent worldwide demand for reform and efficiency. The historian is left with the need to pose questions in order to understand Wilson's dilemmas in Mexico and elsewhere. Given his long-held convictions and his growing doubts, could Wilson have resisted pressures for intervention if Carranza had actually stopped oil production or nationalized the wells, as he often threatened to do? In that case, would he have accepted the argument that Carranza was motivated by orders from Berlin?

The National Security Adviser, his staff, and their intimidating position papers would not appear inside the White House for another half century. But intragovernmental committees were already functioning. In 1919, one of these decided that "the confiscation or destruction of petroleum properties controlled by United States interests or the existence of conditions which make impossible their operation, is an injury to the national interests and an injury which cannot be remedied by apologies or pecuniary compensation after the damage has occurred."[113]

Wilson would have permitted the *British* to intervene to keep Mexican oil flowing to the British navy, which depended on it. Carranza apparently understood this point or feared that Wilson would intervene himself. Policy makers who thought Wilson too soft would have intervened in various ways with far less excuse in war or peace. Many critics consistently blamed Wilson for the sad state of affairs because he had not recognized Huerta at the beginning of all the trouble in 1913. Experience in Russia and then in China in the 1920s demonstrated, however, that intervention was fraught with more peril than "watchful waiting." In the beginning Wilson believed that he could control events in Mexico by using nonrecognition, economic boycotts, and even clandestine aid to Huerta's opponents. He never completely abandoned that idea, but he appreciated the significance of the revolution not only to Mexico's future, but to America's as well, and he attempted to work with it rather than to stifle change.

Wilson did not resolve his dilemmas, and he made errors. Later Presidents would have done well to study these. But they would also have done well to ponder his insistence that "INTERVENTION (that is the rearrangement and control of Mexico's domestic affairs by the U.S.) there shall not be either now or at any other time if I can prevent it."

NOTES

1. I would like to thank the following colleagues who read and commented on the first draft of this paper: Professors Sam Baily, Warren Kimball, and Mark Wasserman of Rutgers, and Walter LaFeber of Cornell. Charles C. Cumberland, *Mexican Revolution: The Constitutionalist Years* (Austin, Tex., 1972), pp. 414–20. For information on the revolutionary years, I have relied throughout on Cumberland and other standard works such as Frank Tannenbaum, *Peace by Revolution: Mexico after 1910* (New York, 1966), and John Womack, Jr., *Zapata and the Mexican Revolution* (New York, 1968). In addition, the brief account in Eric Wolf, "Mexico," in *Peasant Wars of the Twentieth Century* (New York, 1969), pp. 3–50, is simply superb. The standard overview of Mexican-American relations remains Howard F. Cline, *The United States and Mexico* (rev. edn.; New York, 1963). It is the source for many specific points not footnoted individually below.

2. Quoted in Wolf, "Mexico," p. 3.

3. *Ibid.*, p. 26.

4. The view that Mexico was an unfinished revolution is the thesis of writers in *Mexico: The Limits of State Capitalism*, a special issue of *Latin American Perspectives*, II (Summer 1975). Arno J. Mayer, *Wilson vs. Lenin: Political Origins of the New Diplomacy, 1917–1918* (Cleveland, Ohio, 1964), has become the standard work on the "new" diplomacy. Among the first to suggest the need for such an approach was the still very helpful Elie Halévy, *The World Crisis of 1914–1918* (London, 1930). Two interpretations of Wilson's role are N. Gordon Levin, Jr., *Woodrow Wilson and World Politics* (New York, 1968), and Arthur S.

Link, *Woodrow Wilson: Revolution, War, and Peace* (Arlington Heights, Ill., 1979).

5. United States Senate, Committee on Foreign Relations, *Investigation of Mexican Affairs: Preliminary Report and Hearings*, 66th Cong., 2d sess., 2 vols. (Washington, 1920), II, 2251.

6. Robert Freeman Smith, *The United States and Revolutionary Nationalism in Mexico, 1916–1932* (Chicago, 1972), p. 6. See also United Nations, Economic Commission for Latin America, *External Financing in Latin America* (New York, 1965), pp. 5–19.

7. Wolf, "Mexico," pp. 19–22.

8. *Ibid.*, pp. 22–25.

9. Senate, *Investigation of Mexican Affairs*, II, 2253.

10. *Ibid.*, p. 2256.

11. Edith O'Shaughnessy, *A Diplomat's Wife in Mexico* (New York, 1916), p. 162.

12. Marvin D. Bernstein, *The Mexican Mining Industry, 1890–1950* (Albany, N. Y., 1964), pp. 78–83.

13. B. H. Ridgely to Assistant Secretary of State, July 21, 1908, the Records of the Department of State, National Archives, 4021/16; hereinafter cited as State Department Records.

14. Wolf, "Mexico," p. 31.

15. James D. Cockcroft, *Intellectual Precursors of the Mexican Revolution, 1900–1913* (Austin, Tex., 1968), p. 55. Cockcroft's study is essential for understanding the diversity of the revolutionary movement and how it developed.

16. See n. 109 *infra* for citation.

17. Senate, *Investigation of Mexican Affairs*, II, 2258.

18. Sir Francis Stronge to Sir Edward Grey, Feb. 18, 1913, Papers of the Foreign Office, Public Record Office, 371/1671 [7950/6269]; hereinafter cited as the Foreign Office Papers.

19. Stronge to Grey, Feb. 21, 1913, *ibid.*, 371/1671 [8498/6269].

20. Stronge to Grey, Feb. 24 and 25, 1913, *ibid.*, 371/1671 [8950 and 9099/6269].

21. See Peter Calvert, *The Mexican Revolution, 1910–1914: The Diplomacy of Anglo-American Conflict* (Cambridge, Eng., 1968), p. 171. Calvert's study was the first to use British Foreign Office records.

22. For negotiations with Huerta during the Taft administration, see Kenneth J. Grieb, *The United States and Huerta* (Lincoln, Neb., 1969), pp. 36–37. My own interpretation is somewhat different; I do not believe that the evidence is conclusive that Taft would have extended diplomatic recognition without making demands that Huerta would probably have refused.

23. Knox to Wilson, Feb. 17, 1913, *Papers Relating to the Foreign Relations of the United States, 1913* (Washington, 1920), p. 717; hereinafter cited as *FR*, followed by year.

24. Grieb, *United States and Huerta*, p. 192.

25. "Memorandum: The Mexican Situation, May 4, 1914," cited in Smith,

United States and Revolutionary Nationalism, p. 86. See also, Calvert, *Mexican Revolution*, p. 248.

26. "Present Nature and Extent of the Monroe Doctrine, and Its Need of Restatement," June 11, 1914, State Department Records, 710.11/185½.

27. Henry Wilkinson Bragdon, *Woodrow Wilson: The Academic Years* (Cambridge, Mass., 1967), pp. 179–80.

28. John M. Mulder, *Woodrow Wilson: The Years of Preparation* (Princeton, N. J., 1978), p. 60.

29. Wilson articles cited in Lloyd C. Gardner, ed., *A Different Frontier: Selected Readings in the Foundations of American Economic Expansion* (Chicago, 1966), pp. 129–32. The milieu of Wilson's writings of this period can be assessed from other selections in this volume.

30. Quotations from William E. Diamond, *The Economic Thought of Woodrow Wilson* (Baltimore, 1943), pp. 133, 141.

31. Bragdon, *Wilson: The Academic Years*, p. 117.

32. Hobson's defense of Cobden against contemporary critics seems to me to offer insights into the Wilsonian world view not fully developed as yet. See John Hobson, *Richard Cobden* (London, 1919).

33. *Imperialism* (3d rev. edn.; London, 1938), p. 361.

34. Bragdon, *Wilson: The Academic Years*, p. 260.

35. *FR, 1913*, p. 7.

36. Stephen Gwynn, ed., *The Letters and Friendships of Sir Cecil Spring Rice*, 2 vols. (London, 1929), II, 196.

37. The Diary of Edward M. House, April 1, 1913, in the Papers of Edward M. House, Yale University Library; hereinafter cited as the House Diary and the House Papers.

38. *Ibid.*, May 2, 1914.

39. Josephus Daniels, *The Wilson Era: Years of Peace, 1910–1917* (Chapel Hill, N. C., 1944), p. 182.

40. Wilson to W. J. Bryan, May 15, 1913, State Department Records, 812.00/7652.

41. Wilson to Bryan, March 11, 1913, *FR, 1913*, pp. 762–63.

42. See, for example, Womack, *Zapata*, pp. 194–211.

43. Hansard, LXI, col. 23.

44. Quoted in Grieb, *United States and Huerta*, p. 81.

45. Grey to Stronge, March 12, 1913, Foreign Office Papers, 371/1671 [10335/6269]. My interpretation varies on this point from Calvert, pp. 163–64.

46. Desmond Young, *Member for Mexico: A Biography of Weetman Pearson* (London, 1966), pp. 150–51.

47. Senate, *Investigation of Mexican Affairs*, II, 2320.

48. Grieb, *United States and Huerta*, p. 109.

49. The Mobile address is handled in impressive fashion by Calvert, pp. 248–53.

50. *Ibid.*

51. House Diary, Oct. 27, 1913. The Egyptian example was discussed by

French Foreign Office officials in conversations with the American Ambassador. See Myron Herrick to Bryan, Dec. 17, 1913, State Department Records, 812.51/100. House, however, could rely on his own imagination for the example he wanted. In 1912 he had written a novel entitled, *Phillip Dru: Administrator*, in which, after saving the United States from a capitalistic oligarchy, Dru turns to foreign problems, first among them, Mexico. In spite of repeated warnings, the novel's narrator explains, Mexico and Central America had "obstinately" continued their "old-time habit of revolutions without just cause, with the result that they neither had stable governments within themselves, nor any hope of peace with each other." Dru confronts a Mexican dictator on the battlefield, and, after lecturing him on the need to protect the millions that foreigners had invested in good faith in his country, vanquishes the illegal revolutionary. "In another generation," predicts Dru, "this beautiful land will be teeming with an educated, prosperous and contented people, who will regard the battlefield as the birthplace of their redemption" (pp. 279–81). In August 1915, *The New Republic* ran an editorial that might have been written by Dru himself, denying that intervention in Mexico would ruin Wilson's Latin American policy. "They [the Latin Americans] are never likely expressly to approve the dispatch of American soldiers to Mexico, but provided they can be convinced of the necessity of the measure they will tacitly acquiesce, because as practical men they will realize that a continuation of Mexican anarchy is a threat to the whole fabric of American Civilization." *The New Republic*, IV (Aug. 14, 1915), 28–29. Certainly Wilson did not have a monopoly on moral "imperialism."

52. Quoted in Arthur S. Link, *Wilson*, 5 vols. to date (Princeton, N. J., 1947–   ), II, 386–87. The Tyrell visit is covered extensively in *ibid.*, pp. 374–77.

53. Tyrell to Grey, Nov. 23, 1913, Foreign Office Papers, 371/1678 [53167/626g]. Wilson had personally drafted instructions to a personal emissary to Carranza and warned that, if the Constitutionalists failed to protect lives and property, "we foresee we shall be forced to do it," i.e., intervene. See Link, *Wilson*, II, 382.

54. Tyrell to Grey, Nov. 14, 1913, Foreign Office Papers, 371/1678 [52367/626g].

55. Lansing to Edward N. Smith, draft, March 3, 1917, and Lansing, "Method of Determining a Course of Action when an International Dispute Becomes Acute," Nov. 17, 1919, the Papers of Robert Lansing, Library of Congress; hereinafter cited as the Lansing Papers.

56. This is the conclusion of Grieb, *United States and Huerta.*

57. Cabrera to William Phillips, Jan. 27, 1914, the Papers of William Jennings Bryan, Library of Congress.

58. House to Wilson, March 5, 1914, House Papers.

59. Robert E. Quirk, *An Affair of Honor: Woodrow Wilson and the Occupation of Vera Cruz* (New York, 1964).

60. Memorandum by Hohler, Feb. 11, 1914, Foreign Office Papers, 371/2025.

61. *Ibid.*

62. Spring Rice to Grey, March 2, 1914, the Papers of Sir Edward Grey, Public Record Office, Foreign Office Papers, 800/84.

63. See Edward P. Haley, *Revolution and Intervention: The Diplomacy of Taft and Wilson in Mexico, 1910–1917* (Cambridge, Mass., 1970), pp. 130–31.

64. Grey to Spring Rice, April 8, 1914; Arthur Nicolson to Spring Rice, April 9, 1914; Spring Rice to Grey, April 8, 1914, Foreign Office Papers, 371/2026 [15749/19].

65. April 23, 1914. See also, Link, *Wilson*, II, 398–400.

66. House Diary, May 8, 1914; Grey to Spring Rice, May 6, 1914, Foreign Office Papers, 371/2028 [20329/19].

67. Draft of an article, enc. in John Reed to J. P. Tumulty, June 30, 1914, Arthur S. Link, David W. Hirst, John E. Little *et al.*, eds., *The Papers of Woodrow Wilson*, 37 vols. to date (Princeton, N. J., 1966–   ), vol. 30, pp. 234–35; hereinafter cited as *PWW*.

68. *Ibid.*

69. Bryan to American Consul, Tampico, June 19, 1914, State Department Records, 812.6363/111. The discrepancy suggests again not only two aspects of Wilson's policy toward the revolution, but also a developing struggle within the administration between the President and the nascent policy-making apparatus of later years. See *infra*, n. 113.

70. "Address of President Wilson at Independence Hall, July 4, 1914" (Washington, 1917).

71. Press Conference, Nov. 24, 1914, *PWW*, vol. 31, pp. 351–52. See also Wilson to Bryan, Nov. 23, 1914, the Wilson-Bryan Correspondence, National Archives.

72. See, for example, Bryan to Silliman, July 23, 1914, and Silliman to Bryan, July 31, 1914, *FR, 1914*, pp. 568–69, 575–77.

73. Bryan to Silliman, July 31, 1914, *ibid.*, pp. 575–77.

74. House Diary, Aug. 30, 1914. See also Clarence C. Clendenen, *The United States and Pancho Villa: A Study in Unconventional Diplomacy* (Ithaca, N. Y., 1961), and Larry D. Hill, *Emissaries to a Revolution* (Baton Rouge, La., 1973).

75. Cited in Link, *Wilson: Revolution, War, and Peace*, pp. 9–11.

76. Womack, *Zapata*, pp. 197–200; Joe C. Ashby, *Organized Labor and the Mexican Revolution under Lazaro Cardenas* (Chapel Hill, N. C., 1967), p. 10.

77. On oil problems, see Mark T. Gilderhus, *Diplomacy and Revolution* (Tucson, Ariz., 1977), especially pp. 77–86, and Lorenzo Meyer, *Mexico and the United States in the Oil Controversy, 1917–1942*, Muriel Vasconcellos, trans. (Austin, Tex., 1977).

78. Smith, *United States and Revolutionary Nationalism in Mexico*, pp. 102–104.

79. *Ibid.*

80. Link, *Wilson*, III, 490–94. Lansing's belief that Wilson would approve the solution may well have been strengthened by their recent exchanges on Haiti. On August 3, 1915, the new Secretary of State wrote to Wilson that everyone he had talked with wanted the United States to impose a provisional government on Haiti, until arrangements could be made that would "stick."

"We have no excuse of reprisal as we had at Vera Cruz," Lansing reminded the President, and Lansing could justify such action only on "the humane duty of furnishing means to relieve the famine situation." Wilson replied the next day: "We must give all who now have authority there or who desire to have it or who think they have it or are about to have it to understand that we shall take steps to prevent the payment of debts contracted to finance revolution; in other words, that we consider it our duty to insist on constitutional government there and will, if necessary (that is, if they force us to it as the only way) take charge of elections and see that a real government is erected which we can support." Lansing informed the Navy Department of the President's wishes, and Admiral William S. Benson promptly carried them out. See Lansing to Wilson, Aug. 3, 1915; Wilson to Lansing, Aug. 4, 1915, State Department Records, 838.00/1275B and 838.00/1418; and Josephus Daniels to Wilson, Aug. 3, 1915; and Lansing to Wilson, Aug. 7, 1915, the Papers of Woodrow Wilson, Library of Congress; hereinafter cited as the Wilson Papers. The proposed conference of revolutionary leaders was also similar—at the other extreme—to the abortive Prinkipo conference idea accepted by Wilson in 1919 to deal with the Russian Revolution. Wilson may not have gone ahead with the plan in 1915 for another reason. As Lansing was proceeding, the President heard from Colonel House that Lincoln Steffens was preparing a new exposé on the Mexican situation. This may have influenced the President, or at least have stimulated his own second thoughts. See House to Wilson, Aug. 9, 1915, enclosing Steffens to House, Aug. 7, 1915, *ibid.*

81. Wilson to Lansing, Aug. 11, 1915, State Department Records, 812.00/15753½.

82. See also Tannenbaum, *Peace by Revolution*, chap. 9.

83. An important new insight into the tangled web of Mexican affairs is Frederich Katz, "Pancho Villa and the Attack on Columbus, New Mexico," *American Historical Review*, LXXXIII (Feb. 1978), 101–30. The irony of Villa's action was in his attempt, according to Katz, to reinvigorate the revolution, believing as he did that Woodrow Wilson's decision to recognize Carranza was part of a deal. He had good reason to be suspicious, if only because Wilson had kept emissaries with the various Constitutionalist leaders. If Carranza had not made concessions, reasoned Villa, why had he been recognized? Villa also knew from his agents in the United States that high level State Department officials were involved in various intrigues to this end.

84. Wilson to House, June 22, 1916, the Papers of Ray Stannard Baker, Library of Congress. See also the article that Wilson wrote for the *Ladies Home Journal*, XXXIII (Oct. 1916), 9.

85. House to Wilson, June 25, 1916, Wilson Papers.

86. Jan. 22, 1917, *FR, 1917*, pp. 947–57.

87. Thurston to Foreign Office, Jan. 22, 1917, Foreign Office Papers, 371/2958 [142/17940].

88. Smith, *United States and Revolutionary Nationalism in Mexico*, pp. 105–109; and Harold Walker to Fletcher, Aug. 12, 1919, the Papers of Henry P. Fletcher, Library of Congress; hereinafter cited as the Fletcher Papers.

89. Fear of the Mexican example spreading is reflected in a message that

Lansing sent to the American Minister in Colombia, Hoffman Philip, in reference to recent Senate actions on the outstanding Panama Canal issue: "American Senate feared that Mexico would be heartened by Colombia's attitude and would be more persistent in forcing her plan of nationalization of oil lands on the ground that it was justifiable as proven by Colombia's action. That this belief has foundation is shown by a telegram from American Embassy, Mexico City which states: 'Local press today features associated press report that Colombia has declared petroleum producing lands the property of the Government.' If Colombia enforces nationalization we must expect other Latin American countries to follow suit and this should be averted." State Department Records, 821.6363/58. Here the interesting point would seem to be the rebound effect. Mexico acts and influences Colombia; Colombia, in turn, influences Mexico.

90. Reading to Foreign Office, Feb. 15, 1918, Foreign Office Papers, 371/ 3242 [A31213/2429/26].

91. Smith, *United States and Revolutionary Nationalism in Mexico*, pp. 117–26.

92. *FR, 1918*, pp. 577–80.

93. *Ibid.*; Smith, *United States and Revolutionary Nationalism in Mexico*, p. 120.

94. Smith, *United States and Revolutionary Nationalism in Mexico*, p. 111.

95. Undated "Memorandum" (July 1918), Foreign Office Papers, 371/ 3245 [A136685/2429/26].

96. Henry Bruère to Frank L. Polk, Feb. 7, 1919, State Department Records, 812.51/497.

97. *Ibid.*

98. Paul M. Warburg to F. M. Huntington Wilson, Feb. 14, 1913, State Department Records, 812.51/58.

99. Cabrera to Bruère, May 14, 1919, Fletcher Papers.

100. "Interview with the Mexican Ambassador regarding Jenkins Case," Nov. 28, 1919, Lansing Papers; and the Diary of Breckinridge Long, Nov. 28, 1919, the Papers of Breckinridge Long, Library of Congress.

101. Wilson Papers.

102. *Ibid.*

103. Smith, *United States and Revolutionary Nationalism in Mexico*, pp. 180–89, finds that Colby picked up where Lansing left off, though without challenging Wilson directly; whereas Daniel Smith, *Aftermath of War: Bainbridge Colby and Wilsonian Diplomacy* (Philadelphia, 1970), pp. 110–16, is at pains to exonerate Colby. The difference is partially explained by assumptions about the way policy is made. However, much depends upon whether one believes Colby over Creel and the British Ambassador.

104. Edgar Turlington, *Mexico and Her Foreign Creditors* (New York, 1930), pp. 280–82.

105. Davis to Wilson, July 21, 1920, enclosing memorandum of July 9, 1920, Wilson Papers; and "Memorandum of a Conversation with Mr. Pesqueira," Sept. 23, 1920, the Papers of Norman Davis, Library of Congress.

106. Geddes to Foreign Office, May 6, 1920, Foreign Office Papers, 371/ 4492 [A2897/65/26].

107. Morgenthau to Wilson, Sept. 23, 1920, the Papers of Bainbridge

Colby, Library of Congress. See also, Wilson to Colby, Sept. 24, 1920, and Colby to Wilson, Sept. 25, 1920, *ibid.*

108. Smith, *United States and Revolutionary Nationalism in Mexico*, p. 176.

109. Senate, *Investigation of Mexican Affairs*, II, 2255. Wilson's testimony included evidence that the impact of racism on Mexican nationalism had little to do with ignorance or Aztec dreams of glory. Anti-Americanism was noticeable, he said, "in the last stages of the Díaz regime, when Rodriguez, a Mexican, was hung, or boiled or something, by a mob in Texas." Committee counsel preferred "lynched." But Wilson wished to be precise: "There are lots of ways of lynching. I think he was boiled. It resulted in widespread protests in Mexico. In the City of Mexico mobs invaded the streets and burned the American flag, assaulting Americans everywhere." *Ibid.*, p. 2257.

110. Creel to Colby, Nov. 12, 1920; Wilson to Colby, Nov. 20, 1920; and Colby to Wilson, Nov. 20, 1920, Wilson Papers.

111. Quotations (as well as the interpretation) from the following documents: Geddes to Foreign Office, Oct. 29, Nov. 16, Nov. 27, and Dec. 2, 1920, Foreign Office Papers, 371/4497 [A7553, 8091, 8286, 8460/65/26].

112. Wilson's final article, "The Road Away from Revolution," is often cited as a final hardening of his position against Bolshevism and socialism. My own view would be that Wilson's doubts about capitalism being able to reform itself had grown as a result of his experiences with war and revolution. The article was, obviously, a criticism of Republican "normalcy," but, even accounting for the political content, this sentence would indicate just how deep the former President's self-questioning had gone: "Everyone who has an intelligent knowledge of social forces must know that great and widespread reactions like that which is now unquestionably manifesting itself against capitalism do not occur without cause or provocation; and before we commit ourselves irreconcilably to an attitude of hostility to this movement of the time, we ought frankly to put to ourselves the question, Is the capitalistic system unimpeachable? which is another way of asking, Have capitalists generally used their power for the benefit of the countries in which their capital is employed and for the benefit of their fellow men?" Wilson invoked the spirit of Christianity to insure the highest and purest standards of justice; but, he concluded, the Christian conception of justice had to go much higher than it had in the past. He was not a man at ease with himself or his country. Ray Stannard Baker and William E. Dodd, eds., *The Public Papers of Woodrow Wilson*, 6 vols. (New York, 1925–27), VI, 536–39.

113. Economic Liaison Committee, "Petroleum Policy of the United States," n.d. (1919), the Papers of Frank L. Polk, Yale University Library.

Chapter Two

WOODROW WILSON AND THE

RUSSIAN REVOLUTION

BETTY MILLER UNTERBERGER

Woodrow Wilson's response to the Russian Revolution can best be
understood in the light of the principles which guided his foreign
policy throughout his presidency, the experience and wisdom that he
derived from dealing with both the Mexican and the Chinese revolutions, and, finally, the war aims which he formulated upon America's
entry into the First World War. His policies rested firmly upon a body
of principles and assumptions drawn from the beliefs and ethical
values of the Christian tradition and from his deep commitment to
democracy as the most advanced, humane, and effective form of
government. He had an abiding faith in the capacities of all peoples
for self-government because of their inherent character and capacity
for growth. Thus, the Declaration of Independence, with its clarion
call for national self-determination, was for him not merely a statement of political ideals but also a program for action. It was a vital
piece of "practical business, not a piece of rhetoric." Now that the
United States had become rich and powerful, it was important to use
that influence, not for "aggrandizement and material benefit only,"
but to support, through moral influence, the legitimate aspirations of
struggling peoples for self-government throughout the world.[1]

Although Wilson believed in self-determination, he also recognized
the importance of noninterference in the affairs of other nations. His
difficult experiences in formulating policies during the Mexican
Revolution had made him highly sensitive to the limitations of interference in the domestic affairs of other nations.[2] He came to recog-

nize that the Mexican Revolution was not merely a personal struggle for power and profit but also a major social upheaval comparable to the French Revolution. After Huerta abdicated, Wilson saw the wisdom of permitting the Mexicans to settle their own internal affairs. There were in his judgment "no conceivable circumstances which would make it right for us to direct by force or by threat of force the internal process of what is a profound revolution."[3] In a draft of an address to Congress in 1916, Wilson wrote: "It does not lie with the American people to dictate to another people what their government shall be or what use shall be made of their resources, what laws or rules they shall have or what person they shall encourage and favor."[4] Wilson was also opposed to the economic exploitation of weak peoples. He believed in the Open Door, not for the oppressive exploitation of underdeveloped areas, but for the slow and steady improvement of humanity through the expansion of a "reformed and socially responsible democratic capitalism." He would not "help any man acquire a power which he ought not to exercise over fellow beings." Wilson regarded foreign financiers, from whatever quarter they came, as poor guardians of national independence; he utterly detested the exploitative imperialistic system that dominated the international arena in the prewar period.[5]

Wilson, who displayed great sympathy for China throughout his administration, sought to apply these principles to the Chinese Revolution of 1911. He believed that the six-power consortium of bankers, the Japanese Twenty-one Demands, and Japanese efforts to exploit the chaos of the Chinese revolutionary situation to exercise "practical suz[e]rainty" over China endangered the free development of the revolution there. These efforts, Wilson thought, might have been mitigated if Great Britain and tsarist Russia had exercised "appropriate restraint." He was far more suspicious of Japanese intentions and actions in China than were either of his Secretaries of State, William Jennings Bryan and Robert Lansing. Wilson agreed fully with his friend and political patron, Charles Richard Crane, that "with China we must keep entirely clear of anything that gives Japan the slightest leverage for a claim to suz[e]rainty."[6]

It was not surprising that the Russian Revolution would have repercussions in the Far East which would make even more difficult Wilson's task of devising a policy toward Russia that would square with his own most deeply held principles. Indeed, by the end of 1917,

Lansing himself admitted that the Far East "was the hardest and most complicated of all our problems."[7] The major concepts guiding Wilson's policies toward the Russian Revolution—self-determination, nonintervention, antiimperialism, and the Open Door—were principles that were fully compatible with American war aims in 1917. As it turned out, the revolution and the whole question of intervention in Russia became a test of Wilson's rationale for entering the war.

The first Russian Revolution of March 1917, which established a "liberal" provisional government, was hailed with enthusiasm in the United States. American sympathy for the new government was far stronger and more genuine than in Europe.[8] Wilson, reluctant to enter the war with an autocratic Russia, now found in a democratic Russia a "fit partner for a league of honor."[9] The United States was the first nation to grant formal recognition to the Russian Provisional Government.[10]

Wilson agreed with his adviser, Colonel Edward M. House, and Crane, an expert on both Russia and China, that the United States should aid in every way the advancement of democracy in Russia, for it would end the peril of a possible German-Russian-Japanese alliance.[11] Wilson hoped with all his heart that the new forces in Russia would be guided by the principles and objectives which liberals had set forth by the end of May 1917—principles and objectives that bore a strong resemblance to his own.[12]

Wilson's hopes were doomed to disappointment. In November 1917, revolution again rocked Russia, and the Bolshevik leaders, Lenin and Trotsky, seized power. By November 29, 1917, military operations on the Russian front had ceased, and preliminary peace negotiations between Russia and Germany were scheduled to begin on December 2. The Bolsheviks sought "a democratic peace without annexations and contributions, with the right of all nations to self-determination." The German supreme command consented, and all of the Allies were invited to participate to negotiate a speedy armistice on all fronts and to secure a universal democratic peace. None accepted.[13] In late 1917, the Bolsheviks frequently used the concept of self-determination as a basis of peace. Moreover, Trotsky demanded, "before the face of the whole of humanity," that the Allies "declare, clearly, precisely, and definitely in the name of what aims must the nations of Europe shed their blood during the fourth year of war."[14]

Wilson had been deeply concerned about the entire issue of war aims long before America's entry into the war. He was therefore disappointed when House returned from Paris in December 1917 with the news of his failure to persuade the Allies to cooperate in a broad and liberal declaration of war aims.[15] Instead, in response to the Bolshevik appeal, the Allies informed their respective ambassadors in Petrograd that they "were willing to reconsider their war aims in conjunction with Russia" as soon as she "had a stable government with whom they could act."[16] Lansing tended to agree with the Allies. He favored a declaration which announced the impossibility of recognizing Lenin's and Trotsky's regime as a *de facto* government on ideological, social, political, and strategic grounds.[17]

Wilson disagreed. As he pondered the impact of the Bolshevik peace appeal, certain things became clear. The problem was "in the main a psychological one." First, Wilson wanted to determine a course of action "which commended itself to the great majority of the American people whose interpreter he was."[18] Second, he could scarcely be unsympathetic with the Bolshevik appeal to the peoples of the belligerent nations over the heads of their governments, since he had made a similar appeal to the German people "with the full consent of the American people." Wilson also recognized the tremendous power of the Bolshevik appeal and its potentially devastating effect on the morale of the peoples of Italy, England, and France. He believed that, if nothing was done to counteract the Bolshevik statement, "the effect would be great and would increase." Third, while Wilson sympathized with the desire of the Bolsheviks to settle the war on the basis of self-determination, he had no illusions concerning the German response to it. The Ukraine, Finland, and the Transcaucasus were then in the process of declaring themselves independent, while self-determination, as the Germans understood it, justified the severance from Russia of the territories that they occupied: Russian Poland, most of the Baltic provinces, and parts of Byelorussia (White Russia). If Petrograd was to have peace according to the German interpretation of self-determination, it was to be purchased at the price of the dismemberment of Russia.

Finally, Allied policy itself complicated Wilson's position. He believed that the Allies would find it extremely difficult to agree on any definite program which "did not look on the face of it as if its main objective was aggression and conquest." His own program, therefore, had to represent the highest principles for which the United States was fighting in order to evoke the enthusiastic approval of the American people. He had to oppose the aggressive war aims for which the Germans were fighting. He also had to distinguish between American war aims and those of the Allies; to make clear to the Russian people continued American sympathy and support for them; and to pledge noninterference in their affairs.[19]

On January 8, 1918, Wilson, in his Fourteen Points Address, made a powerful appeal to the Russian people with a memorable statement of American war aims. He praised the Russian representatives for insisting, "very justly, very wisely, and in the true spirit of modern democracy," on full publicity for the peace parleys then "in progress at Brest Litovsk."[20] Wilson also made it clear that he approved the Bolshevik appeals for a restatement of war aims. His concern about Russia's plight is revealed in the eloquence of his response:

> There is . . . a voice calling for these definitions of principle and of purpose which is, it seems to me, more thrilling and more compelling than any of the many moving voices with which the troubled air of the world is filled. It is the voice of the Russian people. They are prostrate and all but helpless, it would seem, before the grim power of Germany, which has hitherto known no relenting and no pity. Their power, apparently, is shattered. And yet their soul is not subservient. They will not yield either in principle or in action. Their conception of what is right, of what is humane and honorable for them to accept, has been stated with frankness, a largeness of view, a generosity of spirit, and a universal human sympathy which must challenge the admiration of every friend of mankind; and they have refused to compound their ideals or desert others that they themselves may be safe. They call to us to say what it is that we desire, in what, if anything, our purpose and our spirit differ from theirs; and I believe that the people of the United States would wish me to respond, with utter simplicity and frankness. Whether their present leaders believe it or not, it is our heartfelt desire and hope that some way may be opened whereby we may be privileged to assist the people of Russia to attain their utmost hope of liberty and ordered peace.

Wilson did not call for the overthrow of the Bolsheviks as a condition for renewed cooperation; indeed, he even seemed to hold out the hope of American assistance to Russia's present rulers. Moreover, he indicated his determination to continue his crusade for a just peace regardless of all suggestions for a negotiated peace. In other words, he refused to abandon Russia's border lands to the Central Powers.

The moving and confident language of Point Six, concerning Russia, is convincing evidence that Wilson was profoundly impressed with the importance and seriousness of the recent regeneration of Russia. Point Six represented the official policy of the United States Government toward Russia. Point Six read:

> The evacuation of all Russian territory and such settlement of all questions affecting Russia as will secure the best and freest cooperation of the other nations of the world in obtaining for her an unhampered and unembarrassed opportunity for the independent determination of her own political development and national policy and assure her of a sincere welcome into the society of free nations under institutions of her own choosing; and, more than a welcome, assistance also of every kind that she may need and may herself desire. *The treatment accorded to Russia by her sister nations in the months to come will be the acid test of their good will, of their comprehension of her needs as distinguished from their own interests, and of their intelligent and unselfish sympathy.*[21]

The Fourteen Points Address was at once telegraphed to Ambassador David R. Francis with instructions to have it conveyed unofficially to Trotsky.[22] It was also sent to the Committee on Public Information's agency in Russia and was, by a "successful maneuver," published in full in *Pravda* and liberally quoted by other Russian newspapers. Three days later, the embassy replied that Lenin had "approved of message and thought it a potential agency promoting peace." Moreover, Lenin had agreed to telegraph Wilson's entire speech to Trotsky at Brest.[23] The Bolsheviks were particularly sensitive to the respect with which Wilson had treated Bolshevik peace principles. They were also struck by his "friendly tone," which contrasted so strikingly with the incessant anti-Bolshevik denunciations coming from almost all other Allied quarters.[24] However, in view of their past attacks on Wilsonian bourgeois pacifism and their strong doctrinal convictions, the Bolsheviks combined their brief friendliness toward Wilson with a deep running distrust of his noble words. Nevertheless, they were only too eager to use Wilson's Fourteen Points Address in their dangerous diplomatic encounter with the Central Powers. According to

Edgar Sisson, associate director of the Committee on Public Information, Lenin hailed the speech "as a great step ahead toward the peace of the world."[25] The Bolsheviks were equally quick to notice the difference between the Russian policies of Lloyd George and of Wilson. They feared that the Allies might be seeking "to have German demands satiated in the east so her requirements be minimized in the west."[26] Throughout liberal and socialist circles in Europe, Wilson was widely applauded for refusing to sacrifice Russia.[27]

Wilson's address, when it arrived in Petrograd, inspired a new atmosphere of harmony. As Arthur Bullard, director of the Russian Division of the Committee on Public Information, noted, "It was just what everybody here wanted." A large number of people claimed that they had influenced Wilson to deliver it, including not only Ambassador Francis, but also General William V. Judson, the military attaché, Raymond Robins, head of the American Red Cross Commission, and Sisson. According to Bullard, as far as the "aims of the war and the ideals of peace are concerned," Wilson seemed to be more in accord with Trotsky than with the Foreign Ministers of some of the Allied governments. Wilson's statement met "very exactly the policy recommended by all the heads of American missions in Petrograd." "The crowd here is especially glad of the explicit instructions not to encourage any separatist movements," Bullard noted. He then added a cryptic but interesting comment: "I hope the Department of State will follow the President's policy and remove the idle and vexatious prohibitions against practical relations with the *de facto* government."[28]

On January 1, Wilson had instructed Lansing to investigate "the most possible and least objectionable way" to establish "unofficial relations with the Bolscheviki."[29] Lansing, however, was very reluctant to do so. He believed confidently that the Bolshevik government could not last and that the United States should have nothing to do with "Lenin and his crowd." On January 10, Lansing drafted a proposed public statement that indicated the American rationale for refusing formally to recognize the Bolshevik government. Ambassador Francis had been "firm" in avoiding any suggestion of recognition, and Lansing supported his position.[30] By late January, however, Wilson was sympathetic to a proposal from Senator Robert L. Owen of Oklahoma to recognize the Bolsheviks as a *de facto* government. Basil Miles, the head of the State Department's Russian Division, prepared a memorandum about Owen's proposal for Wilson, in which he asserted, like

Lansing, that it was impossible "to recognize as *de facto* authorities a Government which includes among its extreme views a repudiation of all foreign obligations."[31] Nevertheless, Miles acknowledged the friendly tone of Wilson's address on January 8, and he indicated that the time had come to deal unofficially with all parties in Russia, including the Bolsheviks. Miles, along with Lansing, considered it likely that the Bolsheviks might lose control in Petrograd and that anarchy might prevail; nevertheless, Miles wanted to communicate with shifting parties in all parts of the country—to "play with all of them."[32]

Wilson, by now highly suspicious, wrote to his Secretary of State on February 4: "As I understand it, our official representative in Petrograd *is* keeping in touch with the Bolshevik leaders informally. Am I not right?"[33] The question threw Lansing and the Russian Division into something of a panic, for the State Department had steadfastly refused to permit the embassy or the consulate at Petrograd to enter into any relations whatsoever with the Bolshevik authorities. Francis had used Raymond Robins as a channel of information, but certainly not of communication. Indeed, from December 6, 1917, until February 1, 1918, the State Department had instructed, not only the Russian embassy, the consul at Petrograd, and the European missions, but also Tokyo, Peking, and Bangkok to have no official relations or indeed direct communication with the Bolshevik government or its officials. Lansing informed Wilson of the Department's previous policy on February 9; Lansing also indicated that a change was in process and that new and modified instructions were being sent to Francis.[34] Miles himself admitted that all observers returning from Russia seemed to agree that the Department's earlier policy had been aggravating and had "even tended to throw the Bolsheviks into the hands of the Germans."[35]

The first months of 1918 were a period of great crisis for the United States and the Allies. Bolshevik peace negotiations with the Central Powers threatened to make possible the withdrawal of numerous divisions of German troops from Russia and a powerful German offensive on the western front. Rumania was on the verge of collapse and about to sign a separate peace; Italian morale was low; and a new Austrian offensive was anticipated in the wake of enthusiasm which Austria's apparent victory in the East had generated. The allies desperately sought a renewal of the Russian war effort through conflicting policies. On the one hand, while the Bolsheviks attempted to negotiate a peace with the Central Powers and invited their former allies to participate, the British and French sought to negotiate with the Bolsheviks at Petrograd for their continued participation in the war. At the same time, the British and French extended financial aid to anti-Bolsheviks and counterrevolutionary groups in southern Russia and Siberia who appeared willing to continue the fight against the Germans. Russia's withdrawal from the war caused a near panic and resulted in a flood of proposals from the Allies to the United States for Japanese intervention in Siberia, either alone or with other forces. Meanwhile, chaotic conditions in Vladivostok and along the line of the Trans-Siberian Railway encouraged rumors of lone Japanese intervention in Siberia and northern Manchuria.[36]

Perhaps a bit of discussion about geography would be helpful here. The Chinese Eastern Railway formed a part of the great Trans-Siberian line which linked Asia with Europe. The Chinese Eastern, over 1,000 miles long, crossed northern Manchuria between the crucial cities of Irkutsk and Vladivostok. The railway, owned and operated by the Russian government, and the zone through which it ran had, in effect, become a Russian crown colony in China, despite the fact that Chinese authority had never been renounced. The Russian director of the Chinese Eastern Railway was also the military governor of northern Manchuria. For the Japanese, who controlled southern Manchuria, the Bolshevik Revolution provided a splendid opportunity to extend their control not only to northern Manchuria, but to eastern Siberia as well. These possibilities aroused deep anxiety in the United States, not simply because of America's traditional interest in China and the Open Door, but also because of Wilson's commitment to Russian self-determination in Point Six and his entire antiimperialist war aims.[37]

Wilson faced a dreadful dilemma. France and, to a lesser extent, Great Britain had never agreed with him in adopting a considerate attitude toward the Russian Revolution in its later phases. The Russian defection destroyed all the plans of the Allies and rescued Germany from what promised to be certain defeat. The German eastern army now threatened the safety of Paris and the Channel ports, and the leading French and British statesmen believed, consequently, that they were entitled to adopt any protective measures to compensate for Russia's defection. Their first objective was to reestablish an eastern front, and thus draw off enough German troops to restore the military balance in the West. They believed that a military expedition into Siberia could best accomplish this goal, and, if the job was to be done effectively, a large Japanese army would have to be sent in with the smallest possible delay. They regarded a new eastern front as indispensable to military victory; the only real alternative, as many of them saw it, was a peace which left Germany with a free hand in the East.

Wilson stood in the way. He refused to consent to Japanese military intervention, and he insisted on fighting for the freedom of Russia no less than for the freedom of France and Belgium. Wilson, however, was deeply aware of the terrific strain which a German offensive in the West would place on the morale and military resources of France and Great Britain; he would naturally wish to adopt any measure which, in their opinion, would help their situation. Yet, in the present instance, he had excellent reasons for hesitancy. His own military advisers agreed completely with him that it was not feasible to re-establish the eastern front. Moreover, even if the military advantages of Japanese intervention were indisputable, Wilson would, by consenting to it, compromise the great international objectives that he had enunciated in his war message and other declarations. Japanese military intervention on a scale sufficiently large to have a chance to restore an eastern line could be purchased only at a high price. It would mean the promise to Japan of at least a free hand in China and, to a certain extent, in Siberia, which would mean the repudiation of Wilson's international, antiimperialist program. Such an intervention would be incompatible with a just and enduring peace and with any trustworthy international organization strong enough to guarantee the future security and liberties of all nations. This, in brief, was the perspective from which Wilson viewed Allied and Japanese pressures for intervention in Russia.

By January 17, 1918, the Japanese had sent to Vladivostok a total of four ships and the British one. The Japanese requested that, if conditions should hereafter require the occupation of Vladivostok and the lines of the Chinese Eastern and Amur railways, this task be left to her alone. This gave Wilson an "uncomfortable feeling."[38] The Japanese Minister of Foreign Affairs had conveyed personally to Wilson his hope that the United States would not send troops to Vladivostok or Harbin for the purpose of keeping order, since this would create "a very unfavorable impression in Japan." He had urged that the matter should be left entirely to the Japanese. If the United States landed troops, the Japanese people would feel that the Americans were doing work "which properly belonged to them."[39] Wilson did not think it "safe or wise to leave the Japanese government in any doubt as to the impression such an attitude on their part makes on us."[40] It seemed to him "very significant of possible coming events." He was particularly concerned over the clear indication of Japan's desire to meet the situation in Siberia "exclusively without the cooperation of other governments."[41]

When the British requested that Japan be invited as a mandatory of the Allies and the United States to occupy the Trans-Siberian Railway, including the Chinese Eastern, Wilson also refused by noting that, if such intervention became necessary in the future, it should "be undertaken by international cooperation and not by any one power acting as a mandatory of the others."[42] It seemed to Wilson "unwise to make a request which would in itself give the Japanese a certain moral advantage with respect to any ultimate desires or purposes she may have with regard to the Eastern Provinces of Siberia."[43] From approximately this time onward, the American and Japanese governments waged a diplomatic duel over the control of both the Trans-Siberian and Chinese Eastern railways. Wilson sought to place the operation of the railways in the hands of John F. Stevens and the Russian Railway Service Corps, a contingent of American railway engineers who had been sent to Russia in 1917 at the request of the Provisional Government to aid in the rehabilitation of the Russian railways.

The British well knew that the United States would "certainly be averse to encouraging the Japanese to establish themselves . . . permanently" in Siberia. The British were also deeply suspicious of Japanese imperialism in Asia and recognized the potent danger of Japan's aggrandizement through the occupation of the Maritime Province. Nevertheless, the British believed that they would have to face this possibility in any case, since conditions in Russia would probably soon make such an occupation unavoidable. On the other hand, they argued that, if Japan was invited to act as the mandatory of the Allies, she would come into the open against Germany; the Allies could then avoid the possibility of a German-Japanese alliance which provided for the division of Russia.[44] These arguments presented a serious challenge to virtually everything that Wilson had said regarding Russia, both in the opening parts of his Fourteen Points Address and in Point Six. He reaffirmed that position in a response to the Japanese request for intervention in late January: "The common interest of all the powers at war with Germany demand from them an attitude of sympathy with the Russian people in their present unhappy struggle and that any movement looking towards the occupation of Russian territory would at once be construed as one hostile to Russia and would be likely to unite all factions in Russia against us, thus aiding the German propaganda in Russia."[45] Wilson also evinced a similar concern over Japanese support of certain factions in China, which he believed obstructed "the impulse for free government in China." He hoped, along with Minister Paul S. Reinsch in Peking, that such democratic impulses would "not die for want of any encouragement from the liberal nations of the world and because of Japanese obstruction." He fully agreed with Reinsch that the ideals and the safety of the United States were "bound up with the free self-government of China."[46] When Wilson was informed of the Japanese proposal to China for intervention against the Bolsheviks through a joint military occupation of Siberia and of the Trans-Siberian Railway to restore order in Siberia, he advised the "Chinese government to take over and guard that part of the Trans-Siberian Railway system which passes through China."[47]

At the height of the Brest-Litovsk crisis in February and early March of 1918, the Allies brought heavier pressure than before to bear on Wilson to invite the Japanese to intervene alone, as a mandatory for the other Allies and the United States. Wilson was led to believe that the Japanese would publicly announce their "disinterestedness" and comply with all Allied-American demands. Lansing urged a reconsideration on the basis of the new proposal. House agreed. Both General Tasker H. Bliss, American military representative on the Supreme War Council, and the War Department, which heretofore had adamantly opposed Japanese intervention, also agreed, if suitable guarantees were obtained from Japan.[48]

Wilson had frequently been at odds with his Allies. Now he was "particularly anxious not to appear as obstructing" all their schemes, especially since so many of his advisers approved them and Japan seemed ready to act alone.[49] When severely pressed, therefore, Wilson agreed not to object to the scheme if the others insisted. However, since he had no confidence in the project, he did not join in issuing the invitation.[50] No sooner had Wilson given this tentative consent than he began to have second thoughts. House had already done so. An examination of the rationale for Wilson's immediate return to his original position reveals his deep commitment to the principles that he had enumerated in regard to Russia. Letters from House and William C. Bullitt, White House adviser and, according to N. Gordon Levin, Jr., the only left-liberal in the State Department, reaffirmed Wilson's original convictions.[51]

Both House and Bullitt agreed that the moral position upon which American participation in the war was based would be "irretrievably compromised" unless the United States protested publicly against Japan's invasion of Siberia.[52] Bullitt stated eloquently the fears of the Far Eastern Division of the State Department: "We believe that Japan will take this step because of her desire to annex eastern Siberia, which she covets so intensely that if she cannot obtain it with the consent of the Allies she will take it with the assistance of Germany." As Bullitt put it: "If the United States assents to the Imperial Japanese army invading territory controlled by the Bolsheviki, for the ostensible purpose of restoring order, the United States cannot object to the Imperial German army" invading Bolshevik territory for the same reason. Bullitt continued: "In Russia today there are the rudiments of a government of the people, by the people, and for the people. The latest news indicates that the Bolsheviki are maintaining their power throughout Russia. . . . Are we going to make the world safe for this Russian democracy by allowing the Allies to place Terauchi in Irkutsk, while Ludendorff establishes himself in Petrograd?"

Wilson was clearly moved by these appeals, which, after all, merely repeated his own opinions concerning lone Japanese intervention. Wilson now withdrew his original telegram and substituted another. It opposed Japanese intervention in Siberia, even if Japan gave explicit assurances that she would not impair the political or territorial integrity of Siberia.[53] Wilson believed that it was necessary to make the American position "quite clear" to the Japanese government.[54] He told Lord Reading, British Ambassador to the United States, that if the United States agreed to Japanese intervention, she would deal the Russian democracy another blow "by invading Russian territory in opposition to the wishes of the Bolshevic authorities."[55]

Wilson's opposition to interference in Russia was not confined to military intervention. Simon Strunsky of the *New York Evening Post*

requested that Wilson issue an outspoken guarantee of democratic
institutions to the people of Russia against both the reimposition
of the "rule of autocracy" as well as "against the Bolsheviks now
in power." Wilson replied: "Mr. Strunsky has entirely misinterpreted
the spirit and principles of this Government, if he thinks it possible
for it to propose to interfere with the form of government in any
other government. That would be in violent contradiction of the principles we have always held, earnestly we should wish to lend every
moral influence to the support of democratic institutions in Russia
and earnestly as we pray that they may survive there and become
permanent."[56]

Wilson reaffirmed his position on March 11, 1918, in a personal
message to the Fourth Congress of Soviets then convening in Moscow
to ratify the Treaty of Brest-Litovsk. Much to the dismay of the State
Department, he extended to the Russian people "the sincere sympathy" of the United States and assured the delegates of his continued determination to secure for Russia "complete sovereignty and
independence in her own affairs." He had worded the message so as
to cover clearly the American position toward Japanese intervention
in Siberia.[57]

When the Japanese government inquired as to how Russia should
be regarded in the future, now that she had signed a separate peace,
Wilson replied that the "utter good faith" of all the governments
associated against Germany demanded that they should continue to
treat the Russians "in all respects as friends and Allies against the
common enemy."[58]

To repeated appeals from London for intervention, Wilson emphasized to Arthur James Balfour, British Foreign Secretary, that he was
unconvinced himself of the need for intervention. In any event, Russian assent to any proposal, even if unofficial, was "an indispensable
feature of American policy."[59] Wilson now believed that the "ideal
arrangement would be for Bolshevikii to request Japanese, American,
and Allied assistance against German aggression."[60] The British now
sought to bring this about, and, by the end of March 1918, it appeared as if the stratagem might succeed, at least partially.

Wilson soon learned that Trotsky had authorized acceptance of
Allied aid. The British had landed marines in northern Russia to
cooperate with the "red army" in defense of Murmansk and the railroad line. A French force was to follow. A Soviet committee had
"expressed regret" that the United States had not had a representa-

tive there to enter into a similar agreement signed by the British and French, but it had emphasized that American aid would be welcome on the same terms as the British and French. Ambassador Francis and Colonel James A. Ruggles, the American military attaché in Petrograd, had wired their approval. The British also requested American naval support. Moreover, Trotsky had informed Ruggles specifically that he would "most welcome" American railroad men. Trotsky at the same time indicated his "fear of Japanese army control in Siberia and of Siberia railroad."[61]

Wilson now agreed to the British request to dispatch an American warship to Murmansk, but he gave strict orders to the commander of the vessel, U.S.S. *Olympia*, not to be drawn into any further venture "without first seeking and obtaining instructions from home."[62] At the same time, Wilson turned a deaf ear to all appeals for intervention in Siberia.[63] He seemed more confirmed than ever that "America should not assent to or take part in intervention of Japanese unless there is at least something in nature of request from Russian government for this assistance."[64] Meanwhile, British Intelligence reported that Trotsky had begun to realize that cooperation with the Allies in the war to free Russia from German domination was the only hope either for Russia or the revolution or possibly the maintenance of his own power.[65] Moreover, both the Allied ambassadors and their military attachés had agreed to permit their officers to continue technically to assist in the formulation of plans for a new red army, with the hope that their discussions would result in Bolshevik consent to Japanese intervention.[66] Trotsky had encouraged such cooperation and had even suggested the possibility of using the Czecho-Slovak legion at that time stationed in the Ukraine for the same purpose. Balfour informed Wilson that the situation was "entirely altered by apparent willingness of Trotsky to invite Allied resistance against German aggression."[67]

Wilson now agreed to reconsider the whole problem in view of "the new light upon it." Nevertheless, he wanted to be sure that he was not being "led into a trap by Trotsky." He agreed to ascertain Japan's views of intervention with the cooperation of American and Allied contingents as soon as Viscount Kikujiro Ishii, the new Japanese Ambassador, arrived in Washington on April 26. Although Wilson still doubted the practicality of the entire proposal, his attitude seemed more favorable than earlier.[68]

Reinsch in Peking had kept Wilson informed of the machinations of the Japanese General Staff. It hoped to secure, through its agents in Siberia and northern Manchuria, special privileges from both General Dmitrii L. Horvat, Russian Governor and General Manager of the Chinese Eastern Railway, and Captain Gregorii Semenov, Cossack leader, in return for military and financial support of their anti-Bolshevik efforts. Moreover, both the Japanese and Russian ministers at Peking had informed Reinsch of their opposition to any American assistance on the Chinese Eastern Railway in northern Manchuria. Horvat and Semenov, in the meantime, reorganized the governing body of the Chinese Eastern Railway and planned military action against the Bolsheviks backed by Japanese forces. Japanese financial and military support was premised upon the acceptance of conditions which Reinsch described as "harsh." He had advised that, if the United States was seeking to help, it was essential to organize Allied action to offset the Japanese and to avoid any contact with Semenov, whose anti-Bolshevik efforts were being supported by Japanese artillery.[69]

Moreover, Wilson had just received reports from Ambassador Roland S. Morris in Tokyo concerning secret interviews with Baron Shimpei Goto, Minister of Home Affairs in the cabinet of Masakata Terauchi. These reports suggested that Japan and Germany were in communication through prominent Japanese officials, possibly looking to German-Japanese agreements in view of the collapse of Russia.[70]

After Lansing presented Ishii to the President, Wilson and Ishii had a brief discussion about intervention. Ishii indicated that, while the Japanese were ready to intervene if they were satisfied that the effect would be beneficial to the common cause, their reports indicated that intervention would make the Russian people hostile to Japan and drive them into better relations with Germany. Naturally, the Japanese were unimpressed either with the Bolshevik offer of cooperation at Murmansk or with the new and friendlier tone to the Allies which the British described. By then, the Bolshevik government had made insistent demands for the withdrawal of Japanese troops, which had landed in Vladivostok in April. Moreover, the Japanese were supporting both Horvat and Semenov against the Bolsheviks along the Chinese Eastern Railway. Ishii doubted Trotsky's good faith and emphasized reports from Tokyo which strongly indicated that the Bolsheviks might turn to Germany for assistance against a Japanese intervention, even if that intervention was supported by the

Allies and Americans.[71] Wilson's position seemed to be completely vindicated.

On May 9, Lieutenant General Giichi Tanaka, Vice-Chief of the Japanese General Staff, presented a somewhat different view. He argued that Allied policy should disregard Lenin and support the bourgeois party. He regarded the Bolsheviks as German tools and was convinced that an Allied anti-Bolshevik movement would obtain the support of an overwhelming majority of Russians. He strongly favored sending an Allied army to occupy all railways up to Irkutsk. Moreover, he indicated that recent Japanese negotiations with China had secured its cooperation once the decision to intervene had been reached. In any case, he made it clear that, "if German influences continue to spread eastward, Japan may find herself obliged to act independently to safeguard her interests at once, though an Allied movement is greatly preferable."[72]

The result of these interviews and reports was a marked hardening of Wilson's position against intervention in Siberia. As Reading informed Balfour, Ishii had only confirmed Wilson's view "that any intervention which brought the Japanese into Siberia would meet with hostile actions both from the Bolshevik government and Soviets and the Russian people." However, the American position toward northern Russia had begun to soften. The reported change in Trotsky's attitude also coincided with American reports. Wilson agreed that there was some indication that Trotsky had turned to the Allies for cooperation and assistance at Murmansk, whereas he placed no credence on similar reports concerning Japanese intervention. Wilson appeared ready to cooperate with the Allies in the North, where there was no question of Japanese involvement. Balfour was so informed. Lansing pointed out that the confusion of the two problems was "unfortunate," and that, while the United States had no objection to securing a request from Trotsky to intervene in Murmansk, he thought that it would be "unwise" to bring Japan into the question.[73] In these circumstances, then, Wilson consented to divert American troops from France to northern Russia upon the approval of Marshal Ferdinand Foch, provided such operations had the "sure sympathy of the Russian people."[74]

At the same time, and in accordance with Trotsky's request, Colonel George B. Emerson, head of the Russian Railway Service Corps, and three assistants were sent from Vladivostok to Vologda on May 19 to confer with Ambassador Francis and Trotsky about the best means of aiding in the rehabilitation of the Russian railways in Europe. Stevens had already arrived in northern Manchuria with 100 engineers, where he was seeking to organize and operate the Chinese Eastern Railway in the face of continuous harassment from the Japanese. At that point, Horvat, with Japanese military assistance, had reorganized the Chinese Eastern Railway with the political aim of reconstituting a government for Siberia.[75]

Once Stevens had succeeded in distributing units of the corps along the entire line of the Chinese Eastern Railway, he reported that the Japanese opposed him constantly, "undoubtedly with a view of controlling the entire transportation system of Manchuria."[76] It was not surprising, then, that, in informing Ambassador Francis of Emerson's impending arrival, Lansing added:

> If, however, as a result of your conference in cooperation with Emerson it might be arranged that any reasonable and proper suggestions or requests by the Soviet authorities be favorably considered by the Embassy and the Railway Corps with the distinct proviso and "quid pro quo" that railway assistance in European Russia should be accompanied by permission for the Corps to extend its activities in Siberia, this program might immediately be commenced with the advantage of the tacit acquiescence of such authorities.[77]

By the middle of June, the Supreme War Council had approved of the transportation of some 20,000 Czechs to the Northwest to defend the Russian Arctic ports, prior to their transfer to France. General Bliss agreed to the proposal only insofar as the forces required would be drawn from Czech units then in Russia and would therefore require the dispatch to northern Russia of no more than two American battalions. The forces were to defend against small enemy operations or, in the event of major enemy operations, to insure the removal or destruction of stores that would be of service to the enemy. The addition of British, French, and Italian, as well as American, troops would strengthen the Czech contingent. When Foch made clear his approval of this limited course of action, Wilson also agreed to the scheme. He had, at the same time, refused to consider a new proposal for a much larger Allied expedition sent to him by Lord Alfred Milner of the British War Cabinet, a plan which had received the approval of neither Bliss nor Foch.[78]

At this crucial point, the outbreak at the end of May of a conflict between the Czecho-Slovak legion and the Bolsheviks drastically altered the situation in Siberia. The Czecho-Slovak force was comprised largely of men who had been taken prisoners or who had deserted from the Austro-Hungarian army and were eager to fight on the Allied side. In the spring of 1918, the Czech legion, as the Czecho-Slovak force was called, had been recognized as an Allied belligerent by the French and, under their auspices, was attempting to make its way from European Russia to the western front via Vladivostok. In April and May, it was strung out in train loads along the Trans-Siberian Railway all the way from the Ukraine to Vladivostok. With the disintegration of the old Russian army, the Czech legion had now become the strongest single armed force in Russia.

Hostilities broke out between the Czechs and the Soviet authorities along the route on May 26. In part, the outbreak was the product of the frictions and misunderstandings caused by incidents which occurred when the Czechs encountered parties of Austrian or Hungarian war prisoners who were, after the conclusion of the Brest-Litovsk Treaty, seeking repatriation along the railway in the opposite direction. The Czech uprising actually came as a setback to the Allied military planners, who had hoped to use a part of the Czech corps in the northern ports and had just made arrangements with the Soviet and Czech authorities to have a portion of the corps routed to the Russian North. The outbreak of the conflict made this arrangement impossible. Moreover, as a result of their uprising, the Czechs, within a few days, seized most of the Trans-Siberian Railway from the Volga to Irkutsk. Another body of some 18,000 Czechs had arrived at Vladivostok, but at the time of the uprising there were no Czech trains in the area between Vladivostok and Irkutsk. This territory thus remained initially in Soviet hands.[79] This situation confronted Colonel Emerson as he sought to make his way via the Trans-Siberian Railway to European Russia, there to negotiate with Trotsky for the operation of the Russian railways. Although he continued his efforts to reach his destination and even to mediate the conflict, Czech-Bolshevik differences soon made his mediation impossible.[80]

By the end of June 1918, Allied pressure on Wilson for intervention in Siberia was intense. British political authorities were impatient at the delay, while Allied military leaders insisted that a Japanese expedition to Siberia was essential if the Allies desired victory in 1919.[81] Moreover, virtually all the American representatives in Russia, Siberia, and China were united in supporting the call of the British, French, and Japanese for immediate intervention.[82] By this time, the Allies were in the process of inviting Japan to intervene alone—a course of action which virtually all persons in the State Department regarded as fraught with hazard for the future of eastern Siberia and Manchuria.[83] At the same time, the threat of independent Japanese action loomed on the horizon. The Sino-Japanese military agreements of May 16, 1918, had already provided the machinery for such action, and both Reinsch in Peking and Consul Charles K. Moser in Harbin warned that Japan was attempting to create a situation which would necessitate its immediate implementation.[84] Yet both Sir William Wiseman, chief British Intelligence agent in the United States, and Reading reported that Wilson was still opposed to both Japanese intervention and Allied intervention on the ground that the latter would be the same thing, since the Japanese would supply the major part of the military force. Wilson was convinced that such a policy would simply throw the Russians completely into the hands of the Germans. Moreover, he still desired an invitation to enter Russia from the Bolsheviks or from somebody who really represented Russian opinion.[85] Professor Thomas G. Masaryk, President of the Czecho-Slovak National Council, who was regarded as one of the world's foremost authorities on Russia, supported Wilson on this position. He told the President that whoever would aid Russia must be on good terms with the Bolsheviks: "You can't work against the Government." Masaryk, who doubted the value of military intervention, had publicly announced his conviction that the Bolsheviks were growing more and more anti-German. He added: "I cannot see that military intervention would be of any use to European Russia even if Siberia could be saved." He had made clear both the weakness of the other parties in Russia—the Monarchists, Cadets, and Social Revolutionaries—and his consistent refusal to permit his legion to join them. However, he agreed that, if the Russians were to be helped, the Russian railways had to be supported and rehabilitated.[86]

Wilson's position was also fully supported by his military advisers, particularly Newton D. Baker, Secretary of War, Peyton C. March, Chief of Staff, and General Bliss, who were pronounced "Western Fronters." They were all adamantly opposed to military intervention through Siberia to reestablish an eastern front. March regarded the plan as "neither practical nor practicable." To the President's military advisers, the essential issue was whether the Japanese should have a "free hand in Siberia." They regarded as "wholly inadmissible solving the Russian problem by giving Japan a portion of Siberia." Moreover, March expressed the views of both Baker and Bliss when he emphasized that "none of the schemes looking to the restoration of the Romanoffs, or a government of that country without the consent of the governed," should "be permitted for a moment." Baker himself would have liked "to take everybody out of Russia except the Russians, . . . and let the Russians settle down and settle their own affairs."[87] Wilson fully agreed.

Yet, in July 1918, new and compelling circumstances forced Wilson to change his mind. He not only agreed to intervention, but took the lead in inviting the Japanese to a limited, joint intervention in Siberia. His first avowed reason was to "rescue" some 70,000 Czecho-Slovaks whom Austro-German prisoners of war, supposedly with Soviet connivance, had allegedly attacked in Siberia. Wilson's second avowed reason was to aid the Russian people in any efforts at self-government that they might desire. In late June, the Czechs in central and western Siberia ordered their compatriots in Vladivostok to return to the West in order to insure the security of the passage of the main body of the Czech corps to the Pacific. At the end of June, therefore, they seized Vladivostok and mounted an operation westward to clear the railway toward Irkutsk. They appealed to the Allied governments, and particularly to the United States and Japan, for military support. They knew that intervention in the internal affairs of the Russian people was strictly in opposition to the specific instructions from President Masaryk, but they emphasized the alleged fact that the opposition which confronted them did not come from Communists but from former German and Austrian prisoners of war who had been rearmed by the Bolsheviks and who now threatened to seize Siberia for the Central Powers. At the end of June, with the capture of Vladivostok by the Czechs, Wilson had to respond both to the request of the Czechs for aid in their efforts to rescue their brethren in the interior of Siberia and to the Allied insistence upon reestablishing the eastern front.[88] The British Foreign Office, which had exhausted virtually all of its arguments in the effort to win Wilson's agreement to Japanese intervention, now saw the plight of the Czecho-Slovaks as a new and powerful lever. It would also seek to put pressure on Wilson through the Supreme War Council.[89] The British immediately sought to "press the matter at once" with Wilson. As Balfour urged: "The Czechs are our Allies, and we must save them if we can. Their position seems to me to render immediate Allied action on their behalf a matter of urgent necessity."[90] Lansing supported the British argument.[91] The Supreme War Council also sent a communication urging both support to the Czechs and the reestablishment of the eastern front.

To Wilson, the plight of the Czechs represented an entirely new development. Here was an Allied force, apparently threatened by German and Austro-Hungarian former prisoners of war in their efforts to remove themselves from Siberia and who were now fighting to keep Siberia out of German hands. Allied as well as American leaders had strongly urged the need for American support. Wilson had acquired friendly feelings for the Czechs and their leader, Masaryk; Wilson could not resist their appeals for assistance. Yet the problem was how to act without associating himself with the political schemes of the Allies or opening the door to full-scale Japanese intervention in eastern Siberia and northern Manchuria.

Wilson arrived at a decision on July 6, 1918, after consultation with his cabinet. While he rejected emphatically the whole Allied notion of restoring the eastern front, Wilson agreed to help the Czecho-Slovaks at Vladivostok to establish contact with their brethren further west. He proposed to send 7,000 American troops, provided that the Japanese would send a force of similar size, to guard the line of communication of the Vladivostok Czechs as they advanced westward along the Trans-Siberian Railway to "rescue" their comrades at Irkutsk. Wilson proposed that a public announcement be made by the American and Japanese governments to the effect that the purpose of sending the troops was specifically to aid the Czecho-Slovaks against German and Austrian former prisoners of war; that there was "no purpose" to interfere in the internal affairs of Russia; and that the United States and Japan would guarantee not to impair the political or territorial sovereignty of Russia.[92] Immediately after the White House conference, Admiral Austin M. Knight, in command of the Asiatic Fleet, was instructed to keep Vladivostok "available as a base for the safety of Czechs and as a means of egress for them."[93]

Wilson's initial decision was a unilateral one and in no way a part of the general Allied decision for intervention in Siberia. Wilson rejected virtually every proposal which the British and French governments and the Supreme War Council had urged upon him. Wilson surely did not consider the action that he was authorizing as intervention against the Bolsheviks; and, in communicating his decision to the Allied governments, he condemned the whole notion of intervention in blunt terms. Although the British and French were furious with him over the entire affair, they continued to hope that, with appropriate pressure, the original plan could later be expanded, once American troops had arrived in Siberia.[94]

During the next month, Lansing was on vacation, and the negotiations for an appropriate agreement with the Japanese were largely in the hands of Wilson and the Counselor of the State Department, Frank L. Polk. Wilson's problem was to provide for the "rescue" of the Czechs in cooperation with a government whose motives he deeply distrusted. Wilson was clearly concerned that, once Japanese forces had arrived in Siberia, it would be difficult to induce them to leave. Japanese military leaders saw little value in intervention unless it was to result in Japanese control of eastern Siberia and northern Manchuria. Wilson now sought in every possible way to limit the size of the Japanese expedition, the geographical area in which it would operate, its specific objectives, the conditions for its withdrawal, and to provide for exclusive *Chinese* control of the Chinese Eastern Railway.[95] Wilson sought to make clear to the Japanese that "a military occupation in Manchuria would arouse deep resentment in Russia, which would be greatly increased by any apparent support by the Allies of plans to restore monarchy." Moreover, the State Department informed the Japanese government that the United States was not prepared to support "any of the factions claiming to govern Siberia."[96]

The month of July 1918 was spent in a useless endeavor to win Japanese agreement to the principle of "joint, equal military action." Despite the State Department's agreement to permit the Japanese to have the high command in return for a definite limitation on the number of Japanese troops to be sent to Siberia, the final Japanese declaration failed to mention the number of troops participating in the venture. Moreover, the Japanese Ambassador made it clear that, in the event of an emergency, Japan might be forced to send additional troops "without consultation."[97] Wilson was "very much put out" by the Japanese reply and instructed Polk to tell Ishii that, while he did not wish to cause Japan "any embarrassment," Japan's plan was so different from his own that he thought it best not to act at all.

Wilson believed that the Japanese plans would give the natural impression to the Russian people that the expedition "had more in view
than merely assisting the Czechs." Wilson also objected to the reference in the Japanese proposal to the "special position of Japan." Such
an assertion also might "create a misunderstanding in the minds of
the Russian people and would be seized on by the Germans as having
much greater significance than intended." Wilson warned that if
Japan and the other Allies concluded that a large expedition was a
military necessity, then the United States "would be compelled to
withdraw as that was not our plan."[98]

Even as Wilson sought to limit the size and scope of the Japanese-
American expedition, Lord Reading sought to gain his support, both
for an enlargement of the expedition and for agreement with the
objectives of the Allies. Reading failed on both counts. He then conveyed to the British Prime Minister the "true" feeling of the American
President in regard to the entire enterprise. Reading pointed out
that, ever since the question of intervention was first broached, Wilson
had feared that friends of the old imperial regime would control the
undertaking and that it would, however disguised, eventually prove
to be reactionary and antirepublican. Furthermore, Reading went on,
Wilson was clearly apprehensive lest any intervention "should be converted into an anti-Soviet movement and an interference with the
right of Russians to choose their own form of government." To Reading, it seemed clear that Wilson's present intentions were "to help the
Czecho-Slovaks." However, Wilson was still "opposed to intervention
and somewhat apprehensive lest the step he is now willing to take
should lead him into a much more extended policy."[99]

When Masaryk indicated his deep gratitude for Wilson's decision to
help the Czecho-Slovak army in Russia, Wilson responded that, although he "greatly appreciated" Masaryk's letter, he "felt no confidence in [his] personal judgment, about the complicated situation in
Russia" and that he was "reassured" by Masaryk's approval of what he
had done.[100] Crane, aware of the complexity of the Russian problem,
sent his approval to Wilson. Crane urged him not to be too disturbed
by the "German bogey" and assured him that "Stevens would probably know how to take over control of the railways" and to maintain
them "without making much fuss or any declaration." Wilson was
"comforted . . . greatly." He wrote: "I have had to do some very lonely
thinking about the Russia business, and to have any assurance from

you, that on the whole, I am handling things properly and as wisely as the circumstances permit gives me the deepest comfort."[101]

Wilson's public announcement (usually referred to as the *aide-mémoire*), which he wrote on his own typewriter and released to the press on the afternoon of August 3, declared once more his strong opposition to military intervention. It "would add to the present sad confusion in Russia rather than cure it, injure her rather than help her, and . . . would be of no advantage in the prosecution or main design to win the war against Germany." The United States would take no part in such intervention or sanction it in principle. Military action was admissible in Russia only to help the Czecho-Slovaks, to steady any efforts at self-government or self-defense in which the Russians themselves might be willing to accept assistance, and to guard military stores which Russian forces might subsequently need. Wilson also announced his approval of the use of American troops at Murmansk and Archangel for these same objectives.[102]

The Committee on Public Information at Vladivostok, headed by Arthur Bullard, publicized the American declaration by emphasizing Wilson's continued adherence to Point Six. Foreign bayonets would not help in the matter. It would be contrary to American ideals to "impose a government of our choosing on Siberia and Russia." The United States, however, would seek to help the Russian people to reorganize their railways and to aid in the economic rehabilitation of the nation without interfering in Russian politics.[103] To the Allied representatives in Washington, Polk continued to reiterate during the following week that American policy was not to be interpreted as intervention, and that American help would be limited to the precise reasons publicly stated.[104]

Actually, Wilson did not want the participation of Great Britain or France in the venture. He had opposed their secret support and encouragement of factions in various parts of Russia. Lansing expressed Wilson's views: "The participation of these two governments will give the enterprise the character of interference with the domestic affairs of Russia and create the impression that the underlying purpose is to set up a new pro-Allied government in Siberia, if not in Russia."[105]

The divergence of views concerning the purpose of the Japanese-American expedition became apparent once the troops had arrived in Siberia. While Great Britain and France attempted to extend the scope of military and political action in Russia, and Japan proceeded with her plans to occupy Manchuria and the Russian Far East, the United States attempted to limit and to restrain the independent operations of its associates. American troops had scarcely arrived in Siberia when the British and French requested that additional troops be sent. They pointed out that the safety of the Czechs was "an obligation of honor resting on all the Allies." When Wilson made clear his opposition to such a proposal, the British suggested that the State Department formally request the Japanese to dispatch the necessary additional troops "to save the Czechs from disaster." The French government suggested that approximately 80,000 men would suffice.[106]

After spending a month seeking to limit the size of the Japanese expedition, Wilson was "irritated beyond words" by the continued British pressure to "invite the Japanese to send additional troops into Siberia."[107] Just before he left for a brief visit to Colonel House, Wilson dropped into Lansing's office and discussed Siberia at length with the Secretary of State. "Indignant" over the British request, Wilson had drafted a "stiff reply" which William Phillips, Assistant Secretary of State, feared "might get the Department into trouble."[108] Wilson instructed Lansing to announce American opposition to the British scheme in clear and unmistakable terms.[109]

When Admiral Knight, deeply concerned over the plight of the Czecho-Slovaks and the pleas for assistance from the commander of the Czech forces, requested that the "assistance to Czechs by Americans and other forces be extended to the Manchuria region instead of being confined to the Ussuri Front,"[110] he was informed that the President's statement had clearly indicated that American forces were "not intended for intervention in Russia but solely for the purposes set forth in that statement." The immediate objective of the small force which the United States had proposed was "first to hold Vladivostok and second to safeguard as far as possible the country in rear of the westward moving Czecho-Slovak troops."[111]

General William S. Graves, commander of the American expedition, had not yet arrived in Siberia. He had served as assistant to General March from December 18, 1917, to June 26, 1918; his unfailing tact, fairness, and quiet determination had won him the respect and confidence of both his immediate chief and the Secretary of War. Graves had been closely associated with March during the period of greatest pressure for intervention. Graves thus both understood and shared March's views about the entire enterprise—views which fully coincided with Wilson's. Graves received his orders for the Siberian command directly from Baker himself. Baker handed him a copy of Wilson's *aide-mémoire* of August 3 and warned him that the Japanese intended to expand on the Asiatic mainland. Graves's instructions forbade any interference in the internal affairs of the Russian people; his army was not to engage in hostile action against anyone. Graves understood and approved his instructions. Baker warned him that he would be "walking on eggs loaded with dynamite."[112]

No sooner had Wilson announced his decision than Great Britain and France sought his cooperation in the establishment of a unified political control of affairs, since the Russians were "too divided amongst themselves to do so effectively and impartially."[113] Wilson agreed with Lansing that these efforts were "simply another move to impress our action in Siberia with the character of intervention rather than relief of the Czechs." When the French suggested that an American high commissioner be appointed as head of an Inter-Allied Civilian Board, Wilson dismissed the proposal as "bait to draw us into a policy which has been so insistently urged by Great Britain for the past six months." Wilson was "not to be hurried into the kind of action the Allies wish in Siberia by this or any other kind of arrangement."[114] To Lansing, he wrote: "Please make it plain to the French Ambassador that we do not think cooperation in *political* action necessary or desirable in eastern Siberia because we contemplate no political action of any kind there, but only the action of friends who stand at hand and wait to see how they can help. The more plain and emphatic this is made, the less danger will there be of subsequent new understandings and irritations."[115] By this time, as Wiseman noted, Wilson was beginning to feel that the Allies were "trying to rush, even trick him," into a policy which he had refused to accept.[116]

When Wiseman later asked Wilson why he had not cooperated in sending a political commissioner to Russia or joined in any of the political conferences with the Allies regarding action to be taken in Russia, he responded: "My policy regarding Russia is very similar to my Mexican policy. I believe in letting them work out their own salvation, even though they wallow in anarchy for a while."[117]

Wilson was also deeply concerned over Allied interference in Russian political affairs in northern Russia. He opposed the arbitrary attitude which the British general, Frederick C. Poole, adopted at

Archangel. Poole, who was in command of the northern Russian expedition, had appointed a French colonel as military governor of Archangel; in turn, the colonel had issued an order to arrest anyone guilty of disseminating Bolshevik propaganda. Since Wilson's policy "had been consistently to allow Russians to work out their own salvation," and since there was a local Russian government at Archangel, Wilson saw no need for a military governor. He informed the British that, "unless there was a change in the high handed attitude adopted by General Poole," he would seriously consider the withdrawal of the United States contingent from General Poole's command.[118]

By the first week in September 1918, it was clear to Wilson that both the northern expedition and the Siberian expedition were being expedited and implemented in the "most striking" manner and in "utter disregard" of the "policy to which we expressly confined ourselves in our statement about our action in Siberia." General Poole had instructed the Czecho-Slovaks to take Perm in western Siberia and to effect a junction with the Allied forces moving down from northern Russia. The Allies thus sought to link up their forces in northern Russia with the Czech forces in the West in the expectation of re-establishing the eastern front. Wilson wrote in exasperation: "It is out of the question to send reinforcements from eastern Siberia . . . and we have expressly notified those in charge of those forces that the Czecho-Slovaks must (so far as our aid was to be used) to [sic] be brought out eastward, not got out westward. Is there no way,—no form of expression,—by which we can get this comprehended?" Wilson feared that there was some "influence at work to pull absolutely away from the plan which we proposed and to which the other governments assented, and proceed to do what we said we would not do, namely form a new Eastern Front."[119]

Communications from Generals Bliss and March which indicated that General Poole was engaging in a campaign which "we have never contemplated nor recommended" soon confirmed Wilson's suspicions. He fully agreed with March's position: Poole should obey his instructions and confine himself "to the defense of the Arctic ports."[120] Both Secretary Baker and Wilson agreed that they would not support a British request to send five additional American battalions to Murmansk, because "yielding to this request would only open the door to further diversion of American forces."[121] Wilson's position was unyielding: the United States would not cooperate in any effort to establish lines of operation and defense from Siberia to Archangel. He would send no more American troops to the northern ports. Moreover, insofar as American cooperation was concerned, he would insist that the other governments give up all military effort in northern Russia except to guard the ports themselves and part of the surrounding countryside.[122]

Given Wilson's hostility to what he knew about Poole's activities, it is highly unlikely that he knew that American units commanded by Colonel George E. Stewart, under Poole's overall command, had been sent almost immediately upon their arrival to cooperate in numerous small-scale engagements with the Bolsheviks. Colonel Stewart did not receive a copy of Wilson's *aide-mémoire* until October, although he suspected that his troops were being used contrary to instructions. In any case, Ambassador Francis, who was an ardent interventionist and anti-Bolshevik, had chosen to interpret the *aide-mémoire* as applying only to Siberia, and he encouraged Stewart to cooperate with Poole.[123]

When General Pierre Janin, French commander in chief of the Czech forces in Siberia, arrived in the United States en route to Siberia with a personal appeal to the President from Georges Clemenceau, French Premier and Minister of War, for the reinforcement of troops at Murmansk and Archangel, Wilson labeled the entire operation as "foolish." Wilson's response to a request for the reinforcement of the Czecho-Slovaks by either American or Japanese troops in eastern Siberia was equally negative.[124]

Meanwhile, the Czech leaders were pleading for immediate assistance so they would not be forced to retire east of the Ural Mountains. Such a retreat would leave defenseless those Russians who had supported them against the Bolsheviks.[125] Lansing was thoroughly distressed and perplexed by the Czech dilemma. He sympathized with "the spirit of the Czecho-Slovaks" who would not abandon their helpful friends to "certain massacre and pillage," particularly since this would leave them "at the mercy of the Red Guards, who have committed such monstrous crimes within the past six weeks in Moscow and other cities." He feared that the United States would be generally criticized if it told the Czechs that it was their duty to join their compatriots in Siberia. Masaryk supported the Czech appeal as well as Lansing's position.[126]

Wilson was concerned over the plight of the Czechs, but he was now also fully aware of what his associates were seeking to do militarily and politically in Russia. It was, therefore, his "clear judgment" that the United States should "insist that the Czecho-Slovaks be brought out eastward to Vladivostok and conveyed to the Western Front in Europe . . . according to the original agreement made with them."[127] Ambassador Morris, then on special detail in Siberia, was to be told very clearly "that the ideas and purposes of the Allies with respect to Siberia and 'the Volga Front'" were "ideas and purposes with which we have no sympathy and that the representatives of the Allies at Vladivostok are trying their best to 'work' General Graves and every other American in sight to achieve their purposes. They should be made to understand that there is absolutely 'nothing doing.'" Moreover, the military, naval, and civilian authorities of the United States Government were to be informed that, notwithstanding any pressure to the contrary, they were expected to be "governed wholly and absolutely by the policy of the United States government." The time had arrived, Wilson concluded, when "we cannot act too soon or speak too plainly."[128] The State Department prepared an appropriate, though modified, draft for Wilson, and it was sent to all the Allied governments.[129]

Lansing now had a long talk with Wiseman and explained Wilson's concern over the difference of policy between the United States and the Allies regarding the Czechs in Siberia. "The Czech forces," Lansing said, "are moving West when they ought to be going East." He emphasized that American policy was clear, unaltered, and in entire accord with the policy of the Japanese government "to rescue the Czechs," after which the Japanese would retire with them and both forces would evacuate Russian territory.[130]

The British Foreign Office responded that the decision of the United States Government to hold its troops in eastern Siberia would not affect British determination to aid the Czechs in holding their position west of the Urals. If the Czechs withdrew to the East, the "loyal" Russians would be left to the mercy of their enemies. Moreover, the British government intended to request the French and Japanese governments to follow British policy in standing by the "loyal Russians against the Bolsheviks." The Foreign Office added that, if the United States was "unable to assist us beyond the point indicated, we hope they will not discourage our other Allies from helping us."[131]

By this time, Wilson was also clashing head on with the Japanese.[132] While Wilson resisted Anglo-French efforts to broaden the scope of the northern Russian and Siberian expeditions, Tokyo followed its own independent course in combating what it described as "the increasingly serious conditions developing in northern Manchuria and eastern Siberia." Although the Chinese government denied repeatedly and emphatically that its borders had been violated either by the Bolsheviks or former German prisoners of war, Tokyo informed Washington of its decision to send an independent Japanese force to protect the Manchurian border from invasion by the Bolsheviks. The action was to be taken under the terms of the Sino-Japanese military agreements of May 16, 1918. Japan insisted that the expedition into the zone of the Chinese Eastern Railway was "entirely different in nature from the present joint intervention in Vladivostok or from military action in Russian territory, and the only nations that have interests involved are Japan and China."[133] By August 21, 1918, the Japanese had stationed 12,000 troops along the line of the Chinese Eastern Railway, and the Chinese Minister had personally called upon Lansing to make clear that these troops had been sent "without agreement." Wilson was "very much disturbed" by these reports and sent an emphatic protest to the Japanese government. Stevens reported that Japan was making every effort to control the operation of the railways and would succeed unless the United States took a firm stand. Without quick action, he said, American railroad men would be "out of business completely."[134] Wilson promptly sought to implement efforts to assist in the reorganization and operation of the Chinese Eastern Railway. Polk urged Stevens to use his best efforts to forward the movement of the Czecho-Slovaks and warned him "to avoid alliance with or support to any political group or faction in Russia."[135] By the middle of September, Wilson was vitally concerned about the disposition of some 62,000 Japanese troops in Siberia and in northern Manchuria. Viscount Ishii was informed orally of the President's displeasure.[136] At the same time, plans were initiated for placing the general direction of the Trans-Siberian and Chinese Eastern railways in the hands of Stevens and the Russian Railway Service Corps.[137]

Since Wilson was concerned about turning over military control of the railways to the Japanese—even if under the technical direction of Stevens and the Russian Railway Service Corps—negotiations were begun to secure Dr. Masaryk's consent for the cooperation of the

Czech military forces in the implementation of an international railway control of both the Trans-Siberian and the Chinese Eastern railways.[138] At the same time, Wilson, who had absolutely forbidden General Graves to establish himself at any point along the Trans-Siberian Railway beyond Vladivostok, now agreed to request permission from China for the stationing of Graves and American troops at Harbin in northern Manchuria, both in order to expedite the eastward movement of the Czechs and to curb Japanese action along the line of the Chinese Eastern Railway.[139]

The Chinese government immediately granted the necessary permission and added informally that it "heartily welcomed" the presence of American troops and railway assistance, although it appeared that Japan might resent any expression of that sort.[140] Wilson at once sent Morris (his former student in whom he had complete confidence) to Vladivostok to negotiate an agreement with the Allied and Russian representatives on the spot.[141]

Japan continued to pour troops into Siberia. By the time that the Armistice was signed on November 11, 1918, Japan had sent three divisions, or some 70,000 men, all of them under the direct control of the General Staff in Tokyo.[142] The United States continued to protest vigorously against Japanese actions; at the same time, it sought to place the railways under international military control and to operate them through the Russian Railway Service Corps. After months of patient negotiation and an internal struggle within the Japanese government, an Inter-Allied Railway agreement was finally reached.[143] Wilson regarded the railway plan as of "inestimable value to the people of Russia and the United States, as well as the world in general."[144] When he advised Congress of American policy, he wrote: "It is felt that this matter can be treated entirely apart from the general Russian problem, as irrespective of what our policy may be toward Russia, and irrespective of further Russian developments, it is essential that we maintain the policy of the Open Door with reference to the Siberian and particularly the Chinese Eastern Railway."[145]

The Inter-Allied Railway agreement changed completely the character of intervention in Siberia. The primary concern of American military forces now became the restoration and protection of the railways instead of the rescue of the Czechs. The latter were now participating in the execution of the railway plan. In effect, the improvement of the transportation system served to aid the anti-Bolshevik cause, and, despite its denials, the United States became an active participant

in the Russian Civil War. Wilson justified this course on the ground
that it was a way to maintain the Open Door in Siberia and northern
Manchuria and to preserve Russia's territorial integrity.[146]

The war was over, but the Russian question continued to cause
Wilson "great anxiety." He still believed in letting the Russians "work
out their own salvation"; he agreed with Secretary Baker that "we
ought simply to order our forces home by the first boat." Nevertheless, Wilson now realized more than ever the importance of cooperation with his associates if he was to achieve any success at the Paris
Peace Conference. Moreover, if he had evacuated eastern Siberia and
northern Manchuria at this time, he would have left Japan in complete control there. He would thereby have nullified all his efforts to
preserve Russian territorial integrity and the Open Door. The question of Russia, therefore, he believed, had to be left to the peace
conference.[147] Wilson was clearly finding it harder to get out of Russia
than it had been to go in.[148]

Wilson's views regarding Russia and intervention were made clear
to the British when he visited London in late December 1918. Lloyd
George observed that the President, "though not pro-Bolshevik," was
very much opposed to armed intervention. "He disliked the Archangel and Murmansk expeditions, and would, no doubt, withdraw his
troops from there." Neither was Wilson "very much in favor of the
Siberian expedition," where "his principal anxiety was as to the conduct of the Japanese, who were apparently taking the whole of eastern Siberia into their own hands . . . and generally behaving as if they
owned the country." Wilson's whole attitude, in fact, was "strongly
anti-Japanese." He favored investigating formally the peace proposals
which Maxim Litvinov, a Soviet plenipotentiary, had sent personally
to him on Christmas Eve. On December 29, Wilson expressed the
same views to C. P. Scott, editor of the *Manchester Guardian*, and indicated his willingness "to open conversations with the Bolsheviks,
whether we recognized them formally or not." "Their invasion," Wilson went on, "was mainly an invasion of ideas and you could not
defeat ideas by armies. . . . We had no right to interfere with the internal affairs of Russia . . . and they had a right to have what internal
polity they liked. His policy all through had been not to attack Russia
but to help her."[149] Shortly thereafter, Wilson sent William H. Buckler, a special assistant at the American embassy in London, to investigate Litvinov's proposals.[150]

From the very outset of the Paris Peace Conference, there was little unity in the views of the Allied statesmen concerning Russia. When the Russian problem was discussed on January 12, 1919, Marshal Foch immediately urged a quick peace with Germany in order to permit the Allies to begin an anti-Bolshevik crusade. He wished to crush Bolshevism with American troops.[151] Wilson strongly opposed the plan. Although Communism was indeed "a social and political danger," he doubted whether it could be checked by force of arms.[152] Wilson had already opposed the creation of buffer states out of Bolshevik territory, refused earlier French suggestions to use American forces in the Ukraine, and declined to intervene against advancing Soviet armies in Estonia, Latvia, and Lithuania. The United States would take no action in these areas in opposition to its various declarations of friendship for Russia and the Russian people.[153] When, in late March, Foch submitted a more grandiose plan to stop Bolshevism by force, Wilson declared, "In my opinion, trying to stop a revolutionary movement by troops in the field is like using a broom to hold back a great ocean."[154]

Wilson proposed to negotiate with the Russians.[155] Lloyd George agreed. As early as January 3, 1919, the British government had dispatched notes to all the Allied and Associated governments which proposed a truce among all the warring factions in Russia for the duration of the peace conference and invited the Russian factions to send delegates to Paris.[156] Although the French Foreign Minister was outraged at the idea of negotiating with the Soviets, Wilson strongly favored the proposal. Indeed, he had just received a report from Buckler which indicated that the Soviet government was eager for a permanent peace and was willing to compromise on all points.[157] Wilson presented Litvinov's peace proposals to his colleagues and urged the French to swallow their pride and revulsion and confer with the representatives of all organized Russian groups.[158]

On January 22, Wilson suggested as a site for the meeting Prinkipo, or Prince's, Island. The invitation, drafted by Wilson, reaffirmed the principles which he had enunciated in Point Six. It once again pledged noninterference in Russian affairs and recognized the absolute right of the Russian people to determine their own affairs "without dictation or direction of any kind from outside." Wilson proposed a free and frank exchange of views which would make the desires of the Russian people known; he hoped that an agreement might be reached in which Russia defined its own intentions and established a basis of cooperation with other nations. The invitation proposed a general armistice between the contending forces in Russia and set February 15 as the date for the conference. The French and Italians yielded very reluctantly to Wilson's insistence.[159]

From Siberia, Archangel, and southern Russia, the invitation to Prinkipo was indignantly rejected. The French had urged White Russian representatives to decline the proposal. "Under no circumstances whatever, would there be any question of an exchange of ideas on this matter with the participation of the Bolshevists, in whom the conscience of the Russian people see only as traitors."[160] The Soviet reply to the Prinkipo proposal was quite conciliatory, albeit insulting.[161] The White Russian governments refused to consider a conference with the Bolsheviks; the Soviets, although willing to confer, would make no specific pledges to stop the advance of their armies, and the Prinkipo démarche thus eventually failed.

On February 15, the day before Wilson left Paris for a trip to the United States, Winston S. Churchill came over from England specifically for the purpose of getting Wilson's views on the Russian problem. What was to be the policy, peace or war? Surely Wilson would not leave Paris without answering so important a question.[162] Wilson had very clear answers on two points. First, he believed that Allied intervention was doing no good in Russia; therefore, he advocated the withdrawal of Allied and Associated troops from all parts of Russian territory. The second point related to Prinkipo. He was not opposed to an informal meeting between American and Bolshevik representatives for the purpose of securing information. He would meet them alone, if necessary. Wilson pointed out that, since official and unofficial reports were conflicting, it was impossible to obtain a coherent picture of Russian affairs. Churchill said that the withdrawal of troops from Russia would place some 500,000 non-Bolshevik troops at the mercy of the Bolsheviks and leave "an indeterminable vista of violence and misery." Wilson replied that, since the existing Allied troops in Russia could not stop the Bolsheviks, and since none of the Allies could reinforce its armies there, withdrawal seemed the best solution. Moreover, he added, even when the Allies supplied non-Bolsheviks with arms, they "made very little use of them."[163]

After Wilson had left Paris, Churchill interpreted Wilson's concluding remarks as indicating a willingness to participate with the Allies in anything necessary and practicable to help the non-Bolshevik Russian armies then in the field.[164] Churchill immediately initiated efforts for joint military action by the Associated powers to aid the White Russian armies to maintain themselves against the Bolsheviks; at the same time, Churchill sought measures to safeguard Finland, Estonia, Livonia, Poland, and Rumania.[165]

Wilson was outraged by Churchill's action and immediately instructed the American peace commissioners to oppose any policy which did not mean the "earliest practicable withdrawal of military forces."[166] He instructed House to make it plain to the Allied statesmen that "we are not at war with Russia and will in no circumstances that we can now foresee, take part in military operations there against the Russians."[167] General Bliss immediately explained Wilson's views to Churchill, and the project was dropped.[168]

The next British and American attempt to deal with the Russian problem was to send a secret diplomatic agent, William C. Bullitt, to talk to the Bolshevik leaders. Although Wilson personally had no objection to American representatives meeting informally with those of the Soviet government, the plan itself was initiated and undertaken after his departure from Paris. House approved of the mission whose purpose was to study conditions in Russia and to procure from the Bolsheviks an exact statement of the terms on which they would agree to a cease fire.[169]

The mission was unofficial and for informational purposes only.[170] Moreover, it remained secret from all of the Allies except the British. House instructed Bullitt to confer with Phillip Kerr, Lloyd George's private secretary, who handed him a letter which suggested terms of settlement, generally similar to the instructions which House gave him. Kerr's letter, Bullitt later testified, was based on consultations with Lloyd George and Balfour.[171] After a week in Russia, Bullitt returned to Paris with a document containing the terms of peace which the Soviet government pledged itself to accept. Bullitt believed that they constituted a practicable basis for peace between the Soviet government and the Allied powers, and he wrote a moving plea to Colonel House urging their acceptance.[172] He also submitted a report to Wilson recommending the acceptance of the peace offer as just and reasonable, and he provided copies of his report and of the Soviet proposals to Kerr. Lloyd George received Bullitt and questioned him closely as to conditions in Russia and the character of the Bolshevik leaders.[173]

The Bullitt proposals were quietly suppressed for a variety of reasons. In the face of strong anti-Bolshevik opinion at home, Lloyd George felt it politically unwise to support them.[174] More important, Bullitt returned to Paris at the height of one of the most severe crises of the conference, a time which Ray Stannard Baker called "the dark period." Wilson and Lloyd George felt that they had yielded all they could to inflexible French demands for security, and the conference appeared to be on the verge of breaking up. Wilson was naturally heavily preoccupied with German issues and deeply concerned as to whether peace in the West could be achieved at all; the question of peace in Russia seemed for the moment a relatively insignificant secondary problem.[175]

Although Wilson agreed to see Bullitt in House's office, he was unable to keep the appointment because of a headache. There is no doubt that Wilson at this time was not only overworked and under a great strain but also physically and emotionally exhausted. A few days later he became violently ill, and the illness lasted for over a week. This was the reason why Wilson did not deal with Bullitt directly.[176] In any case, in view of the hostile attitudes of virtually all of the Allied statesmen, particularly the French, there was little that Wilson could have done to have insured a favorable response to the Soviet offer. The Prinkipo proposal had clearly demonstrated that.

To recapitulate, whenever the question of Russia and intervention was discussed at Paris, Wilson said that the Allied intervention in Russia was a mistake and a failure. He insisted that the Allied forces there were doing no good; that they did not know for whom or for what they were fighting; that they were not assisting any promising effort to establish order; and that they ought to be removed at once. Wilson never changed these opinions. When it became clear that the peace conference could not agree on any policy toward Russia, the British were advised that the United States desired the withdrawal of American forces from northern Russia at the earliest opportunity.[177] This withdrawal could not take place before late spring or early summer, because of ice in the approaches to Archangel. Moreover, the United States could scarcely pull its troops out so abruptly as to cause military embarrassment to the Allied forces with whom it had been associated.

In Siberia, because the French and British during the winter of 1919—before and during the Paris Peace Conference—had succeeded in bringing about the establishment of an anti-Bolshevik authority under Admiral Aleksander V. Kolchak in central and western Siberia, the situation was complicated for Wilson. As the peace conference neared its end, reports arrived in Paris that Kolchak was doing well in his struggle against the Bolsheviks, and heavy pressure was brought to bear on Wilson, both by the British and by his own subordinates, to give support and recognition to Kolchak. Kolchak, however, was supported by independent Cossack leaders who used the chaotic conditions in Siberia as a means of increasing their own wealth and power. The Cossacks also destroyed railway transportation, interrupted telegraphic communications, and terrorized the eastern regions with their irresponsible activities. Japan directly encouraged and supported the Cossacks.[178]

At the same time, the Kolchak authorities were provoked by what they regarded as the "unneutral" policy of American troops. General Graves held to a strict interpretation of his instructions and refused to take action for or against either Kolchak or the Bolsheviks, except insofar as each side might benefit from the protection of the railway sectors and military stores assigned to his command. Kolchak's government at Omsk stated flatly that American troops were accomplishing no useful purpose in Siberia and even accused them of pro-Bolshevik activities. The British and French governments sustained the objections of the Omsk government.[179]

Wilson was obviously deeply troubled about the entire Siberian situation. He presented his problem to the Council of Four in Paris. He pointed out that, although the United States did not believe in Kolchak, the British and French military representatives in Siberia were supporting him. Kolchak, who regarded American soldiers as neutrals, was quite irritated by their presence on the railway. The Cossacks were also antagonistic toward American soldiers. Wilson suspected that the Japanese would be glad to see a collision between the Cossacks and the Americans. In these circumstances, Wilson believed that the United States must either take sides with Kolchak and send a much stronger force to Siberia or else withdraw. If the United States aided Kolchak and increased its forces in Siberia, Japan would increase hers still more. If American troops continued merely to guard the railroad and to maintain a neutral position, collisions would probably occur, which might result in actual war. If American troops were withdrawn, Siberia would be left to the Japanese and Kolchak. Wilson's dilemma was quite evident. Although he favored a neutral policy toward Russia and Siberia, at the same time he did not wish to withdraw American soldiers from Siberia and leave Japan in control. Under heavy pressure, Wilson finally agreed to offer support to Kolchak, although he insisted that democratic pledges be secured from him. Wilson's discussions in the Council of Four, however, clearly indicated that he had no confidence in the entire enterprise, nor in Allied or Japanese motivations for promoting it.[180]

Wilson, above all the man of principle, found himself caught, as had the American nation itself many times since its inception, in a situation in which, despite deep convictions, none of his principles could be absolutely applied. Personally, Wilson had always believed that the proper policy for the Allied and Associated Powers was "to clear out of Russia and leave it to the Russians to fight it out among themselves."[181] American troops continued to remain in Russia for two reasons. For all practical purposes, an American evacuation would have left Japan in virtual control of northern Manchuria and eastern Siberia. Moreover, Britain and France were opposed to withdrawal. Wilson did not wish to jeopardize his program at the peace conference by independent action. Thus, in order to block Japan and to insure support for his League of Nations, Wilson followed a policy which appeared to be totally at variance, not only with the principles which he had enunciated concerning Russia, but also with the principles of his proposed League. As time went on, these differences between what Wilson said and what he did made the American position in Russia even more difficult. Wilson soon found it impossible to keep American troops in Siberia without aiding Kolchak. Whatever may be said concerning America's neutrality in Siberia in 1918, there is little doubt that in 1919 the State Department actively supported and aided Kolchak, particularly after Wilson's illness. But this was Lansing's doing, not Wilson's.

Nevertheless, the Bolsheviks themselves conceded that the United States had been justified in following such a policy when, in 1933, after being shown certain documents concerning American policy, they agreed to drop all claims against the United States for her part in the Siberian intervention.[182] As Cordell Hull pointed out, "These latter documents made clear to Litvinov that American forces had not been in Siberia to wrest territory from Russia, but to insure the withdrawal of the Japanese, who had a far larger force in Siberia with the intent to occupy it permanently."[183]

Wilson's policy toward the Russian Revolution can best be understood within the context of his own moral and ethical principles. He faced the classic dilemma of the moral man seeking to implement principled policies. He had announced to the world in general and to Russia in particular a policy which advocated neutrality and non-interference in Russian affairs, respect for the Russian right of self-determination, and opposition, not only to German imperialism but also, in effect, to Japanese imperialism. He had to devise a Russian policy which would restrain, but not alienate, his associates whose support he required for the realization of his war aims; to endeavor to rescue the Czechs opposed by the Germans and Bolsheviks; to aid the peoples of Russia without interfering in their internal affairs; to prevent his associates from turning the venture into a military endeavor to reestablish an eastern front or an anti-Bolshevik crusade; to preserve the Open Door and protect Russian and Chinese territorial integrity against the ambitions of the Japanese; and to retain the good will of his allies in order to secure the acceptance of his League of Nations. Surely President Wilson faced an impossible task.

NOTES

1. Arthur S. Link, David W. Hirst, John E. Little *et al.*, eds., *The Papers of Woodrow Wilson*, 37 vols. to date (Princeton, N. J., 1966–), vol. 30, pp. 248–55; hereinafter cited as *PWW*; Link, *Woodrow Wilson: Revolution, War, and Peace* (Arlington Heights, Ill., 1979), pp. 4–6.

2. Link, *Woodrow Wilson and the Progressive Era, 1900–1917* (New York, 1954), pp. 107–44.

3. WW to Lindley M. Garrison, Aug. 8, 1914, *PWW*, vol. 30, p. 362; John Reed, interview with WW, *ibid.*, pp. 231–38. See also Wilson's remarks at a press conference, Nov. 24, 1914, and his Jackson Day Address, Jan. 8, 1915, in the Papers of Woodrow Wilson, Library of Congress; hereinafter cited as the Wilson Papers.

4. Draft of address to Congress, c. June 25, 1916, *ibid.*

5. Draft of address to Congress, c. Oct. 31, 1913, *ibid.*; Link, *Woodrow Wilson and the Progressive Era*, pp. 7–8.

6. WW to Lansing, Dec. 5, 1915, with enclosure from Paul S. Reinsch, Dec. 4, 1915, Wilson Papers; Crane to WW, March 28, 1917, the Papers of Charles R. Crane, Columbia University Library; hereinafter cited as the Crane Papers; Thomas La Fargue, *China and the World War* (Stanford, Calif., 1937), pp. 186–87; Link, *Wilson*, 5 vols. to date (Princeton, N. J., 1947–), III, 292–308.

7. The Diary of Breckinridge Long, Jan. 15, 1918, the Papers of Breckinridge Long, Library of Congress; hereinafter cited as the Long Diary and Long Papers.

8. *Literary Digest*, xiv (March 31, 1918), 885–87; Lord Reading to D. Lloyd George, July 12, 1918, the Papers of Sir William Wiseman, Yale University Library; hereinafter cited as the Wiseman Papers.

9. Lansing to D. R. Francis, April 3, 1917, *Foreign Relations, 1918, Russia*, 3 vols. (Washington, 1931–32), I, 17.

10. Francis to Lansing, March 22, 1917, *ibid.*, p. 13.

11. House to WW, March 17, 1917, Wilson Papers; E. David Cronon, ed., *The Cabinet Diaries of Josephus Daniels* (Lincoln, Neb., 1963), pp. 119–20. Crane had written that "with Russia and China directed by their peoples we shall not have to concern ourselves so much about the military autocracies of Germany and Japan." Crane to WW, March 28, 1917, Crane Papers.

12. WW to Lansing, June 1, 1917; William Phillips to Lansing, May 28, 1917; the Russian Minister of Foreign Affairs to the American Chargé d'Affaires, May 8 and 21, 1917, the Records of the State Department, 861.00/362½, National Archives; hereinafter cited as State Department Records.

13. Francis to Lansing, Nov. 29 and Dec. 6, 1917, *Foreign Relations, 1918, Russia*, I, 253, 258.

14. Francis to Lansing, Dec. 6, 1917, *ibid.*, p. 258.

15. The Diary of Edward M. House, Dec. 18, 1917, the Papers of Edward M. House, Yale University Library; hereinafter cited as the House Diary and the House Papers.

16. House to WW, Dec. 1 and 2, 1917, House Papers; Charles Seymour, ed., *The Intimate Papers of Colonel House*, 4 vols. (Boston, 1926–28), III, 285, 278–90.

17. Wilson, after several conferences with Lansing, decided to postpone action until they were more fully in possession of the facts. A long public statement, which Lansing had drafted as a diatribe against the Bolshevik government, was put away with a handwritten note by Lansing: "President did not use it." Lansing, memorandum, Dec. 4, 1917; Lansing typescript of "Memoirs," p. 361, both in the Papers of Robert Lansing, Princeton University Library; hereinafter cited as the Lansing Papers, Princeton.

18. At the beginning of the year, Wilson had instructed his Secretary, Joseph P. Tumulty, to survey with care the editorial comments in the principal journals of the country to determine, if possible, their attitude toward a reformulation of war aims. The results of Tumulty's survey indicated that those newspapers which favored a reply to Trotsky did so almost exclusively on the ground of diplomatic expediency. Papers such as the *Baltimore Sun*, the *New York Sun*, the *Newark Evening News*, and the *Boston Globe* agreed that "the Allies must meet the powerful peace offensive of the Central Powers promptly and courageously with a unified and a high-minded policy." J. P. Tumulty, memorandum for the President, Jan. 3, 1918, Wilson Papers; see also Arno J. Mayer, *Political Origins of the New Diplomacy, 1917–1918* (New Haven, Conn., 1959), p. 352.

19. C. A. Spring Rice to A. J. Balfour, Jan. 4, 1918, the Papers of Arthur James Balfour, Public Record Office; hereinafter cited as the Balfour Papers. Wilson expressed many of these views to Spring Rice, the British Ambas-

sador, so that they might be conveyed to Balfour, although he preferred that they not be transmitted to David Lloyd George, the British Prime Minister. Balfour to Spring Rice, Jan. 5, 1918, Balfour Papers; Cronon, ed., *Cabinet Diaries of Josephus Daniels*, p. 243; the Diary of William Phillips, Dec. 18, 1917, the Papers of William Phillips, Harvard University Library; hereinafter cited as the Phillips Diary; memorandum for the Secretary of State by Basil Miles, Acting Chief of the Russian Division, Jan. 1, 1918, State Department Records, 861.00/935½; WW to Lansing, Jan. 1, 1918, *ibid.*, 861.00/936½. Except for Lansing, key members of the State Department also agreed that it was "urgent" for Wilson and, indeed, for all the Allies to state their case. Phillips Diary, Jan. 2 and 3, 1918; the Diary of Frank L. Polk, Jan. 3, 1918, the Papers of Frank L. Polk, Yale University Library; hereinafter cited as the Polk Diary; memorandum for the Secretary of State by Basil Miles, Jan. 1, 1918, State Department Records, 861.00/935½.

20. Lansing noted that Wilson's address was a reply to Trotsky's communication "because some of the Bolshevik terms are clearly endorsed." In view of the fact that Wilson had refused to make a public declaration of the sort which Lansing had earlier desired and had not disclosed his reasons for doing so, Lansing now saw in the Fourteen Points Address what Wilson's real position was. Lansing typescript of "Memoirs," pp. 361, 365, Lansing Papers, Princeton.

21. My emphasis. Ray Stannard Baker and William E. Dodd, eds., *The Public Papers of Woodrow Wilson*, 6 vols. (New York, 1925–27), v, 159–60.

22. Lansing to Francis, Jan. 9, 1918, State Department Records, 763.72119/1072; *Foreign Relations, 1918, Russia*, I, 426.

23. Francis to Lansing, Jan. 12, 1918, State Department Records, 763.72119/1123; George F. Kennan, *Russia Leaves the War* (Princeton, N. J., 1956), pp. 258–60; Edgar Sisson, *One Hundred Red Days* (New Haven, Conn., 1931), pp. 208–9; George Creel, *How We Advertised America* (New York, 1920), pp. 377, 379; *Literary Digest*, LVI (March 2, 1918), 17; and *Foreign Relations, 1918, Russia*, I, 426.

24. Jacques Sadoul, *Notes sur la révolution Bolchévique* (Paris, 1926), p. 194.

25. Sisson, *One Hundred Red Days*, pp. 206–11; Kennan, *Russia Leaves the War*, p. 262.

26. *Foreign Relations, 1918, Russia*, I, 425.

27. *Foreign Relations, 1918, The World War, Supplement One*, I (Washington, 1933), 19, 34; Mayer, *Political Origins of the New Diplomacy*, p. 376.

28. Francis to WW, Jan. 3, 1918 (sent to Wilson on Jan. 7, 1918), Lansing Papers, Princeton; Arthur Bullard to Maddin Summers, Jan. 11–24, 1918, the Papers of Arthur Bullard, Princeton University Library; hereinafter cited as the Bullard Papers; Polk Diary, Jan. 8, 1918. The press of the country was equally favorable. The Fourteen Points Address was hailed as "one of the great documents in American history." *New York Herald Tribune*, Jan. 9, 1918; Ray Stannard Baker, *Woodrow Wilson: Life and Letters*, 8 vols. (Garden City, N. Y., 1927–39), VII, 456; Mayer, *Political Origins of the New Diplomacy*, pp. 376–81.

29. WW to Lansing, Jan. 1, 1918, State Department Records, 861.00/936½.

30. Lansing to WW, Jan. 10, 1918, with enclosure, Wilson Papers. Wilson did not accept Lansing's proposal. Polk Diary, Jan. 10, 1918; Lansing to Polk, Jan. 21, 1918, Lansing Papers, Princeton.

31. Memorandum for the Secretary of State on Senator Owen's letter concerning Russia, Jan. 29, 1918, Wilson Papers. This was the position also taken by the Secretary of the Treasury, William G. McAdoo. McAdoo to Lansing, Jan. 17, 1918; McAdoo to WW, Jan. 17, 1918; Lansing to Polk, Jan. 21, 1918, *ibid*. Although Wilson recognized that McAdoo's concern was wise and necessary for the protection of the American Treasury, Wilson was nevertheless reluctant to permit this aspect of the Bolshevik program to determine the response of the United States to the revolutionary situation in Russia. WW to Lansing, Jan. 20, 1918, Lansing Papers, Princeton. For Wilson's anger and confrontation with the Allies over a statement issued by the Inter-Allied Council on War Purchases and Finance, which indicated Allied opposition to the recognition of the Bolsheviks because of their repudiation of tsarist debts, see WW to Lansing, Feb. 4, 1918, Wilson Papers; Sharp to Lansing, Feb. 2, 1918, *ibid.*; Lansing to WW, Feb. 16, 1918, State Department Records, 861.51/272; draft telegram to Balfour, Feb. 26, 1918, Wiseman Papers; Balfour to Reading, Feb. 22, 1918, *ibid.*; Lansing to WW, Feb. 22, 1918, State Department Records, 763.72SU/32½.

32. WW to Lansing, Jan. 24, 1918; Owen to WW, Jan. 22, 1918, Wilson Papers; memorandum for the Secretary of State on Senator Owen's letter concerning Russia, Jan. 29, 1918, State Department Records, 861.00/1048½.

33. WW to Lansing, State Department Records, 861.01/14½.

34. Lansing to WW, Feb. 9, 1918, *ibid.*, 861.00/4212A. Wilson approved the altered instructions.

35. Basil Miles, "Policy toward Bolshevik government," Feb. 5, 1918, State Department Records, 861.01/14½.

36. The Chinese Minister was deeply concerned over Japanese actions and told Polk: "Japanese wish to land in Russian Siberia. . . . They were not so much afraid of Russians as they were glad of opportunity to land." Polk Diary, Jan. 9, 1918.

37. Betty Miller Unterberger, *America's Siberian Expedition, 1918–1920* (New York, 1969), pp. 13–14; "The Approaching Crisis," *The New Republic*, xv (June 22, 1918), 217–20; "Russia and Recognition," New York *Nation*, cvi (June 22, 1918), 727–28.

38. WW to Lansing, Jan. 20, 1918, *Foreign Relations, The Lansing Papers*, 2 vols. (Washington, 1939–40), ii, 351; hereinafter cited as *The Lansing Papers*.

39. Polk to WW, Jan. 24, 1918, State Department Records, 861.00/1047A.

40. WW to Polk, Jan. 28, 1918, *ibid.*, 861.00/1047½.

41. *Foreign Relations, 1918, Russia*, ii, 32; *The Lansing Papers*, ii, 352; WW to Lansing, Jan. 28, 1918, State Department Records, 861.00/985½.

42. *Foreign Relations, 1918, Russia*, ii, 42; La Fargue, *China and the World War*, p. 166.

43. WW to Lansing, Feb. 4, 1918, with memorandum prepared by E. T.

Williams, Chief of the Division of Far Eastern Affairs, and to Breckinridge
Long, Feb. 9, 1918, State Department Records, 861.00/1097; Polk Diary, Feb.
4, 1918; Lansing to WW, Feb. 9, 1918, Wilson Papers.

44. War Cabinet 316, Jan. 7, 1918, CAB 23/25, 23/24; War Cabinet 350,
Feb. 20, 1918, CAB 23/5, Public Record Office; Balfour to Wiseman, Jan. 30,
1918, handed to House for presentation to Wilson, enclosure in House to
WW, Jan. 31, 1918, Wilson Papers; William G. Sharp to Lansing, Feb. 20 and
28, 1918, *Foreign Relations, 1918, Russia*, II, 52, 58–59.

45. WW to Lansing, Jan. 20, 1918, *The Lansing Papers*, II, 351; Polk to
Roland S. Morris, Jan. 20, 1918, *Foreign Relations, 1918, Russia*, II, 31.

46. Reinsch to Lansing, "for the President," Feb. 12, 1918, Wilson Papers.

47. Long Diary, Feb. 26, 1918; Reinsch to Lansing, Feb. 21, 1918; Lansing
to Walter Hines Page, Feb. 27, 1918, *Foreign Relations, 1918, Russia*, II, 53–54,
57–58. See also Long to Lansing, Feb. 27, 1918, Lansing Papers, Princeton,
for the State Department's awareness of the secret documents published by
the Bolsheviks regarding Japanese territorial expectations. In the meantime,
Stevens had returned to Harbin to confer with General Dmitrii L. Horvat,
Russian governor and general manager of the Chinese Eastern Railway, about
the best means of utilizing the services of the Russian Railway Service Corps.
Stevens to Lansing, Feb. 1, 1918, *Foreign Relations, 1918, Russia*, III, 218–19.
Charles K. Moser, the American Consul at Harbin, had warned that unless the
United States took over the direction of the railroad, Japan would do so. The
Japanese naturally had watched the Americans very closely. Moser to Lan-
sing, Feb. 3, 1918; Stevens to Lansing, Feb. 10, 1918, *ibid.*, pp. 219–22.

48. Benedict Crowell, Acting Secretary of War, to WW, March 2, 1918,
Wilson Papers; Lansing to WW, Feb. 27, 1918, *The Lansing Papers*, II, 353–55;
House Diary, Feb. 25, 1918; Morris to Lansing, Feb. 27, 1918, *Foreign Rela-
tions, 1918, Russia*, II, 57; Final Report of Tasker H. Bliss, Joint Note #16,
Feb. 18, 1918, State Department Records, 763.72SU/99.

49. Sir William Wiseman to Sir Eric Drummond and A. J. Balfour, Feb. 4,
1918, Wiseman Papers; Polk Diary, March 1, 1918; *The Lansing Papers*, II,
393–94.

50. Draft telegram to the Ambassador in Japan, *The Lansing Papers*, II, 355.
Lord Reading, British Ambassador to the United States, pointed out that the
United States could not join the Allies in requesting Japan to act as their
mandatory in Siberia, since such an arrangement would be in the nature of a
treaty, which would require the approval of the Senate. Moreover, the Wilson
administration was "not prepared to risk the opening of the whole Japanese
question in a public debate at this time." Reading to Foreign Office, March 1,
1918, the Papers of the Foreign Office, 115/2445, pp. 97–98, Public Record
Office; hereinafter cited as the Foreign Office Papers; Kennan, *Russia and the
West under Lenin and Stalin* (Boston, 1960), p. 99.

51. House to WW, March 3, 1918, Wilson Papers; the Diary of Gordon
Auchincloss, March 3, 1918, the Papers of Gordon Auchincloss, Yale Univer-
sity Library; hereinafter cited as the Auchincloss Diary; House to Balfour,
March 4, 1918, Wiseman Papers; see also Seymour, ed., *Intimate Papers*, III,

392–93, and Bullitt to Polk, March 2, 1918, State Department Records, 861.00/1290½; N. Gordon Levin, Jr., *Woodrow Wilson and World Politics* (New York, 1968), p. 90.

52. Bullitt to Polk, March 2, 1918, State Department Records, 861.00/1290½, and in the Wilson Papers. For a similar view also sent to Wilson, see the *Manchester Guardian*, March 1, 1918.

53. Auchincloss Diary, March 3, 1918; House to WW, March 3, 1918, House Papers; Polk to Morris, March 5, 1918, *Foreign Relations, 1918, Russia*, II, 67; see also Long Diary, Feb. 25, 1918; Cronon, *Cabinet Diaries of Josephus Daniels*, p. 285; Anne W. Lane and Louise H. Wall, eds., *Letters of Franklin K. Lane* (Boston, 1922), pp. 266–67.

54. Reading to Foreign Office, March 5, 1918, Wiseman Papers; Polk Diary, March 6, 1918. Wilson was unmoved by Reading's argument that, if the Allies invited Japan to act as their mandatory while the United States refused to assent, the Germans would misrepresent Allied aims as not being disinterested because "otherwise America would have joined." Wiseman to Drummond, March 6, 1918, Wiseman Papers. Balfour continued to emphasize the argument that Germany hoped that the question of Japanese intervention would "cause friction between America and her co-belligerents." Balfour to Wiseman, March 17, 1918, *ibid.*, also in Balfour Papers.

55. Notes for a cable from the Ambassador to the Foreign Office, March 9, 1918, Wiseman Papers. For the distrust of Japanese motives and the fear of a German-Japanese coalition, see Long Diary, Feb. 25, 1918.

56. WW to J. P. Tumulty, Feb. 23, 1918; memorandum on Russia by Simon Strunsky, Wilson Papers.

57. House Diary, March 11, 1918; Polk to Summers, March 11, 1918, *Foreign Relations, 1918, Russia*, I, 395–96. Polk was concerned about the desirability of sending the address to the meeting of the Soviets and had suggested a few changes which Wilson accepted. Polk to WW, March 9, 1918, enclosing draft declaration, Lansing Papers, Princeton; Polk Diary, March 11, 1918. Jean Jules Jusserand, the French Ambassador, criticized the message. Polk Diary, March 12, 1918. For the State Department's revision of Wilson's initial draft, see Eugene P. Trani, "Woodrow Wilson and the Decision to Intervene in Russia: A Reconsideration," *Journal of Modern History*, XLVIII (Sept. 1976), 451. While House had enthusiastically endorsed Wilson's initiative, Lansing believed that the message should have been followed by "a definite announcement of policy toward Bolshevism," but he found Wilson unwilling "to make such a declaration." House Diary, March 11, 1918; typescript of "War Memoirs," p. 361, Lansing Papers, Princeton.

58. WW to Polk, March 10, 1918; Polk to WW, March 9, 1918, enclosing memorandum of Imperial Japanese Embassy, handed to Long, March 7, 1918, Lansing Papers, Princeton; Polk Diary, March 11 and 12, 1918. Japan had requested this statement so as to determine its future policy toward Russia. See also Polk to W. H. Page, March 12, 1918, *Foreign Relations, 1918, Russia*, I, 397. All of the allies were so informed. Polk Diary, March 11 and 12, 1918.

59. Wiseman to Drummond, March 14, 1918; Reading to Balfour, March 27, 1918, Wiseman Papers. Francis had already made clear to Wilson the Soviet fears of Japanese intervention without Soviet *de facto* approval. Francis to Lansing, March 12, 1918, *Foreign Relations, 1918, Russia*, I, 396.

60. Japanese Foreign Office to Balfour, March 27, 1918, Foreign Office Papers, 115/2445, pp. 219–20; Reading to Balfour, March 27, 1918, Wiseman Papers; Balfour to House, April 3, 1918, Wiseman Papers, original in Balfour Papers.

61. Lansing to WW, March 25, 1918, enclosing Ruggles to Warcolstaf, Petrograd, March 12, 1918, Lansing Papers, Princeton; British Embassy to Department of State, March 4, 1918, *Foreign Relations, 1918, Russia*, II, 469.

62. WW to Lansing, April 4, 1918, Wilson Papers. For the confusion and misleading information surrounding these events, see Kennan, *The Decision to Intervene* (Princeton, N. J., 1958), pp. 46–49; and Richard H. Ullman, *Intervention and the War* (Princeton, N. J., 1961), pp. 113–19.

63. Lansing to WW, March 24, 1918, *The Lansing Papers*, II, 357–58; WW to Lansing, March 22, 1918, State Department Records, 861.00/1433½, enclosing Lansing to WW, March 21, 1918, *ibid.*, 861.00/1432½, with enclosures; Lansing to WW, March 24, 1918, *ibid.*, 861.00/1433½A. Wilson's views were solidified by a report from Admiral Austin M. Knight, Commander of the Asiatic Fleet, which he found both "interesting and sane." Wiseman to Drummond, March 21, 1918, enclosing cable from Admiral Knight to Navy Department, March 18, 1918, Wiseman Papers. Wilson had not changed his mind by April 4, when Lansing sent him additional memoranda. Wilson found nothing in them "at all persuasive." WW to Lansing, April 4, 1918, State Department Records, 861.00/1439½, enclosing documents 1435½, 1436½, 1437½, and 1438½.

64. Reading to Balfour, April 7, 1918, Foreign Office Papers, 115/2445, p. 261.

65. Balfour to Reading, April 18, 1918, the Papers of Lord Reading, Public Record Office; hereinafter cited as the Reading Papers.

66. Paraphrase of a telegram from R. H. Bruce Lockhart, head of the Special Mission to the Bolshevik government, March 28, 1918, handed by Lord Reading to Department of State, April 2, 1918, State Department Records, 861.00/1438½; Francis to Lansing, April 4, 1918, *Foreign Relations, 1918, Russia*, I, 493; James Bunyan, *Intervention, Civil War, and Communism in Russia* (Baltimore, 1936), p. 62; Ullman, *Intervention and the War*, p. 121; Eduard Beneš, *My War Memoirs* (London, 1928), pp. 357–58, 365–66.

67. Balfour to Reading, April 23, 1918, Reading Papers, original handwritten note in Balfour Papers; see also Ullman, *Intervention and the War*, pp. 160–61.

68. Reading to Balfour, April 25, 1918, Foreign Office Papers, 115/2446, pp. 8–11. Lansing, too, thought that Trotsky's attitude made a considerable difference and seemed to be more favorably inclined toward cooperation than Reading had yet seen him.

69. Moser to Lansing, April 4, 1918; Reinsch to Lansing, April 8, 1918, for

the President; Reinsch to Lansing, April 25, 1918, Wilson Papers.

70. Morris to Lansing, Jan. 10 and 22, 1918; Lansing to WW, April 25, 1918, *ibid.*

71. British Embassy to Foreign Office, May 1, 1918, Foreign Office Papers, 115/2445, pp. 412–15; Lansing to WW, April 29, 1918, State Department Records, 861.00/1674A; Reading to Balfour, May 2, 1918, Foreign Office Papers, 115/2445, p. 426.

72. Reading to Lansing, May 13, 1918, Foreign Office Papers, 115/2446, pp. 55–57; Reading to Lansing, May 17, 1918, and attached handwritten note, *ibid.*, 115/2446, p. 58. The Department had received only a brief note on Tanaka's statement through the American military attaché. *Ibid.*, p. 59.

73. Lansing to WW, May 11, 1918, State Department Records, 861.00/1795A; Reading to Foreign Office, May 12, 1918, Foreign Office Papers, 115/2446, pp. 48–52; Lansing to WW, May 16, 1918, *The Lansing Papers*, II, 360–61; Reading to Foreign Office, May 23, 1918, Foreign Office Papers, 115/2446, pp. 338–40; Balfour to Reading, June 11, 1918, Wiseman Papers. Major General Frederick C. Poole, the British commander of the North Russian expedition, had already been designated for duty at those ports. He was to have available three warships and their crews, a few hundred French, 1,500 Serbian, and 1,200 British troops. The British Foreign Office had not yet abandoned the hope that the initial force might be strengthened considerably by the Czecho-Slovak troops if they succeeded in reaching the northern ports. Lord Milner, British Secretary of State for War, to Reading, June 11, 1918, Newton D. Baker Papers, Library of Congress; hereinafter cited as the Baker Papers.

74. WW to Lansing, May 20, 1918, *The Lansing Papers*, II, 361; Balfour to Reading, June 11, 1918, Wiseman Papers; memorandum of the Secretary of State, June 3, 1918, *Foreign Relations, 1918, Russia*, II, 484–85; Reading to Lansing, May 29, 1918, *ibid.*, p. 476.

75. Lansing to WW, May 10, 1918; WW to Lansing, May 20, 1918; memorandum for Secretary of State by Basil Miles, May 21, 1918, handed to Wilson by Lansing, May 21, 1918, Wilson Papers.

76. Stevens to Lansing, April 10 and 29, 1918, *Foreign Relations, 1918, Russia*, III, 229, 231.

77. Lansing to Francis, May 29, 1918, State Department Records, 861.00/2079½.

78. Joint Note #31, Supreme War Council, Military Representatives, June 3, 1918, *ibid.*, 861.00/6731; Bliss to Baker, June 19 and 22, 1918, Baker Papers; Bliss, Final Report, 126–127, State Department Records, 763.72SU/99; Baker to WW, June 20, 1918, Baker Papers; Colville A. Barclay, Counselor of the British Embassy at Washington, to D. Lloyd George and Lord Milner, June 22, 1918, Balfour Papers; the Diary of Robert Lansing, June 22, 1918, the Papers of Robert Lansing, Library of Congress; hereinafter cited as Lansing Diary and Lansing Papers, LC.

79. Kennan, *The Decision to Intervene*, pp. 149–53.

80. Emerson to Francis, June 21, 1918, Emerson Report, State Department

Records, 861.77/541, p. 55. For a description of the efforts of both Consul General Ernest L. Harris at Irkutsk and Emerson to negotiate the conflict, see Unterberger, "The United States and the Czech-Bolshevik Conflict, 1918," *Proceedings of Conference on War and Diplomacy* (Charleston, S. C., 1976), pp. 145–53, and Kennan, *The Decision to Intervene*, pp. 282–91.

81. C. E. Callwell, *Field-Marshal Sir Henry Wilson: His Life and Diaries*, 2 vols. (London, 1927), II, 109; Seymour, ed., *Intimate Papers*, III, 412; Joseph Noulens, *Mon ambassade en Russie soviétique, 1917–1919*, 2 vols. (Paris, 1933), II, 114; Baker, *Woodrow Wilson*, VIII, 215, 233; Tom Bridges, British military representative at Washington, to Reading, June 18, 1918, Reading Papers; Morris to Lansing, June 22, 1918, *Foreign Relations, 1918, Russia*, II, 219.

82. Long reported that "a general sentiment of persons all over the Northern Hemisphere seemed setting towards Allied intervention." Long Diary, May 31, 1918; see also Unterberger, *America's Siberian Expedition*, pp. 48–49, 60.

83. Lansing Diary, June 11, 1918; Morris, Tokyo, to Lansing, June 13, 1918, State Department Records, 861.00/1992.

84. Sir John Jordan, British Minister at Peking, to the Foreign Office, June 13, 1918, Foreign Office Papers, 371, W 38, file 106087/50420; memorandum of a conversation with Mr. Anderson by E. T. Williams, June 13, 1918, State Department Records, 861.00/2082; Reinsch to Department of State, June 13, 1918, *ibid.*, 861.00/2014; Lansing Diary, June 14, 1918; Moser to Department of State, June 14, 1918, *Foreign Relations, 1918, Russia*, II, 208–209; Reinsch to Lansing, June 26, 1918, *ibid.*, pp. 231–32.

85. Wiseman to Drummond, June 14, 1918, Wiseman Papers; Reading to Balfour, June 16, 1918, Balfour Papers. Wilson was confirmed in his fears when intelligence revealed that Trotsky's recent Russian mobilization had been dictated by his fear of Japanese intervention and that he was collaborating with Germany to offset such an event. Ira Morris, Minister in Stockholm, to Lansing, June 17, 1918, State Department Records, 861.00/2062.

86. *New York Times*, May 27, 1918; Masaryk to Crane, April 10, 1918, State Department Records, 861.00/2721; Richard Crane to WW, May 7, 1918, with Masaryk enclosure, Wilson Papers; White House Appointment Book, June 19, 1918; Chicago *Denní Hlasatel*, June 21, 1918; Baker, *Woodrow Wilson*, VIII, 218; Thomas G. Masaryk, *The Making of a State: Memories and Observations* (New York, 1927), pp. 299–300.

87. Bliss to Baker, June 18, 1918, Wilson Papers; Baker to WW, June 19, 1918, Baker Papers; WW to Baker, June 19, 1918, *ibid.*; March to Baker, June 24, 1918, Wilson Papers; Bliss to March, June 24, 1918, the Papers of Tasker H. Bliss, Library of Congress; hereinafter cited as the Bliss Papers; March to WW, June 24, 1918, in Peyton C. March, *Nation at War* (New York, 1932), pp. 116–20; Frederick Palmer, *Newton D. Baker: America at War*, 2 vols. (New York, 1931), II, 321. Wilson had already indicated earlier his "great interest" in similar statements presented by two American military officers who had had extensive experience in Russia. WW to Benedict Crowell, March 6, 1918, responding to enclosures of General W. V. Judson, chief of the American Mili-

tary Mission at Petrograd, to Acting Chief of Staff, March 4, 1918; memorandum by Lieutenant Colonel Sherman Miles, General Staff, to General Judson, March 4, 1918, all in Wilson Papers.

88. Flagship *Brooklyn* to Secretary of the Navy, June 21, 1918, State Department Records, 861.00/2165½; John K. Caldwell, American Consul at Vladivostok, to Lansing, June 20, 1918, *ibid.*, 861.00/2083; Caldwell to Lansing, June 25, 1918, *Foreign Relations, 1918, Russia*, II, 226–27; Knight to the Secretary of the Navy, June 26, 1918, *ibid.*, p. 235.

89. David R. Woodward, "The British Government and Japanese Intervention in Russia during World War I," *Journal of Modern History*, XLVI (Dec. 1974), 680–81.

90. Balfour to Reading, June 21, 1918, Foreign Office Papers, 371/3324, No. 110145, p. 16.

91. Lansing to WW, June 23, 1918, *The Lansing Papers*, II, 364; paraphrase of a telegram from Lockhart to the Foreign Office, June 20, 1918, State Department Records, 861.00/2164½.

92. Memorandum of the Secretary of State of a conference at the White House in reference to the Siberian situation, July 6, 1918, *Foreign Relations, 1918, Russia*, II, 262–63; Baker, *Woodrow Wilson*, VIII, 256. The American proposals were issued to the Allied governments in an *aide-mémoire* on July 17, 1918. *Foreign Relations, 1918, Russia*, II, 287–90.

93. Lansing to Morris, July 6, 1918, *ibid.*, p. 263.

94. Lansing to WW, July 9, 1918, *ibid.*, pp. 269–70; Phillips Diary, July 9, 1918; Auchincloss Diary, July 9, 1918; Reading to Lloyd George and Balfour, July 9, 1918; Reading to Lloyd George and Balfour, July 10, 1918, Wiseman Papers; *Denní Hlasatel*, July 11, 1918. Wilson's position was to some extent offset by the comments of Lansing to Lord Reading who reported: "In conversation Lansing said this expedition may well be the means eventually of creating a Russian Front." Reading to Lloyd George and Balfour, July 10, 1918, Wiseman Papers. In any case, the British immediately proceeded to act on their own with a view to realizing the plans which they had conceived. Foreign Office to British Embassy in Washington, July 10, 1918, Wiseman Papers; Sir Arthur C. Murray to Wiseman, July 9, 1918, *ibid.*; Woodward, "The British Government and Japanese Intervention in Russia during World War I," pp. 676–82. Yet to Wiseman it seemed apparent that Wilson believed that the interventionists were "reactionaries under another name." Wiseman to Reading, July 19, 1918, Wiseman Papers.

95. WW to Long, July 26, 1918, Long Papers; Auchincloss Diary, July 24 and 25, 1918; WW to Josephus Daniels, Aug. 1, 1918, Wilson Papers; Seymour, ed., *Intimate Papers*, III, 415; *Foreign Relations, 1918, Russia*, II, 297–98, 301–302, 304–305, 314; Unterberger, *America's Siberian Expedition*, pp. 82–86.

96. Polk to Morris, July 9, 1918, *Foreign Relations, 1918, Russia*, II, 297; La Fargue, *China and the World War*, p. 169.

97. Polk Diary, July 16 and Aug. 3, 1918; *Foreign Relations, 1918, Russia*, II, 292, 324–26.

98. Auchincloss Diary, July 25, 1918; Polk to Morris, July 27, 1918, *Foreign*

Relations, 1918, Russia, II, 306–307; Baker, *Woodrow Wilson*, VIII, 297–98. Wilson told Lansing that the Japanese government was trying to alter the whole plan in a way "in which we cannot consent and for the time being, at any rate, the whole matter is in suspense." *Ibid.*, pp. 310–11.

99. Reading to Lloyd George, July 12, 1918, Wiseman Papers.

100. Masaryk to Polk, Aug. 5, 1918, Polk Papers; Polk to Masaryk, Aug. 6, 1918, *ibid.*; Masaryk to WW, Aug. 6, 1918, Wilson Papers; Baker, *Woodrow Wilson*, VIII, 322–23.

101. WW to Crane, July 29, 1918, Wilson Papers.

102. Polk to Morris, Aug. 3, 1918, *Foreign Relations, 1918, Russia*, II, 328–29; Baker, *Woodrow Wilson*, VIII, 286.

103. Leading editorial from first number of weekly bulletin of American Committee on Public Information, Vladivostok, Bullard Papers.

104. Polk Diary, Aug. 1 and 8, 1918; Reading to Polk, July 29, 1918, Foreign Office Papers, 115/2448, pp. 322–23.

105. Lansing to Polk, Aug. 3, 1918, Lansing Papers, LC.

106. *Foreign Relations, 1918, Russia*, II, 341–42; *The Lansing Papers*, II, 376–77; WW to Lansing, Aug. 14, 1918, State Department Records, 861.00/2501; Balfour to Barclay, Aug. 10, 1918, Wiseman Papers; *Foreign Relations, 1918, Russia*, II, 341–42; Barclay to Foreign Office, Aug. 12, 1918, Foreign Office Papers, 371/3324, No. 139748, pp. 435–36. Barclay to Foreign Office, Aug. 13, 1918, *ibid.*, 371/3324, No. 140117, p. 449; and Barclay to Foreign Office, Aug. 14, 1918, *ibid.*, 371/3324, No. 141371, pp. 453–54. The British were worried about putting too much pressure on Wilson. They feared that, since he had consented to American participation with such reluctance, he might, if pressed too hard, withdraw his cooperation altogether. Therefore, they thought that it perhaps might be wiser in the future to let the Japanese deal directly with the Americans concerning the expansion of the expedition to Siberia. Foreign Office to Reading, Aug. 10, 1918, Wiseman Papers.

107. Phillips Diary, Aug. 12, 1918.

108. Lansing Diary, Aug. 14, 1918; Phillips Diary, Aug. 14, 1918.

109. WW to Lansing, Aug. 14, 1918, State Department Records, 861.00/2501; Lansing to Barclay, Aug. 14, 1918, *Foreign Relations, 1918, Russia*, II, 344–45; Unterberger, *America's Siberian Expedition*, pp. 91–92. Reading also sought to appeal to Wilson through Colonel House. Reading to Wiseman, Aug. 20, 1918, Wiseman Papers. House, now woefully out of touch with Wilson's policy, suggested that, since the Japanese had the military direction of the expedition, they were the "right people to press U.S.G. to increase the expedition to whatever size they consider necessary in order to enable the Czecho-Slovaks to retire in safety." Wiseman to Reading, Aug. 22, 1918, Wiseman Papers.

110. Knight to Secretary of the Navy, Aug. 15, 1918, *The Lansing Papers*, II, 377–78.

111. Opnav to Commander in Chief, Asiatic Fleet, Aug. 17, 1918, WA6, Naval Records Collection, National Archives; hereinafter cited as NRC. Wilson later gave exactly the same reasons for his decision to C. P. Scott, editor of

the *Manchester Guardian*. He had "approved what he regarded as the limited object of the Vladivostok expedition, namely to rescue the Czecho-Slovaks." In addition, he had agreed "to assist the inhabitants of the area by supplying them with necessaries and by sending small detachments of troops to escort these supplies and see that they were properly distributed." The Japanese, he said, had agreed to this limited objective, but had then sent 60,000 troops in violation of the agreement. *The Political Diaries of C. P. Scott, 1911–1928*, Trevor Wilson, ed. (London, 1970), p. 365.

112. "Major General William S. Graves," *United States Army Recruiting News*; tribute by Frank H. King, Associated Press correspondent with the A. E. F. Siberia, both in the Papers of William S. Graves, United States Military Academy; Graves, *America's Siberian Adventure, 1918–1920* (New York, 1931), pp. 2–4.

113. *Foreign Relations, 1918, Russia*, ii, 349–50, 354–55.

114. WW to Lansing, Sept. 2, 1918, Long Papers; *Foreign Relations, 1918, Russia*, ii, 339–41. Officials in the State Department differed in their response to the Anglo-French request. Both Phillips and Long favored an affirmative response. Phillips to Lansing, Aug. 22, 1918, State Department Records, 861.00/2659; Long to Lansing, Aug. 17, 1918, *ibid.*, 861.00/2601½. Ambassador Morris in Tokyo and Consul Caldwell at Vladivostok agreed. *Foreign Relations, 1918, Russia*, iii, 139–40; *ibid.*, ii, 360, 364; Lansing to WW, Aug. 22, 1918, *The Lansing Papers*, ii, 378. See also Wilson's negative response to the proposal for the creation of an "Allied Military Council at Vladivostok." WW to Lansing, Sept. 17, 1918, State Department Records, 861.00/2672½.

115. Lansing to WW, Aug. 22, 1918; WW to Lansing, Aug. 23, 1918, *The Lansing Papers*, ii, 378–79; Lansing to Jusserand, Aug. 31, 1918, *Foreign Relations, 1918, Russia*, ii, 362. Apparently, Lansing indicated Wilson's irritation, for he delivered the message "somewhat sharply" to Barclay who, in turn, reported this to the Foreign Office. Barclay to Foreign Office, Sept. 4, 1918, Foreign Office Papers, 115/2449, p. 260.

116. Wiseman to Reading, Aug. 23, 1918, Wiseman Papers.

117. Notes of an interview with the President at the White House, Oct. 16, 1918, the Papers of Sir Eric Geddes, Public Record Office, Add. MSS., 116/1809; also reproduced in Wilton B. Fowler, *British-American Relations, 1917–1918: The Role of Sir William Wiseman* (Princeton, N. J., 1969), pp. 283–90.

118. Barclay to Foreign Office, Sept. 9, 1918, Foreign Office Papers, 115/2449, p. 352; also in Wiseman Papers.

119. WW to Lansing, Sept. 5, 1918, State Department Records, 861.00/1381. John Van A. MacMurray, Chargé in China, to the Secretary of State, Aug. 30, 1918, *ibid.*, 861.00/2617; also in Wilson Papers. See also WW to Lansing, Sept. 17, 1918, State Department Records, 861.00/3009.

120. Bliss to March, Sept. 7, 1918, RG 120, War Records Collection, National Archives; hereinafter cited as WRC; WW to March, Sept. 18, 1918, RG 120, Supreme War Council, WRC. March also sent a copy of the instructions given by the British War Office to General Poole.

121. Baker to WW, Sept. 15, 1918, Baker Papers.

122. WW to Lansing, Sept. n.d., 1918, Long Papers.

123. See "Extracts from Correspondence Files of Allied G.H.Q., Archangel," the Papers of George E. Stewart, United States Military Academy; Francis to Lansing, Aug. 27, 1918, *Foreign Relations, 1918, Russia*, II, 515–16.

124. Jules Legras, ed., "Fragments de mon Journal Siberien," *Le Monde Slave*, II (Dec. 1924), 2–5; British Embassy to Foreign Office, Sept. 20, 1918, Foreign Office Papers, 371/3324, No. 160450, p. 572A; British Embassy to Foreign Office, Sept. 20, 1918, *ibid.*, 115/2450, p. 58.

125. Morris to Lansing, Sept. 23, 1918, *Foreign Relations, 1918, Russia*, II, 387–90.

126. Masaryk to Lansing, Sept. 23, 1918, enclosed in Lansing to WW, Sept. 24, 1918, Wilson Papers; Lansing to WW, Sept. 24, 1918, *The Lansing Papers*, II, 386–87.

127. WW to Lansing, Sept. 17, 1918, State Department Records, 861.00/3009.

128. WW to Lansing, Sept. n.d., 1918, Long Papers; Lansing to Barclay, Sept. 27, 1918, Foreign Office Papers, 115/2450, pp. 141–43, 147, enclosing a memorandum; WW to Lansing, Sept. 18, 1918, State Department Records, 861.00/3010; Phillips Diary, Sept. 20, 1918; Lansing Diary, Sept. 20, 1918; Lansing to Morris, Sept. 26, 1918, *Foreign Relations, 1918, Russia*, II, 392–94.

129. The Department found it difficult to draft a memorandum, since its chief officers did not agree with Wilson's position and, as they pointed out, his statement in the *aide-mémoire* of July 17 had been modified by the Department to indicate that the American position was not intended as a criticism "of any independent action which the other governments might care to take." Long Diary, Sept. 20, 1918; Phillips Diary, Sept. 20, 1918; Lansing Diary, Sept. 20, 1918. For the exchanges and negotiations surrounding the drafting of this memorandum, see Lansing to WW, Sept. 2, 1918, State Department Records, 861.00/2783, partially reproduced in Baker, *Woodrow Wilson*, VIII, 419; Lansing Diary, Sept. 21, 1918; Long Diary, Sept. 21, 1918; Lansing to WW, Sept. 21, 1918, State Department Records, 861.00/3010; WW to Lansing, Sept. 23, 1918, *ibid.*, 861.00/3013. For the final note, see *Foreign Relations, 1918, Russia*, II, 394.

130. Wiseman to Reading and Drummond, Sept. 21, 1918, Reading Papers. Wilson had agreed that Lansing was "quite right" about the manner in which the American position should be stated. He agreed that they could "merely . . . urge the advisability" of what was, "in our judgment, a wise and necessary course." WW to Lansing, Sept. 23, 1918, State Department Records, 861.00/3013.

131. Barclay to Lansing, Oct. 3, 1918, *Foreign Relations, 1918, Russia*, II, 403–404. For the controversy surrounding the British response to Wilson's memorandum, see Wiseman to Reading, Oct. 2, 1918, Wiseman Papers; War Cabinet, 481, Oct. 2, 1918, CAB 23/8, Public Record Office.

132. CAB 23/7; War Cabinet 475/32; meeting held Sept. 23, 1918; Fowler, *British-American Relations*, p. 195.

133. Polk Diary, Aug. 10, 1918; *Foreign Relations, 1918, Russia*, II, 330–31,

334, 335, 343–46, 348–49, 378; Tatsuji Takeuchi, *War and Diplomacy in the Japanese Empire* (New York, 1935), p. 209; see also the *New York Times*, Aug. 18, 1918. For the Japanese version of the dangers from Bolsheviks and former prisoners of war, see Ishii to Lansing, Aug. 17, 1918, State Department Records, 861.00/2602½.

134. Lansing to Morris, Sept. 6, 1918, *Foreign Relations, 1918, Russia*, III, 242–43; V. K. Wellington Koo, Chinese Minister at Washington, to Lansing, Sept. 13, 1918, *ibid.*, II, 378; Lansing Diary, Aug. 21, 1918; Caldwell to Lansing, Aug. 26, 1918, *ibid.*, III, 239. For a report of Koo's conversation with Long, see *ibid.*, II, 353.

135. Polk to Moser, Aug. 10, 1918, *Foreign Relations, 1918, Russia*, III, 237.

136. Basil Miles to Lansing, Sept. 23, 1918, State Department Records, 861.00/2763½.

137. Willing Spencer, Chargé in Japan, to Lansing, Sept. 18, 1918, *Foreign Relations, 1918, Russia*, III, 257–58; Morris to Lansing, Sept. 18, 1918, *ibid.*, III, 258–59; MacMurray to Lansing, Sept. 19, 1918, *ibid.*, III, 259–60; Morris to Lansing, Sept. 20, 1918, *ibid.*, III, 262.

138. Long Diary, Sept. 19, 1918; memorandum of conversation with Dr. Masaryk, Sept. 23, 1918, Long Papers; Long Diary, Sept. 23, 1918; Long to American Legation at Peking, Sept. 23, 1918, Long Papers.

139. WW to Lansing, Sept. n.d., 1918, Long Papers; Lansing to Morris, Sept. 26, 1918, *Foreign Relations, 1918, Russia*, II, 392–94; Lansing to Barclay, Sept. 27, 1918, Foreign Office Papers, 115/2450, pp. 141, 143–47; Lansing to MacMurray, Sept. 26, 1918, State Department Records, 861.00/2791a; MacMurray to Lansing, Sept. 28, 1918, *Foreign Relations, 1918, Russia*, II, 396.

140. Lansing to MacMurray, Sept. 26, 1918, State Department Records, 861.00/2791a; MacMurray to Lansing, Sept. 28, 1918, *Foreign Relations, 1918, Russia*, II, 396.

141. Unterberger, *America's Siberian Expedition*, p. 110; the Diary of Cary T. Grayson, Dec. 9, 1918, in possession of Cary T. Grayson, Jr.; hereinafter cited as Grayson Diary.

142. Knight to Daniels, Nov. 4, 1918, WA 6, Russian situation, NRC; Ingersoll to F. Leonard, Nov. 17, 1921, State Department Records, 861A.00/131; memorandum on the Japanese role in the intervention in Siberia, Oct. 15, 1918, Wiseman Papers. The Japanese occupation of eastern Siberia was quite thorough and was aptly described as "a commercial invasion under military convoy."

143. Polk Diary, Dec. 23, 1918; *Foreign Relations, 1919, Russia* (Washington, 1937), p. 239.

144. *Foreign Relations, 1919, Russia*, pp. 246–48.

145. *Ibid.*, pp. 244, 250–51.

146. *Ibid.*, p. 494; memorandum of John F. Stevens, Railway Service Corps Papers, Hoover Institution on War, Revolution, and Peace; notes of a meeting held at President Wilson's house in the Place des États Unis, Paris, May 9, 1919, *Foreign Relations, 1919, Russia*, pp. 345–47.

147. Wiseman, "Notes of an Interview with the President at the White House," Oct. 16, 1918, Wiseman Papers, in Fowler, *British-American Relations*,

p. 196; Baker to WW, Nov. 27, 1918, Baker Papers; Palmer, *Baker*, II, 395; *Foreign Relations, 1918, Russia*, II, 433–37, 440–41. Moreover, the British saw no reason "for criticizing from their point of view" the mere presence of considerable bodies of Japanese troops in Russian territory. *Ibid.*, pp. 456–57; Bullard to House, Oct. 21, 1918, House Papers.

148. WW to Granville MacFarland, Nov. 27, 1918, Wilson Papers.

149. Draft minutes of a meeting held at 10 Downing Street, Dec. 30, 1918, at 3:30 p.m., discussing President Wilson's visit, Wiseman Papers; report of interview with President Wilson, Dec. 29, 1918, Wilson, *Political Diaries of C. P. Scott*, p. 365; John M. Thompson, *Russia, Bolshevism, and the Versailles Peace* (Princeton, N. J., 1966), pp. 90–91.

150. Thompson, *Russia, Bolshevism, and the Versailles Peace*, p. 92; House Diary, Jan. 1, 1919; *Foreign Relations, 1919, Russia*, p. 4.

151. Supreme War Council, Ninth Session, Jan. 12, 1919, Records of the Supreme War Council, WRC.

152. Baker, *Woodrow Wilson and World Settlement*, 3 vols. (New York, 1922), I, 166.

153. *Foreign Relations, 1918, Russia*, II, 839–42, 851–52, 856–61; Arthur Walworth, *America's Moment: 1918* (New York, 1977), p. 202.

154. Paul Mantoux, *Les Délibérations du Conseil des Quatre*, 2 vols. (Paris, 1955), I, 55, as quoted in Arthur S. Link, *Wilson the Diplomatist* (Baltimore, 1957), pp. 117–18.

155. WW to Lansing, Jan. 10, 1919, Wilson Papers.

156. Barclay to Polk, Jan. 3, 1919, *Foreign Relations, 1919, Russia*, pp. 2–3; see also pp. 10–14.

157. Buckler to Lansing, Jan. 18, 1919, *Foreign Relations, 1919, Russia*, p. 15; David Lloyd George, *Memoirs of the Peace Conference*, 2 vols. (New Haven, Conn., 1939), I, 225.

158. *Foreign Relations, 1919, Russia*, pp. 18–25. In deference to Clemenceau, Wilson suggested that the British proposal be modified to permit the Russian representatives to meet at some other place besides Paris.

159. *Ibid.*, p. 31; Callwell, *Sir Henry Wilson*, II, 167; Lady Algernon Gordon Lennox, ed., *Diary of Lord Bertie of Thame, 1914–1918*, 2 vols. (London, 1924), II, 314–15. For the opposition of certain key Foreign Service officers such as Francis, Poole, and Polk, see *Foreign Relations, 1919, Russia*, pp. 27–30, 32, 37–39, 42, 44–46, 54–55; and the *New York Times*, Jan. 24 and 25, 1919.

160. Russian Embassy in France to Secretary General of the Paris Peace Conference, Feb. 12, 1919, *Foreign Relations, 1919, Russia*, pp. 53–54; *New York Times*, Feb. 20, 1919. For replies of other Russian groups, see C. K. Cumming and W. W. Pettit, eds., *Russian-American Relations, March 1917–March 1920, Documents and Papers* (New York, 1920), pp. 298–306.

161. George V. Chicherin, Acting Soviet Commissar for Foreign Affairs, to the principal Allied and Associated governments, Feb. 4, 1919, *Foreign Relations, 1919, Russia*, pp. 39–42.

162. Winston S. Churchill, *The Aftermath* (New York, 1929), pp. 173–74.

163. Minutes of the Fourteenth Session of the Supreme War Council held in M. Pichon's Room at the Quai d'Orsay, Paris, Feb. 14, 1919, *Foreign Rela-*

tions, 1919, Russia, pp. 57–59; Callwell, *Sir Henry Wilson*, ii, 170.

164. Churchill, *The Aftermath*, p. 174.

165. Lansing to Polk, Feb. 17, 1919, *Foreign Relations, 1919, Russia*, pp. 68–69; Lloyd George, *Memoirs of the Peace Conference*, i, 242. The American representatives opposed the adoption of this resolution.

166. WW to Commission to Negotiate Peace, Feb. 19, 1919, *Foreign Relations, 1919, Russia*, pp. 71–72.

167. Seymour, ed., *Intimate Papers*, iv, 348. Lloyd George also protested against Churchill's project. Lloyd George, *Memoirs of the Peace Conference*, i, 243–44.

168. Commission to Negotiate Peace to Polk, Feb. 23, 1919, *Foreign Relations, 1919, Russia*, p. 73; Seymour, ed., *Intimate Papers*, iv, 348; Bliss to House, Feb. 17, 1919, Bliss Papers, not sent.

169. William C. Bullitt, *Bullitt Mission to Russia: Testimony before the Committee on Foreign Relations, United States Senate* (Washington, 1919), p. 4; Lincoln Steffens, *Autobiography* (New York, 1931), pp. 790–91; Thompson, *Russia, Bolshevism, and the Versailles Peace*, pp. 151–52; Levin, *Woodrow Wilson and World Politics*, p. 213.

170. Bullitt, *Testimony*, pp. 35–37; the Commission to Negotiate Peace to Polk, Feb. 24, 1919, *Foreign Relations, 1919, Russia*, p. 74. Instructions for the mission can be found in *Senate Document 106*, 66th Cong., 1st sess., p. 1234.

171. Seth P. Tillman, *Anglo-American Relations at the Paris Peace Conference of 1919* (Princeton, N. J., 1961), p. 142.

172. Bullitt to House, March 18, 1919, *Foreign Relations, 1919, Russia*, p. 84.

173. *Foreign Relations, 1919, Russia*, pp. 85–89; Kerr to Sir R. Graham, July 11, 1919, E. L. Woodward and Rohan Butler, eds., *Documents on British Foreign Policy, 1919–1939*, 1st series, 21 vols. (London, 1947–78), iii, 426; Bullitt, *Testimony*, pp. 65–73.

174. Bullitt, *Testimony*, pp. 65–66; Thompson, *Russia, Bolshevism, and the Versailles Peace*, pp. 242–44.

175. *Foreign Relations, 1919, The Paris Peace Conference*, 13 vols. (Washington, 1942–47), xi, 124–25. Both Kerr and Lloyd George later denounced Bullitt's testimony before the Senate as a "tissue of lies." *New York Times*, Sept. 16, 1919.

176. House Diary, March 28, 1919; Grayson Diary, March 11, 16, 26, and 27, and April 3–7, 1919; Bullitt, *Testimony*, p. 73; Thompson, *Russia, Bolshevism, and the Versailles Peace*, p. 235.

177. Bliss to WW, Feb. 12, 1919, Wilson Papers; *Foreign Relations, 1919, Russia*, pp. 617–18.

178. Reinsch to Polk, Dec. 9, 1918; Polk to Lansing, Jan. 2, 1919; Morris to Lansing, Jan. 10, 1919, State Department Records, 861.00/3368, 861.00/3617b, and 861.00/3622.

179. Omsk government to Boris A. Bakhmetev, Ambassador to Washington of the Provisional Government, April 24, 1919, *Foreign Relations, 1919, Russia*, pp. 494–96.

180. Grayson Diary, May 27, 1919; *Foreign Relations, 1919, Russia*, pp. 345–47, 351–53, 367–70.

181. Notes of a meeting held at President Wilson's house in the Place des

États Unis, Paris, May 9, 1919, *Foreign Relations, 1919, Russia*, pp. 345–47.

182. N. W. Graham, "Russian-American Relations, 1917–1933: An Interpretation," *American Political Science Review*, xxviii (June 1934), 408–409. For an analysis of the documents that led to this position, see Stanley K. Hornbeck, "The American Expeditionary Forces in Siberia," Hornbeck Papers, Hoover Institution on War, Revolution, and Peace.

183. Cordell Hull, *Memoirs*, 2 vols. (New York, 1948), I, 299.

Chapter Three

WOODROW WILSON AND THE

REBIRTH OF POLAND

KAY LUNDGREEN-NIELSEN

Although the Polish state was reestablished more than sixty years ago, the debate over the factors that were decisive for Poland's restoration has raged for years. Many factors contributed to the creation of a Polish state. The policy of President Wilson was one of them.

During the First World War, as in the Second World War, the American leaders avoided participating in discussions on territorial problems, especially those which concerned eastern Europe, before the war was over.[1] In both cases, the vital, direct American interests in that part of the world were not great.[2] However, even though the United States did not have a large stake in the Italian-Yugoslavian conflict, it became deeply involved in this affair. The problem was that, in Wilson's opinion, American policy toward Italy was becoming a threat to his vision of a peace settlement. Although he was not a rigid doctrinaire, neither on the problem of Italy nor on other questions, it is worth briefly mentioning his general principles, for his policy on Poland is not clear without reference to them.[3]

Wilson favored the worldwide development of self-governing, democratic states. He believed that a world consisting of such states, organized within a League of Nations, would be the best guarantee for peace in the future. As far as new frontiers were concerned, therefore, the principle of national self-determination should guide the postwar settlement. These democratic states in the League of Nations would work for disarmament; the new order would preserve the peace more effectively than the old diplomacy, which relied on the

balance of power, military and secret alliances, annexations, armaments, strategic frontiers, and hard economic conditions imposed on
the defeated. Wilson did not regard the Allied European states as
wholly and loyally committed to these ideals. In 1917–1918, the
Americans acquired an unfavorable impression of the policy of Italy
and later also of France.[4] In January 1918, Wilson was already aware
of the danger of a Latin bloc as a counterweight to a presumed Anglo-
Saxon bloc, and Wilson was ready to fight such a combination.[5]

The implementation of Wilson's principles raised many problems. Even if the complex situation in Europe after the war had not
added to the difficulties, some of the principles, such as national self-
determination, left many practical problems unsolved. The mixed
nationalities in eastern Europe posed a special problem, but, on the
other hand, Wilson always had reservations concerning this principle:
he realized that, in some cases, other considerations—diplomatic,
strategic, or economic—might be important.[6] Although Wilson
wanted the new states and the defeated autocratic states to emerge as
democracies, his belief in self-government and self-determination at
times placed him in a dilemma. What should happen if a people did
not want a democratic system? Did the victors have the right to impose
it from the outside? Wilson faced this dilemma in Russia and in Germany's transition from an autocratic imperial government to a democratic parliamentary republican system.[7] In both cases, the "Mexican
lesson" influenced Wilson; he perceived that military intervention
would not solve internal problems which required a national or popular resolution.[8]

Despite this realization, Wilson preferred the development of democracies; and he did, at times, encourage it by using other means,
such as food relief. Even so, democratic states might very well be
anything but peaceful; public opinion and the parliaments might be
nationalistic. A strong and aggressive nationalism erupted in most
countries after the First World War. Public opinion in the United
States, led by the Republicans, was certainly no exception to this development. Wilson's appeal in April 1919 to the Italian people was a
failure because of popular pressure for national aggrandizement.
Strong and aggressive nationalism, which public opinion supported,
also existed in most of the new or reestablished states in eastern and
southeastern Europe.[9]

The implementation of Wilson's principles met other difficulties.

While the war was fought and won by the United States together with the Allies, an American peace was not possible unless Wilson used the overwhelming financial power of the United States to press his views on the Allies. But such a policy entailed the risk of breaking the alliance and wrecking the whole work of the peace conference, including the establishment of the League of Nations, the most important element in the Wilsonian peace structure.[10] The Americans did not use their financial weapon, and Wilson's political position in the United States, after the congressional elections in November 1918, was weakened. The peace was therefore a compromise between different interests.

The problems which surrounded the reestablishment of Poland added to these ambiguities. Before the peace conference, Wilson did not have specific ideas about the reestablishment of Poland. His policy on Polish problems developed gradually during 1917 and 1918. In his public declarations, he made only vague pronouncements. In a famous statement in the speech of January 22, 1917, Wilson recognized the principle of a Polish state, just as the Central Powers, in their Manifesto of November 5, 1916, had stated that they would do. "Statesmen everywhere are agreed that there should be a united, independent and autonomous Poland," Wilson declared.

These few words on Poland were the only words in that speech about territorial settlements. On the other hand, his laconic remarks fell very much short of the Polish desires that one of the Polish leaders in the United States, the famous pianist Ignacy Jan Paderewski, expressed in a long memorandum to Wilson. Paderewski favored a big Poland, a federation of the United States of Poland.[11]

Wilson made his statement in January probably in reaction to the international situation and not in response to any pressure by Polish Americans. Most historians maintain that, during both the First World War and the Second World War, pressure from Polish Americans had a large influence upon American Presidents. Wilson, of course, was well aware that the Poles in America constituted a part of the electorate, but it is remarkable that his statement in January 1917 came *after* the presidential election of 1916. Polish-American organizations were rather weak and divided. Later, Wilson did not let Italian or Jewish opinions influence his policy.[12]

Paderewski was a leading member of one of the Polish groups in the United States. Through his acquaintance from late 1915 onward with

Colonel House, Paderewski hoped to influence American policy toward Polish problems. There is no doubt that he charmed and flattered House. Yet it is quite another question as to how far this acquaintance influenced political decisions. When the Allied debate on the Polish problem was most acute—that is, during the Paris Peace Conference—the influence of Colonel House was declining.[13] The problem of the importance of personal acquaintances also has another dimension, since Wilson and the American leaders could and *did* try to influence Paderewski to induce Policy policymakers to follow *their* principles.

In 1917, plans existed to create a Polish government and a Polish army in America. The French also permitted the establishment of a Polish army in France and, later, the formation in 1917 of the Polish National Committee (KNP), which was soon seated in Paris. The American government, however, was the last of the great powers to recognize the KNP in 1917. The Americans complained that the KNP was reactionary and unrepresentative; it included no socialists, peasants, or Jews.[14] The KNP, which Roman Dmowski headed, did not represent democratic ideals in the eyes of most Americans.

During the war, The Inquiry, which Wilson established in 1917, did detailed work on Polish problems and future frontiers. As Wilson phrased it, these experts would establish the factual basis for a "scientific peace." Recent scholarship has established that these experts, most of whom were academics, were more conservative than Wilson and were more concerned with America's economic and strategic position than with the principle of national self-determination.[15] The leading experts in the United States on Poland were Professors Robert H. Lord of Harvard University and Isaiah Bowman of The Johns Hopkins University. Most of the literature on the peace conference has overemphasized the influence of the American experts and their preparatory work. The British, for example, were also very well prepared. Moreover, Wilson's advisers frequently disagreed on Polish affairs, and Wilson did not always follow their advice, especially when they departed from Wilson's own principles. Wilson's independent attitude concerning Poland was embodied in Point Thirteen of his Fourteen Points Address.[16] The vagueness of his statement was deliberate, for the diplomatic situation was far from clear, and he also had to consider the views of the Allies. American policy toward Austria-Hungary was not clarified before the middle of 1918. Until then,

Wilson did not dismiss the possibility of the continued existence of Austria-Hungary. Polish Galicia was part of the Hapsburg Empire; in 1918, the Allies still had plans for a separate peace with Austria-Hungary, and, in 1917, for a Polish state within a federalized new Austria-Hungary.[17]

When the Allies abandoned their attempts at a separate peace with Austria-Hungary in April 1918, the path lay clear for statements of support for the subject nationalities of the Austro-Hungarian Empire. The Versailles Declaration of June 3, 1918, demonstrated that all the Allies and the United States now favored a united and independent Polish state with access to the sea. The final defeat of the Central Powers in the autumn of 1918 forced the Poles and the great powers to make their ideas about Poland more concrete.

The situation in and around Poland was confused at the time of the Armistice. Russia was in chaos and was experiencing both civil war and foreign intervention; Germany had a revolution; and Austria-Hungary had disintegrated. In Galicia (Austrian Poland), fighting broke out in November 1918 between Poles and Ukrainians. The German troops withdrew in an orderly fashion from Russian Poland, but German soldiers were still in territories east of Poland, from the Ukraine to the Baltic states. When the Polish state emerged in November 1918, the problem of the representation of Poland at the Paris Peace Conference was unsolved. In Warsaw, Józef Piłsudski took power from the Regency Council—the Polish agency which the Central Powers had established—and soon formed a socialist government. The Allies did not support this regime, since they had recognized Dmowski and the KNP since 1917. Dmowski and his National Democratic party now had aspirations to seize power in Poland.

The State Department was well aware of the internal quarrels of the Polish factions.[18] Officially, however, it had recognized only Paderewski in America during the war, and it was not involved in these internal problems as much as the French and the British governments. On the other hand, the American peace commissioner, General Tasker H. Bliss, tended to support Piłsudski; he thought that Dmowski was a reactionary.[19] Wilson stated in December 1918, on board the *George Washington*: "As for the form of Poland's government he would only say that he was in favor of their having any government they damned pleased."[20] He had learned his "Mexican lesson" well. This statement meant that Wilson would not prevent the ruling government—that is, the government appointed by Piłsudski and headed by Jędrzej Moraczewski, from remaining in power, and that Wilson had assumed a position against the KNP's pretensions to power in Poland.

In the middle of January 1919, an agreement made between Paderewski and Piłsudski in Warsaw solved the problem of Polish representation. Dmowski reluctantly approved it in Paris, and Piłsudski remained as Chief of State and Paderewski as Prime Minister and Minister of Foreign Affairs. The American leaders probably hoped that Paderewski could and would influence Poland in a democratic direction. They were the first to recognize the new Polish government, just as they were the first to recognize the new government of Yugoslavia. Colonel House eagerly recommended this to Wilson, who at once approved.[21]

There is no evidence that shows direct American involvement in the formation of the Paderewski government. Herbert Hoover's later explanation that his food mission to Poland had an important influence is not sufficient or necessary. Piłsudski had considered a change of government for weeks before the food mission arrived, and there were many reasons for the compromise with Paderewski.[22] Piłsudski hoped to gain Allied help and recognition by nominating Paderewski and by placing the KNP under his control. On the other hand, Hoover certainly had a political aim in sending food to Central and East Central Europe: he wanted to stop Bolshevism. The first ships with food landed at Danzig in the middle of February 1919.[23]

The Polish compromise, just before the peace conference opened in January 1919, meant that Dmowski and Paderewski were the Polish plenipotentiaries, and that representatives from Piłsudski were incorporated into the KNP. The expanded KNP represented Polish interests in Paris until normal state agencies were established. During the conference, however, this formal compromise was not carried out. Dmowski and his men did not regard themselves as subordinate to the Polish authorities in Warsaw, and, since they held different ideas on more questions than did Piłsudski and Paderewski, a dualism in the conduct of Polish foreign policy existed. The great powers were aware of these differences and used them for their own ends.[24]

It is essential to examine the attitude of President Wilson himself to understand completely the American policy toward the reestablishment of Poland. Very often, however, it is impossible to learn much about his position. His opinions are frequently recorded, not by himself, but by others—his close collaborators, foreign visitors, Polish or Allied politicians, and ambassadors. This type of evidence must be examined very carefully. Wilson rarely gave precise instructions to his delegates, either about Poland or about many other problems.[25] The various plans that his advisers and experts favored were, therefore, not necessarily identical to his own ideas. In the autumn of 1918, Lansing, House, and The Inquiry favored including Danzig as part of Poland. When Dmowski and Paderewski presented the Polish territorial demands to Wilson in September and October 1918, Wilson found them excessive. He told Dmowski in clear terms that arguments about strategic frontiers carried little weight with him, and that Poland would have to rely on the League of Nations for security. Dmowski was taught the same lesson as the Italians, who also spoke as representatives of the "old diplomacy."[26]

One of the most difficult questions concerned the interpretation of Wilson's phrase, "with access to the sea," which appeared in Point Thirteen. Wilson's French, Polish, and American listeners provide most of the sources concerning his views, but all the scant evidence points to the conclusion that, before the conference and at its beginning, Wilson did not favor giving Danzig to Poland. As late as January 21, 1919, the American experts in The Inquiry advocated giving Danzig to Poland. However, on the next day Wilson told his Allied colleagues that "Danzig must remain an open question."[27]

Wilson wanted to be sure that the great powers wrote the peace settlement; otherwise his policy would be very difficult to execute. But the divergent views among the great powers created a host of problems. In close cooperation with the British, Wilson wanted to stop the tendency toward local military *faits accomplis*, which threatened to decide many questions *before* the peace conference had discussed them. An Allied warning of January 24, 1919, was based on Anglo-American cooperation, and the French only reluctantly adhered to it. The statement was "a solemn warning that possession gained by force will seriously prejudice the claims of those who use such means. If they expect justice, they must refrain from force and place their claims in unclouded good faith in the hands of the Conference of Peace." The British and Americans were thinking of the Poles, the Rumanians, the Italians, the Serbs, the Hungarians, and, possibly also, the French, who, through military force and *coups*, could forestall the decisions of the conference.[28] Neither the British nor the Americans had their own vital interests in specific Polish frontiers. In principle, both wanted to create a strong and viable state, but, in their opinion, that meant, as far as possible, a state within ethnographical lines. The French leaders had another definition of a strong Poland and of its function in the French security system.

Since the disappearance in 1917–1918 of France's old ally, Russia, Poland, in French planning, gradually assumed the role of an anti-German barrier. Because of the civil war in Russia, the French hoped that Poland would be an anti-Bolshevik bulwark.[29] The French leaders were prepared to use economic, historical, and strategic arguments to further these aims and to establish precedents for their own borders with Germany. The problem of Danzig was a good example.

Since November 1918, the French and the Poles had proposed to transport the Polish Army in France, under the command of Colonel Józef Haller, to Poland through Danzig, and accompanied by Allied troops. In January and February 1919, common American and British opposition blocked this proposal. Wilson and Bliss certainly understood that Haller might use his troops against both Germany and the new Polish government. Wilson pointed out that, in dispatching Polish troops to Poland, "we should not only be sending armed men, but strong partisans on Polish questions." He certainly had no desire for a right-wing coup in Poland; he steadfastly refused to send American troops to Poland to accompany Haller's army, and he avoided supporting the French policy, which tended to favor military solutions to political problems.[30] Ferdinand Foch, Dmowski, and Dmowski's close associate, Count Jan Horodyski, tried, unsuccessfully, to win Anglo-American support for the transport of Haller's army by using anti-Bolshevik arguments. This stratagem failed totally. Wilson firmly rejected the use of military weapons to fight Bolshevism. Instead, his solution lay in the food weapon; his instrument was Hoover's Relief Organization.[31]

The attempt to forestall the decisions of the peace conference regarding Danzig did not succeed. But during February and March 1919 the territorial problems were discussed both informally between the American and British experts and formally in the territorial commissions of the conference. Most of this time Wilson was not in Paris, and, apparently, he left his delegation without precise instructions. When he returned on March 14, he discovered that Colonel House had compromised on several issues with the British and the French and that the territorial commissions were ready with their proposals.

Did the work of the American experts, Lord and Bowman, and of Colonel House correspond to Wilson's policy on Polish problems? Lord, Bowman, and House, like the British experts, Sir Esme Howard, Hamish James Paton, and Frederick H. Kisch, maintained that Danzig should be part of Poland, a position which was contrary to the prevailing view in the Foreign Office during 1917 and 1918, and which was contrary to Wilson's previous statements. Part of the British delegation expressed doubt and opposition in February, but, by the middle of March, all the British experts, including Foreign Secretary Balfour, accepted the proposal to award Danzig to Poland. Whether Wilson approved of this decision is not known, but he probably left House in Paris without instructions, and House favored giving Danzig to Poland.[32] In his memoirs, Dmowski states that House told him that Wilson was in favor of including Danzig as part of Poland.[33] This evidence must, however, be used cautiously, since House very often was not loyal to Wilson.[34]

When he returned to Paris, Wilson may have accepted the report of the Polish Commission. He pointed out—in accordance with his general view—that it was not entirely possible to follow the ethnographical principle, there or elsewhere. Wilson also drew attention to the general situation in Poland: "The Allies were creating a new and weak state, weak not only because historically it had failed to govern itself, but because it was sure in future to be divided into factions, more especially as religious differences were an element in the situation."[35] Wilson talked about the religious situation, but he could also have been thinking of the severe political schism. Remarkably enough, however, he very quickly changed his mind and took the same position as did Lloyd George, who in the beginning had not questioned the proposal on Danzig. In fact, American activity with respect to Danzig and other Polish problems was much greater than the existing treatments of the question have thus far indicated.

After his return to Paris in March, Wilson concluded that the proposals for the peace treaty with Germany, as House had negotiated them, and the behavior of the new states of eastern Europe, did not correspond to his principles and policy. He viewed the policy of the French and the Italians as being in large measure responsible for the fight between the old order and the new order. The character of the peace was at stake. House's concessions were one of the factors to blame for this development,[36] and both Lloyd George and Wilson probably, already on March 27, began to think of revising the proposal on Danzig.[37]

For Wilson, the same principle governed the issues that surrounded Teschen, the Saar, Fiume, and Danzig. If he agreed to Polish economic claims on Danzig, he had to agree to Czech claims to Teschen, French claims to the Saar, and so on.[38] If Wilson permitted the Poles or the Ukrainians to forestall the decisions of the peace conference—contrary to the declaration of January 24, 1919—by military force in eastern Galicia, or if he permitted the Poles to use Haller's army either against the Ukrainians or against the Germans in Danzig, he thought that his principles for a peace settlement would be gravely injured.

At the end of March and the beginning of April 1919, therefore, Wilson reacted strongly. His activity on both the Italian and Polish problems was so great because these states were weaker than France and Great Britain. In April, he compromised frequently with the French and the British, but on Italy and Poland he tried to impose his principles, in the last case in close cooperation with the British. He worked eagerly on the details of the frontiers and of the status of Danzig. He took time for meetings with the American and British experts and made handwritten proposals.[39] In fact, Wilson disapproved of the work of his own experts and did not take their advice. Lord and Bowman were still firmly in favor of Danzig going to Poland and of strong measures against the Ukrainians in eastern Galicia. Wilson worked hard to make Danzig a free state, and he avoided unilateral actions in the Polish-Ukrainian conflict; in fact, in response to the reports of an American representative in Poland, General Francis Joseph Kernan, Wilson acted against what he thought was Polish militarism and imperialism.[40] Kernan, in several letters to General Bliss, sharply criticized the French in Poland, and he contradicted the frequent Polish contentions about the Bolshevik threat. On the contrary, General Kernan reported that the real threat was Polish militarism and imperialism. In Paris, Bliss and Wilson wholeheartedly supported Kernan's interpretations, and not those of Lord. Wilson and Bliss were disappointed at the behavior of the new states, which behaved very much like the worst among the existing states—for instance, France and Italy.[41] This mood was reflected in Wilson's actions on Polish affairs.

Wilson's active part in establishing the Free State of Danzig has been mentioned. He was just as active in working out a solution for the transport of Haller's army which would make military *faits accomplis* impossible either at Danzig or in eastern Galicia. Foch's attempts to persuade the Council of Four to approve either a route for Haller via Rumania to eastern Galicia or via Danzig would have had quite the opposite effect. The French proposals strengthened the American-British suspicion of the underlying motives and led to the final solution which wholly satisfied American-British policy: Haller's army was to go through Germany by railway. This solution was identical to a British proposal of October 1918; in March 1919, the Germans also favored it.[42] From the middle of April 1919 onward, Haller's troops gradually arrived in Poland without untoward episodes. The British and the Americans clearly stated that their transport had no connection with decisions on frontier problems and that its purpose was purely defensive; moreover, they had frustrated Foch's intention to use Haller's army for a war against Russia or the Ukrainians.[43]

The Americans persistently warned the Poles to stop their military activities in eastern Galicia or else to risk drastic American pressure. In April 1919, the Americans and British agreed that the commission in Paris which should force the Poles and the Ukrainians to stop fighting ought not to have a French chairman.[44] Telegrams were sent from the peace conference after March 19 on British and American initiative to stop the fighting in eastern Galicia. But the Poles—unknown to the peace conference—after that day were on the offensive, and these orders worked to their disadvantage. Bliss and Wilson were well aware that the new states were very much dependent on American aid. Thus Wilson halted trains with supplies to Poland, and he personally tried to influence Paderewski in Paris.[45] At the end of April, Bowman plainly told the Poles the essence of the American policy: the United States feared that Poland was going to be an aggressive and imperialistic state.[46] The existence of the government of Paderewski was at stake, and the Americans seemed willing to risk its collapse. Just as the British and the Americans discussed at the end of April whether the Ebert-Scheidemann regime in Germany ought to give place to a government more amenable to Allied aims, they also discussed the value of the Piłsudski-Paderewski regime. In both cases, the alternatives were not enviable. British and American leaders feared that extremist parties from the right (in Germany, the military; in Poland, the Dmowski group) or the left (Bolshevism) would take power. Moreover, Poland was an Allied country. Therefore, Paderewski, on the explicit recommendation of the first American Minister in Poland, Hugh Gibson, got more than warnings and pressures from the Council of Three before he left for Poland in the beginning of May. The Big Three thanked him for his efforts in Paris, and he was promised a much needed loan.[47]

Dmowski in Paris had closely cooperated with the French. The work in the territorial commissions and the sending of a French military mission to Poland seemed to show that his policy was right—and he himself certainly had no doubts about that.[48]

Piłsudski's envoys for weeks had criticized Dmowski's alliance with the French and his deliberate ignoring of the British and Americans.[49] Thus, Paderewski journeyed to Paris at the beginning of April to repair important but badly tended fences. Paderewski in Paris and Piłsudski in Poland tried to make Polish policy fit British and American principles. Paderewski stressed the democratic character of the new Polish state, but he tried in vain to obtain a revision of the Allied decisions on Danzig, Marienwerder, and eastern Galicia. Paderewski made a last attempt to propose a plebiscite in Danzig, at a much later date, but Wilson and Lloyd George turned it down.[50] On the other hand, Wilson's tendency to defend his principles after his return in March worked to the advantage of the Poles in their conflict with Czechoslovakia over Teschen. No explicit instructions from Wilson about this problem exist, but it is hardly a coincidence that the American experts after March 25 tried to revise the pro-Czechoslovak decision, which was based on economic and historical arguments.[51] It is not known whether Wilson knew that most of the Poles in Teschen who would suffer from a pro-Czechoslovak decision were workers, but, as Klaus Schwabe has shown concerning the Saar and Upper Silesia, he was very concerned about the fate of the workers.[52] The result was that, during April, Lansing succeeded in postponing a pro-Czechoslovak decision, and, for the time being, the problem was left to direct Polish-Czech negotiations. This move had a clear anti-French tendency.[53] Piłsudski and Paderewski tried to appeal to Anglo-Saxon ideas on national self-determination concerning the eastern frontiers of Poland. On April 19, when Piłsudski conquered Wilno, he soon issued a declaration in this sense which favorably impressed the American representatives. In Paris, Paderewski openly criticized Dmowski's annexationist proposals and instead advanced a federal solution.[54] During the meetings in the expanded KNP in Paris, for instance, on March 2, the Poles had discussed their disagreement on the eastern frontiers of Poland and on the future rule in these areas. Dmowski had prevented this disunity from appearing in public, but in April the Polish groups did not hide their internal conflicts.[55]

Wilson's views on the exact line of Poland's eastern frontiers are not known. According to his principles, only indisputably Polish populations belonged to Poland. The chaos in Russia, however, made Allied decisions difficult. General Bliss, who usually had the same views on Polish problems as Wilson, wanted to determine the Polish eastern frontier very quickly in Paris. He intended to make it quite clear to the Poles that the conference would not recognize any expansion beyond that frontier. The views of the British delegates were exactly the same. Both Wilson and Bliss disagreed with those people, especially some French military leaders, who thought that Bolshevism could be stopped through military means. Instead, good government, social reforms, and food were the essential means to stop Bolshevism.[56] General Kernan, who in March had visited the eastern areas of Poland, had seen no sign of a Bolshevik threat to Poland. His analysis, which very much impressed the Americans in Paris, was that the real threat consisted of Polish militarism and imperialism, which was encouraged by French officers in Poland.[57] Wilson's advisers, Lansing, Bliss, and Henry White, agreed with Kernan, and Wilson took their advice. He ordered Bliss to talk with Paderewski. It is interesting to note that the Polish account of their meeting stresses the anti-Bolshevik arguments, while the American account hardly takes any notice of this part of Paderewski's exposition. Bliss interpreted Polish military expansion in eastern Galicia exactly as did General Kernan.[58]

The Americans and British, in April and May 1919, tried energetically to stop Polish military expansion in eastern Galicia. Nonetheless, in Paris, Lord and Bowman—contrary to the position of the British and of Wilson—were willing to discuss during the meetings of the territorial commissions final frontiers which far exceeded borders drawn according to strictly ethnographical principles. In fact, Lord was very much in agreement with the French representative, General Henri Le Rond, and both perceived the need for strategic frontiers. Probably Lord was without clear instructions from Wilson and followed his own pro-Polish tendency, just as he had done in February 1919 in the Lord-Howard agreement. Because of the British attitude, the proposal of the Polish Commission on a provisional minimum border line closely followed ethnographical principles, and this line was the origin of the boundary later known as the "Curzon Line."

Piłsudski, who was not interested in the whole of eastern Galicia, wanted to obey the orders from the peace conference to stop the Polish offensive, but both he and Paderewski in April and May faced opposition among leading generals and from Dmowski's followers in the Sejm (the Polish parliament) and in the press. Dmowski's negative attitude in Paris toward Anglo-American pressure and his confidence in French support and in the strength of his followers in Poland led the Anglo-Americans to doubt the value of promises that Paderewski and Piłsudski gave. The actual dualism in the conduct of Polish foreign policy made the Anglo-Americans suspicious of Polish policy.[59]

However, in May 1919, Wilson was less willing than the British to press the Poles too hard and to risk the fall of the Paderewski government. Wilson thought, after all, that that government was a bulwark against anarchy. Just as Wilson negotiated with Clemenceau and Lloyd George and made compromises with them, even though he disagreed with them on many issues, so he accepted the Polish regime as better than the possible alternatives. The fear of the coming into power of chauvinistic groups in all those countries determined his actions, since the existence of such governments imperiled a Wilsonian peace. In Poland, Wilson also feared that extreme leftist groups might seize power.[60] Both Paderewski and Piłsudski in Poland used the Allied pressure to convince their political opponents. In the important debate in the Sejm, Paderewski exposed his policy as being in accordance with Wilson's principles.[61]

Another delicate problem also drew the Allies' attention to internal Polish problems and differences of policy. Pogroms and anti-Semitism were well-known phenomena in parts of eastern Europe. The Allies quickly realized that they had to make some guarantees for minorities, particularly Jews. The American Jewish organizations were in close cooperation with east European Jews. Pressure on Wilson to make arrangements to make Jews secure in the new states, including Poland, was therefore very strong. The demands of Polish Jews amounted, in effect, to the creation of a separate Jewish nation within the Polish state. It is remarkable that Wilson did not yield to this demand, for the British and American policy to protect Jews in Poland was in response to the strong position in Poland of Dmowski's National

Democratic party. Dmowski's anti-Semitism was well known to Wilson, Lloyd George, and their advisers. Indeed, Dmowski never concealed his anti-Semitism in his conversations with Allied leaders or with American Jews.[62] Paderewski's and Piłsudski's statements respecting tolerance for the Jews were not enough to permit the Allies, especially the Americans and the British, to drop the project of a special treaty for minorities between Poland and the Allies. On the other hand, neither Wilson nor Lloyd George wanted to support Jewish demands for what amounted to a state-within-a-state in Poland. In spite of strong Jewish pressure, frequent rumors in the Western press on pogroms in Poland, demonstrations in New York, and questions in Congress, Wilson stuck to his original position.

Hugh Gibson, the first American Minister to Poland, investigated the problem. His reports, however, were pro-Polish, as were those of his British and French colleagues: they carefully explained the reasons for some of the episodes and tried to minimize the importance of them. The great difference, however, was that, while the British advisers in London and Paris did not believe these reports, the Americans were impressed, and Gibson, at the end of June, traveled to Paris to explain his case. Much against the advice of American Jews, Wilson accepted a plan worked out by his advisers, Lord, Hoover, and Gibson, and approved by Paderewski, for an American mission to Poland to investigate the Jewish problem. The Jews did not want the prominent American Jew, Henry Morgenthau, to head the mission, but Wilson stubbornly stuck to his decision to name him. According to Morgenthau, Wilson "did not want zionism dragged in." One of Piłsudski's men in Paris, Kazimierz Dłuski, was introduced to Morgenthau by Lord, who informed him that Dłuski was an opponent of Dmowski and a pro-Semite. Dłuski in July accompanied Morgenthau in the train to Warsaw.[63] The French, in cooperation with Dmowski, were strongly suspected of obstructing the Anglo-American initiatives for guarantees to the Jews, but the Americans and the British stuck to the idea of special protection.[64]

Although Wilson sided with the British concerning Polish problems during most of the peace conference, the final debate on the fate of Upper Silesia resulted in a sharp disagreement between Wilson and Lloyd George. There had been no discussion in the Polish Commission on the problem of Upper Silesia; in March, Lloyd George had not attacked that decision. But in May 1919, the Germans showed signs of refusing to sign the peace treaty without revisions, especially concerning the eastern frontier of Germany. Their desire for revision, with which Lloyd George sympathized, very much annoyed Wilson. He did not want to alter the territorial decisions and tried vainly, through Lord, to counter the British policy by collaborating with the French and the Italians over the Polish settlement. The British proposal of a plebiscite was not against Wilson's principles, although he reminded Lloyd George that a plebiscite did not necessarily follow his interpretation of Point Thirteen. Wilson and Lord were also convinced that the Poles would win the plebiscite, at least in the mining districts. The concession for the sake of Allied unity was, therefore, in the eyes of the Americans not great. It is worth noting that neither Wilson nor Lloyd George in 1919 questioned the decision, later controversial in western Europe, to give the Polish Corridor to Poland. Both leaders and their advisers did not favor that solution in 1917–1918, but in 1919, with the great German defeat, they faced a different situation.[65]

The settlements at the Paris Peace Conference were the results of compromises between the great powers. With respect to Polish problems, Wilson for the most part cooperated with the British, since his ideas on the territorial and political settlement in Europe coincided more often with British than with French policy. Because the British and the Americans were without military means of pressure in eastern Europe, it was essential for them to have local governments with ideals as close as possible to their own.[66] The lack of military means and the chaos in Russia made some of the American and British advisers favor Polish schemes for federalism in the East; and such a solution was in accordance with the principle of self-determination. This frontier was, however, not determined by the great powers, but by the Polish-Soviet War in 1920.

Disillusionment quickly replaced Wilson's belief in the new democratic states. The new strong nationalism was a danger as great as the so-called Bolshevik threat. Wilson was aware of Polish domestic problems; both British and American policy on Poland was based on intimate knowledge of the Polish situation, not, as has often been stated, on ignorance. Wilson saw the policy of Dmowski's group as a challenge to his visions: Dmowski was anti-Semitic; reactionaries surrounded him; and he collaborated most closely with the power which Wilson identified most with the old order—France.

Wilson, however, never voiced the same deep distrust of the Poles as did Lloyd George. Wilson drew quite other conclusions from his knowledge of internal weakness and disunity in Poland. He wanted to help and strengthen the new state to make its existence more secure. He often defended Poland against Lloyd George at the conference. Wilson excused Polish participation in the war on the side of the Central Powers. He supported Paderewski and Piłsudski, although at times he used economic pressure to make them comply with his policy. But Wilson regarded this as a prop to Paderewski against his domestic opponent. In this way, Wilson not only supported the reestablishment of Poland but also the creation of a new democratic state which would be an essential part of the fundamental structure of his peace—the League of Nations.

NOTES

1. Geir Lundestad, *The American Non-policy towards Eastern Europe, 1943–47* (Oslo, Norway, 1978).

2. Dagmar Perman, *The Shaping of the Czechoslovak State* (Leiden, 1962); Peter Pastor, *Hungary between Wilson and Lenin* (New York, 1976).

3. Dragan R. Živojinović, *America, Italy and the Birth of Yugoslavia, 1917–1919* (Boulder, Colo., 1972); Klaus Schwabe, *Deutsche Revolution und Wilson-Frieden* (Düsseldorf, 1971); Victor S. Mamatey, *The United States and East Central Europe, 1914–18* (Princeton, N. J., 1957).

4. Živojinović, *America, Italy and the Birth of Yugoslavia*, pp. 112–29.

5. Mamatey, *The United States and East Central Europe*, pp. 199–202.

6. Živojinović, *America, Italy and the Birth of Yugoslavia*, pp. 60, 65, 282, 289, 305; Schwabe, *Deutsche Revolution*, pp. 58, 315, 418, 633; Mamatey, *The United States and East Central Europe*, pp. 369–71.

7. Schwabe, *Deutsche Revolution*, pp. 36, 60–61.

8. Eugene P. Trani, "Woodrow Wilson and the Decision to Intervene in Russia: A Reconsideration," *Journal of Modern History*, XLVIII (Sept. 1976), 444, 460; Schwabe, *Deutsche Revolution*, pp. 60–61.

9. Ivo J. Lederer, *Yugoslavia and the Paris Peace Conference* (New Haven, Conn., 1963), pp. 196–202, 206; Živojinović, *America, Italy and the Birth of Yugoslavia*, pp. 45, 58–59, 211; Schwabe, *Deutsche Revolution*, pp. 497, 510, 576; Perman, *The Shaping of the Czechoslovak State*, pp. 103–109; Sherman D. Spector, *Rumania at the Paris Peace Conference* (New York, 1962).

10. Živojinović, *America, Italy and the Birth of Yugoslavia*, pp. 13, 44; Schwabe, *Deutsche Revolution*, pp. 54, 305–306, 626.

11. For a detailed and documented account of the problems mentioned in this essay, see my book, Kay Lundgreen-Nielsen, *The Polish Problem at the Paris*

Peace Conference: A Study of the Great Powers and the Poles, 1918–1919 (Odense, Denmark, 1979); I. J. Paderewski memorandum, "I. Paderewskiego," *Archiwum Polityczne*, I (1973), 100–109; the Papers of Edward M. House, Yale University Library, Paderewski file; hereinafter cited as the House Papers.

12. Mamatey, *The United States and East Central Europe*, p. 131; Titus Komarnicki, *Rebirth of the Polish Republic* (London, 1957), p. 146; Arthur S. Link, *Wilson*, 5 vols. to date (Princeton, N. J., 1947–), v, 93–164. For another opinion, see Louis L. Gerson, *Woodrow Wilson and the Rebirth of Poland, 1914–1920* (New Haven, Conn., 1953), p. 66; R. Dmowski to Maurycy Zamoyski, Oct. 27, 1918, KNP file 139, Polish State Archives, Warsaw.

13. Inga Floto, *Colonel House in Paris: A Study of American Policy at the Paris Peace Conference 1919* (Princeton, N. J., 1981).

14. Marian Leczyk, *Komitet Narodowy Polski a Ententa i Stany Zjednoczone 1917–1919* [Polish National Committee versus the participating countries, 1917–1919], (Warsaw, 1966), pp. 138–43.

15. Lawrence E. Gelfand, *The Inquiry: American Preparations for Peace, 1917–1919* (New Haven, Conn., 1963); Schwabe, *Deutsche Revolution*, pp. 65–74, 412–20, 444; Irena Spustek, "Sprawa zachodnich granic Polski w okresie przygotowań do Konferencji Pokojowej w świetle materiałów 'Inquiry,'" [Polish western borders during the period of preparations for the peace conference based on materials of The Inquiry], *Przeglad Historyczny* (1972), pp. 651–67.

16. Gelfand, *The Inquiry*, pp. 146–52.

17. Mamatey, *The United States and East Central Europe*, pp. 213–71; Wilfried Fest, *Peace or Partition: The Habsburg Monarchy and British Policy, 1914–18* (London, 1978), pp. 132–219; Kenneth J. Calder, *Britain and the Origins of the New Europe, 1914–18* (Cambridge, Eng., 1976), pp. 124–30, 167–74, 195–99.

18. Lansing to the American Embassy, Paris, Sept. 26, 1918, 86oc 01/222b, State Department Records, National Archives.

19. T. H. Bliss, "Memorandum of the present Polish situation: for the information of American Correspondents," Jan. 13, 1919, the Papers of Tasker H. Bliss, Library of Congress; hereinafter cited as the Bliss Papers; the Diary of Tasker H. Bliss, Dec. 29, 1918, and Jan. 1, 1919, *ibid*.

20. Account by Isaiah Bowman, the Papers of Ray Stannard Baker, Library of Congress; hereinafter cited as the Baker Papers.

21. Gerson, *Woodrow Wilson and the Rebirth of Poland*, pp. 117–18; Mamatey, *The United States and East Central Europe*, pp. 373–75.

22. Herbert Hoover, *The Memoirs of Herbert Hoover*, 3 vols. (New York, 1951–52), I, 357; Piłsudski's instructions of Nov. and Dec. 1918, Archive of Michał Mościcki, No. 12, No. 692, and No. 529, Piłsudski Institute, New York.

23. See Schwabe, *Deutsche Revolution*, pp. 233, 257–79.

24. See my book mentioned in n. 11.

25. Schwabe, *Deutsche Revolution*, pp 131, 164, 178, 622; Perman, *The Shaping of the Czechoslovak State*, pp. 139–41; Floto, *Colonel House in Paris*, p. 126; Živojinović, *America, Italy and the Birth of Yugoslavia*, p. 213.

26. Roman Dmowski, *Polityka Polska* [Polish politics], 2 vols., 3rd edn. (Han-

nover, West Germany, 1947), ı, 250–51; Gerson, *Woodrow Wilson and the Rebirth of Poland*, pp. 94–100; Živojinović, *America, Italy and the Birth of Yugoslavia*, p. 52; Mamatey, *The United States and East Central Europe*, pp. 199–201, 369–70.

27. J. J. Jusserand to S. Pichon, Oct. 20, 1918, Pologne 66/54–55, French Foreign Ministry Archives. For Wilson's statements on the Polish demands, see Paul Mantoux, *Les Délibérations du Conseil des Quatre*, 2 vols. (Paris, 1955), ı, 112; ıı, 282; Wilson, at a meeting of the Council of Ten, Jan. 22, 1919, Department of State, *Papers Relating to the Foreign Relations of the United States, The Paris Peace Conference*, 13 vols. (Washington, 1942–47), ııı, 673. Wilson also disagreed with The Inquiry's proposal to give Fiume to Yugoslavia. See Živojinović, *America, Italy and the Birth of Yugoslavia*, p. 283.

28. Schwabe, *Deutsche Revolution*, pp. 382–83; Živojinović, "The Emergence of American Policy in the Adriatic: December 1917–April 1919," *East European Quarterly*, ı (Sept. 1967), 197–98. On the British initiative, see James Headlam-Morley, *Diary* (London, 1972), pp. 15–16; also George Grahame (British Embassy, Paris) to House, Jan. 2, 1919, House Papers.

29. Janusz Pajewski, *Wokół Sprawy Polskiej Paryż-Lozanna-Londyn 1914–18* [concerning Polish affairs in Paris-Lozanna-London 1914–18], (Poznań, 1970), pp. 229–38; Kalervo Hovi, *Cordon sanitaire or barrière de l'Est? The Emergence of the New French Eastern European Alliance Policy 1917–1919* (Turku, Finland, 1975); Piotr S. Wandycz, *France and Her Eastern Allies, 1919–25* (Minneapolis, Minn., 1962).

30. Memorandum by Major Julian Coolidge, Dec. 11, 1918, *The Paris Peace Conference*, ıı, 414–15; WW in the Council of Ten, Jan. 22, 1919, *ibid.*, ııı, 670–74; Bliss Diary, Dec. 22, 1918.

31. Bliss Diary, Jan. 7, 1919; Wilson to Lansing, Jan. 10, 1919: "The real thing to stop Bolshevism is food." Cited in Schwabe, *Deutsche Revolution*, p. 275.

32. Harold I. Nelson, *Land and Power: British and Allied Policies on Germany's Frontiers, 1916–1919* (London, 1963), p. 145; Headlam-Morley, *Diary*; Balfour minute, Sir Esme Howard to the Foreign Office, Feb. 27, 1919, FO 608/61/468, Public Record Office; meeting between Colonel House and André Tardieu, March 2, 1919, Papiers A. Tardieu, Carton 51, French Foreign Ministry Archives. For the American account of this meeting, see the entry for March 2, 1919, in the McCormick Diary, Yale University Library.

33. Dmowski, *Polityka Polska*, ıı, 22.

34. Cf. Floto, *Colonel House in Paris*, *passim*.

35. Council of Ten, March 19, 1919, *The Paris Peace Conference*, ıv, 404–19.

36. Floto, *Colonel House in Paris*, p. 170; Schwabe, *Deutsche Revolution*, pp. 446–47; Živojinović, *America, Italy and the Birth of Yugoslavia*, pp. 201, 265.

37. Cf. the account by Sir Eyre Crowe, March 28, 1919, Eyre Crowe Papers, mentioned in articles by Anna M. Cienciała: Poznań *Studia Historica Slavo-Germanica*, ı (1973), 74; Romae *Antemurale*, xx (1976), 83; *Zeitschrift für Ostforschung* (1978), 435. Headlam-Morley, in the draft of his book on the Peace Conference, comments on the meeting of the Council of Four of March 27,

1919 as follows: "There is no record of what took place except a note to the following effect. President Wilson evinced a strong disposition in favour of overriding the report of the Polish Commission and creating a free port of Danzig instead of annexing it to Poland." Public Record Office.

38. Mantoux, *Les Délibérations du Conseil des Quatre*, I (March 28, 1919), 68–69.

39. Headlam-Morley, *Diary*.

40. Lord to Bowman, March 19, 1919, Records of the Commission to Negotiate Peace, 181.21302/70, National Archives.

41. Kernan to Bliss, Feb. 20 and 28, 1919; Bliss to Mrs. Bliss, Feb. 26, 1919; Kernan to Bliss, March 20, 1919; Wilson to Bliss, March 28, 1919, all in the Bliss Papers.

42. A. Parker to Eric Drummond, Oct. 22, 1918, FO 371/3282, Public Record Office (seen by Cecil and Balfour); minute by Edward H. Carr, Oct. 30, 1918, on letter from Ambassador Derby (Paris) to Balfour, Oct. 20, 1918, FO 371/3277, *ibid*. Schwabe, *Deutsche Revolution*, pp. 460–68, emphasizes the importance of the German proposals.

43. See the accounts of the meetings since March 17, 1919, in Mantoux, *Les Délibérations du Conseil des Quatre, passim*, and in *The Paris Peace Conference, passim*. For an opposite view, see Arno J. Mayer, *Politics and Diplomacy of Peacemaking* (London, 1968), p. 603.

44. Undated draft by Bliss, Bliss Papers.

45. Živojinović, *America, Italy and the Birth of Yugoslavia*, pp. 13, 44, 78, 239; Mantoux, *Les Délibérations du Conseil des Quatre*, II (May 14, 1919), 70; Stefan Markowski to Andrzej Wierzbicki, April 30, 1919, KNP file 558, Polish State Archives, Warsaw. See also the House Diary, May 2, 1919.

46. Conversation with Professor Eugeniusz Romer of the Polish delegation; E. Romer to Paderewski, April 28, 1919, Warsaw *Archiwum Paderewskiego*, II (1974), 118–19.

47. Schwabe, *Deutsche Revolution*, pp. 468, 554–59; Wilson to Paderewski, April 26, 1919, Wilson Papers, Library of Congress; Herbert Hoover to Paderewski, May 6, 1919, Warsaw *Archiwum Paderewskiego*, II (1974), 141; Hugh Gibson, American Minister to Poland, to House, April 29, 1919: "There seems to be a great deal of apprehension that unless Paderewski brings back something definite to show that he has been successful in his mission, there will be an attempt to oust him and his government either by the radicals or by the Dmowski group, or possibly by both." House Papers.

48. Roman Dmowski to Stanisław Grabski, March 14, 1919, in Mariusz Kułakowski, *Roman Dmowski w świetle listów i wspomnień* [Roman Dmowski in light of his letters and recollections], 2 vols. (London, 1972), II, 147–51.

49. See the numerous reports of February and March 1919 by Michał Sokolnicki, Stanisław Patek, Leon Wasilweski, K. Dłuski and Wieniawa-Długoszowski, starting with Sokolnicki's report of February 3, 1919, in file 54/402, Adjutantura Generalna Naczelnego Dowództwa, Piłsudski Institute, New York.

50. Account by C. Hurst, legal adviser to the British delegation, May 7,

1919, FO 608/70/148, Public Record Office.

51. See Bowman's new arguments in the meeting of the Polish Commission, *Conférence de la Paix, 1919–20. Recueil des Actes de la Conférence* (Paris, 1924), pp. 92–96. For the English version, see Records of the Commission to Negotiate Peace, 181.213201/14, National Archives.

52. Schwabe, *Deutsche Revolution*, pp. 473, 630, 633.

53. Lansing to Wilson, April 13, 1919, Wilson Papers: The method of direct negotiations between the Poles and the Czechs "removes the impression that France is the ultimate arbiter between the new states of Eastern Europe, an impression which is being industriously spread by the French military clique who are making all sorts of promises to the various nationalities as to political and economic as well as military matters."

54. The Polish Commission, meeting no. 17, April 12, 1919, *Conférence de la Paix, 1919–20. Recueil des Actes de la Conférence*, pp. 109–13; Sub-Commission on the Polish Eastern Frontier, April 17, 1919, *ibid.*, pp. 354–58; "Audition de M. Paderewski," stenographic account, Records of the Commission to Negotiate Peace, 181.2132101/9, National Archives; F. R. Dolbeare (American Legation, Warsaw) to Lord, May 24, 1919, Records of the Commission to Negotiate Peace, 186.3116/63, *ibid.*; M. K. Dziewanowski, *J. Piłsudski: A European Federalist, 1918–1922* (Stanford, Calif., 1969), p. 135.

55. *Sprawy polskie na konferencji pokojowej w Paryżu w 1919 r. Dokumenty i Materiały* [Polish matters at the Paris Peace Conference in 1919: documents and materials], 3 vols. (Warsaw, 1965), I, 77–104.

56. Bliss to Kernan, March 9 and 21, 1919, Bliss Papers; Mantoux, *Les Délibérations du Conseil des Quatre*, I (March 27, 1919), 54–56.

57. Czarnecki, an American journalist, to the American Commission to Negotiate Peace, March 23, 1919, Wilson Papers; memorandum by Kernan, April 11, 1919, *ibid.*

58. Bliss to Wilson, April 18, 1919, *ibid.*; Paderewski to Pichon, April 18, 1919, Fonds Clemenceau, Vincennes Archive. Erazm Piltz (representative of the KNP in Paris) to Pichon, April 19, 1919, Pologne 83/252–53, French Foreign Ministry Archives.

59. Draft of instructions by Piłsudski, December 1918, Archive of Michał Mościcki, no. 692, Piłsudski Institute, New York; General Stanisław Haller to Piłsudski, April 12, 1919, file 3/627, Adjutantura Generalna Naczelnego Dowództwa, *ibid.*; Prof. St. Dąbrowski to Paderewski, April 12, 1919, file 752, Paderewski Archive, Warsaw.

60. Schwabe, *Deutsche Revolution*, pp. 497, 510, 516–17. Hugh Gibson feared the Polish chauvinists (e.g., Dmowski and Grabski) more than the leftists: see Gibson to the American Commission to Negotiate Peace, May 14, 1919, Henry White Papers, Library of Congress. On Wilson's attitude on May 19 and 21, 1919, see Mantoux, *Les Délibérations du Conseil des Quatre*, II, 108, 146–56; and *The Paris Peace Conference*, V, 775–81.

61. Sejm debate of May 22, 1919, *Sprawy polskie na konferencji pokojowej w Paryżu w 1919 r. Dokumenty i Materiały*, I, 178–85.

62. Wilson's statement to Ray Stannard Baker on board *George Washington*,

March 8, 1919, R. S. Baker Diary, Baker Papers; for Wilson's comments on Dmowski's anti-Semitism, see also Mantoux, *Les Délibérations du Conseil des Quatre*, 1, 474–75.

63. Gibson to Secretary of State, May 30, June 2, and June 20, 1919, 860c.4016/57 and 860c.4016/72, State Department Records, National Archives; Henry Morgenthau Diary, June 26, 1919 (interview with Wilson), and July 6, 1919 (interview with Dłuski), Henry Morgenthau Papers, Library of Congress; see also K. Dłuski to Morgenthau, July 6, 1919, *ibid.*

64. James Headlam-Morley to Lewis Namier, June 30, 1919, in Headlam-Morley, *Diary*, pp. 175–77.

65. Schwabe, *Deutsche Revolution*, pp. 570–637; memorandum for the President, June 4, 1919, Wilson Papers. Lord got his instructions from Wilson by telephone.

66. Cf. Marie-Luise Recker, *England und der Donauraum 1919–1929* (Stuttgart, 1976), pp. 37–39, 42, 267.

Chapter Four

WOODROW WILSON: WAR

AIMS, PEACE STRATEGY, AND

THE EUROPEAN LEFT

INGA FLOTO

Since the late fifties, a remarkable development in the study of Wilsonian foreign policy during the First World War and the Paris Peace Conference has taken place. The authors, obviously taking their cue from contemporary political developments, have "rediscovered" the political significance of the ideological elements in Wilsonian foreign policy. This recognition that ideology is an independent and vital factor in the formulation of American foreign policy is closely related to a change in the focus of interest. Whereas research in the years between the wars and the first few postwar years was naturally concentrated on relations with Germany, a new generation of historians felt themselves attracted to what they considered much more pressing problems of communism and revolution. Bolshevik Russia, therefore, became a matter of the highest concern to these authors. A methodological reorientation has also accompanied this change of interest: foreign policy is no longer regarded as an isolated phenomenon but is analyzed in interplay with domestic policy.[1]

The most important and the most representative of these new interpretations is undoubtedly Arno Mayer's *Political Origins of the New Diplomacy*, which to me represents the first real breakthrough in this trend of Wilsonian research. Mayer analyzed the European political situation and showed how, during the war and culminating in 1917,

the left-wing spectrum of European politics, that is, the liberals and
socialists/social democrats, were rising in political influence and
power. And at the same time, he demonstrated that Wilson's war-aims
policy (for instance the Fourteen Points) was shaped by his keen realization of the fact that his real power basis in European politics was
among these left-wing forces in the Allied countries as well as among
the Central Powers. Wilson's several proclamations can only be properly understood in this perspective.

While Mayer's thesis seems extremely convincing in explaining the
nature of wartime politics in Europe—and thus the main target of the
American war-aims policy—it has a fault. It explains in a compelling
way the relationship between the foreign and domestic policies of the
European governments, but it does not treat the American scene in
the same way; indeed, it does not touch on American domestic policies at all, except by hinting that, in America, the roles in the determination of policy were reversed. The policy of the "conservative"
European governments seemed to be identical with the policy of the
American Republican opposition to Woodrow Wilson, and "in particular Theodore Roosevelt and Henry Cabot Lodge, [who] called for
an unequivocal commitment to unconditional victory over Germany
in a language similar to that of the European parties of order." John
Reinertson, in his dissertation, "Colonel House, Woodrow Wilson,
and European Socialism," has made this point. He asked the question
of who the "power groups" were who determined American foreign
policy, and he found at least two important groups who tried to influence Wilson's thinking: Colonel House and his organization, "radical"
in many respects, and the "conservative" Samuel Gompers, President
of the American Federation of Labor, and his advisers. Although we
are still missing a comprehensive analysis of the significance of the
Republican party's stance on foreign policy, and of the connection
between the American and the European "conservatives," we at least
have the beginning of the study of the relationship between the domestic and the foreign policy of the United States.[2]

In his later book, *Politics and Diplomacy of Peacemaking: Containment
and Counterrevolution at Versailles, 1918–1919* (1969), Mayer analyzed
the period of the Armistice and the Paris Peace Conference. Mayer
demonstrated that, whereas in the period 1917–1918 the left-wing
forces had a decisive influence on political and diplomatic developments, the period following the Armistice witnessed a strong move to

the right. Mayer's main thesis, however, was to demonstrate that the central problem of the peace conference was not Germany, but Russia; the dreaded enemy was not the German army, but the spread of the Bolshevik Revolution. Mayer has undoubtedly touched upon a crucial point in his analysis of the political climate of the peace conference. But the question remains whether he has also managed to provide a new interpretation of the diplomatic conflict. I do not think that he has done so. In another connection, I have tried to show that the supposed influence of the fear of revolution on the peacemakers—and not the least its impact on Wilson—is much overrated. But this problem is only of minor concern to my present subject.[3]

To recapitulate: Mayer's thesis was that the well-known proclamations of Wilson during the First World War are best understood as propaganda, part of an ideological war directed, not only at undermining the authoritarian regime in Germany, but also aimed at strengthening the liberal and socialistic/social democratic forces in the Allied and Associated powers (including Russia). Thus, Wilson's purpose was to provide a counterweight to the Bolshevik ideological offensive, which emanated at the same time and was directed toward the same groups. Wilson's policy was essentially revolutionary if implemented properly: it would mean an American attempt to overthrow the existing "conservative" governments of the Allied powers. A policy formulated in the clear perception of the European political constellation, it was probably also under the impression of a too positive evaluation of the political consequences of this situation.[4] In the following paper, I shall try to indicate some of the determining factors behind this policy: in the first place, Colonel House and the circle around him; and second, some of the difficulties inherent both in the conception and the implementation of such a policy.

Edward M. House played an important role in the formulation of the American war aims and peace strategy. He was Wilson's one confidante in most of his important wartime proclamations, and he was the originator of The Inquiry, Wilson's peace-planning staff. But, as a matter of fact, House's influence was circumscribed: he had no influence whatsoever upon the conduct of the war at home and abroad; moreover, Wilson's central propaganda agency, the Committee on Public Information, was in the hands of George Creel. House's main function was the planning of Wilson's war aims and peace strategy.[5] House was not alone: in The Inquiry, he had established a veritable fact-finding and policy-planning "organization" both in the United States and overseas. Informants both outside and inside the traditional State Department channels provided him with useful information about the political developments on the left side of the European political spectrum. And in the United States, he had established close contacts with young radical journalists such as William C. Bullitt, Lincoln Colcord, and Walter Lippmann: bright young men placed either in the State Department, at the *Philadelphia Public Ledger*—which House briefly tried to make a tool for his own policy—or at *The New Republic*.[6]

Now, the problem is which policy did House advocate, to what degree was he able to influence Wilson and/or was there a common consensus between the two men? And, how was this policy implemented—if it was implemented at all?

Both Wilson and House are impervious and elusive persons: for the evaluation of Wilson's policy, we are reduced, mainly, to his public papers and official correspondence; whereas House kept a lengthy diary, which is one of the main sources of the political history of this period. Unfortunately, the problems surrounding this diary are numerous, but for my present purposes it is enough to state that House's diary entries are mainly directed to posterity and therefore concentrated on supposedly "important" discussions with American and foreign politicians, while the real politico/strategic considerations are either left out or are only intimated.[7] To break through this barrier, it is necessary to turn to other channels of information, such as House's correspondence with different members of his "organization."

It is first necessary to illuminate more clearly the political viewpoints and/or differences between Wilson and House by concentrating on their opinion of the ways and means of implementing the liberal peace program. While the Paris Peace Conference seems to provide the first example of House's enthusiasm for manipulation which led him to a policy to the right of Wilson, there are numerous examples during the war years of his taking a far more liberal view than the President, even though there are signs here, too, of a certain ambivalence. Whereas Wilson, after the American intervention, found it essential to make the successful prosecution of the war the guiding theme of his policy, House, "even after the American declaration of war, continued to hope and strive for a peace of compromise." It is, of course, possible to attribute this to House's declared ambition as a mediator, but the fact remains that his persistence in following Wilson's original program was quite in line with the policy of the liberal forces which Wilson had originally represented and on which the implementation of his active peace program would finally depend.[8]

The touchstone and dividing line in the liberal/socialist interpretation of the war was the Russian Revolution and the fate of Russia. House realized this fact very clearly, but it is no exaggeration to state that the Bolshevik seizure of power in Russia placed all liberals/socialists in a serious dilemma. The Wilson administration itself was split over the question. House hoped to bring Russia back to liberal nationalism by liberalizing Allied war aims and by absorbing Bolshevism into a liberal war consensus. The more conservative administration elements which surrounded Secretary Lansing were suspicious of the Allied left and were also more oriented toward an overtly anti-Bolshevik position. As N. Gordon Levin, Jr., writes: "House never intended his Wilson-Lenin fusion to be other than on Wilson's terms, whereby revolutionary-socialist passion would be moderated by the progressive controls of a pro-allied version of anti-imperialism"; Wilson was much more reluctant and much less prepared "to compromise with the left than either House or *The New Republic*-oriented liberals who went much further even than the Colonel in seeking to accommodate the American war effort to the values of radical anti-imperialism."[9]

The reason why this was so can be very easily inferred. Woodrow Wilson was waging a world war, and his task was not only to contemplate the possible future peace, but also the much more urgent problem of prosecuting the war. The German, not the Russian, question had first priority in his day-to-day deliberations, and, equally important, he had to keep a keen eye on the internal political situation in the United States. He not only had to observe a truce with the Republicans, but he also had to engage American labor in the war effort. And here he certainly encountered great difficulties: not in reconciling Samuel Gompers and his allies with the war, but in preventing the fervent nationalism of the American labor movement from hampering his own liberal peace program.[10] Herein lies the core of the Wilsonian dilemma: in order to stimulate the American war effort, so he thought, he had to promote an extreme nationalism that not only involved labor, but also allowed it to be the tool of the European conservative governments and their antiliberal war aims, and thus to undercut his own peace strategy.[11]

As mentioned earlier, there are very few direct references to this strategy in the House Diary itself. Of those references that exist, the following is of singular importance. It shows that there was a strategy, and that it was discussed between the two men:

> We discussed the trend of liberal opinion in the world and came to the conclusion that the wise thing to do was to lead the movement intelligently and sympathetically and not to allow the ignoble element to run away with the situation as they had done in Russia. He spoke of the necessity of forming a new political party in order to achieve these ends.
>
> . . . Again let me say that the President has started so actively on the liberal road that I find myself instead of leading as I always did at first, rather in the rear end holding him back.[12]

Several diary entries during the summer of 1918 also provide clues. House began to conjecture about the most favorable political constellation for the peace conference. He argued that the best thing would be the establishment of "really liberal governments," not only in Germany, but also in Britain and France, and he even went so far as to discuss the matter with the British Ambassador, Lord Reading. Later on, when the peace conference and the British elections were imminent, House again took up the plan, this time trying to influence Lloyd George through more indirect channels.[13]

If we want to get a closer look at this policy, though, it is necessary to turn to more indirect sources of information, such as the letters which Ray Stannard Baker and Lincoln Colcord wrote to House. Baker, the famous journalist, went to Europe in the spring of 1918, at the initiative of Colonel House, to report to Wilson on developments on the left side of the European political spectrum, especially in England, France, and Italy. The result was a series of excellent and well-informed, but at the same time biased and overly optimistic, reports on the strength of European socialism and liberalism, which seem to have influenced both Wilson and House. Before Baker left, Colonel House briefed him about his new task, and the references in Baker's letters and diary indicate that he was well informed about Wilsonian peace strategy and also strongly committed to its implementation. In one of his letters he wrote: "You may not fully realize it, that in sending me over here, but as a matter of fact, you've inaugurated something new! I have had a curious kind of delight in thinking that I was one of the diplomats of the New Order."[14]

Baker stressed one major point in letter after letter:

> Mr. Wilson can never hope for wholehearted support upon
> the reconstructive side of his program from those at the moment
> in power either here (in England) or in France. His true friends,
> the ones he must go to victory with, are the labour and liberal
> groups. I believe that we shall find that we shall have to be as *im-*
> *placable* and *exacting* in securing *our* disinterested purposes—
> if we were to get anything at all out of our investment of blood
> and treasure—as these interests in seeking their purposes. The
> great source of Mr. Wilson's strength is that while each govern-
> ing group over here can command a part of its own people, Mr.
> Wilson, in so far as his policy is disinterested and democratic, can
> command large and powerful groups in all the nations. They can
> never get real unity, because each has a separate policy, while he
> can. Therefore we must never let these democratic forces in
> England and France get away from us.[15]

And, one might well add, Baker's conclusion lay at the heart of the
Wilsonian strategic conception.

The crucial question, however, was how Wilson could translate this
influence upon the liberal and socialist forces of Europe into active
support at the peace conference. Baker, himself, tried to answer this
question in a letter that he sent at the height of the Pre-Armistice
negotiations. He defined the vital points in Wilson's strategy: the
President ought to come to Europe to establish direct, personal contacts with the liberal and socialist leaders, and "when the time comes
he may have to make or threaten to make an appeal direct to the
people over the heads of the obstructors." Baker thought that, "while
they [the Socialists] agree with us, generally, upon the Wilson program, they have a method of their own which they have by no means
given over—to wit—an International Socialist Conference." Baker
also suggested that "the President might throw his support in favor of
some form of international Conference of Workers, not necessarily
socialists, but all workers. . . . The President himself might address
this assembly and bring them to the support of his method." In conclusion, Baker pointed out that "no one of the three countries [the
Allies] is more fluid, or more open to our leadership, than Italy, or
more willing to accept Mr. Wilson's program or to follow him to the
end." Baker strongly recommended a visit to Italy.[16]

Clearly, Baker enumerated the most effective weapons at Wilson's disposal. Wilson might have used these weapons if the political constellation in Europe had been more conducive to his intentions; he would have been able to take full advantage of the ideological campaign of the war years. At the same time, Baker also pointed to the country in which these weapons would be most effective. House thought that this approach was consistent with Wilsonian policy, and he had gladly accepted the offer of the French Socialists to make a huge welcoming demonstration in the streets of Paris at the arrival of the President. The French Socialists were well aware of the advantages of a publicly demonstrated alliance with the American President. But, to the astonishment of House, Wilson turned the demonstration down; he said that he did not wish to be identified with any single element and recalled "the criticisms already made by those interested in opposing his principles with regard to the source of the popular support he was receiving."[17] Wilson shrank from a confrontation with the Allied governments over the International: he refused to use his prestige to arrange an international socialist conference in Paris at the same time that the peace conference took place, and when the International Socialist Conference finally assembled in Bern, the United States had no official representative there. Only William C. Bullitt was there as an unofficial observer, and even his attendance was officially regretted by Samuel Gompers. The tactic Baker had advocated—the use of an international socialist conference as an instrument in Wilsonian foreign policy—was thus ruled out, for domestic political as well as foreign-policy reasons, before the meeting of the peace conference.[18]

Lincoln Colcord, unlike Baker, stayed in America. He was a bright young journalist, who, from 1917 to 1918, was very close to House. The Colonel used him both as a sounding board and a mouthpiece; the two had something of a father-son relationship. The friendship came to a rather abrupt end sometime in 1918, when the radicalism of Colcord became too much for House—or, this radicalism was perhaps no longer useful in House's relationship with Wilson. At any rate, Colcord's letters to House represent a kind of complementary source to Baker's. While Baker stresses the great possibilities of the Wilsonian strategy, Colcord's letters, at least his letters to House after their estrangement, illuminate the shortcomings and inherent dilemmas in Wilson's policy, especially the discrepancy between his domestic and foreign policies, and what Colcord believed was an erroneous policy toward Bolshevism.[19]

In March 1919, when the peace conference was well under way, Colcord wrote a letter to House in which he described his conception of Wilsonian strategy and criticized its implementation:

> Let me begin by laying down the ground from which I take my point of view. I believe that our analysis of the European political situation of a year ago has now been proven to have been true. The Soviet Government in Russia should have been recognized at the time of Brest-Litovsk. The revolution was ready in Germany. The revolutionary factors in England, France and Italy were as estimated; new and unforeseen circumstances, and especially the President's influence in European politics, have affected them in various ways; but in the main they stand as we outlined them, and victory, much to my surprise, has not retarded their development. Lloyd George, Clemenceau and Orlando should have been overthrown in the spring of 1918. The Gompers mission, with its attempt to split the labor and socialist forces of the Entente, should not have been permitted. The President should have played politics in Europe on the opposition side, with the design of placing the British Labor Party and the French and Italian socialists in power. Last but not least, there should have been a serious effort to liberalize the forces of American labor and public opinion.[20]

The same elements of Baker's attitude appear in this quotation, as does the same exaggerated optimism about the power of the left. Colcord also emphasized the domestic obstacles which blocked the implementation of the Wilsonian strategy; again and again, he stressed the "reactionary" stance of the American Federation of Labor, a stance which Wilson seemed neither able nor willing to change, even at the cost of the success of his own peace strategy.

Throughout these letters, Baker and Colcord exhibit what they *thought* was Wilsonian foreign policy—that is, what House had told them about the American strategy. But these letters also suggest something about the nature of Wilsonian strategy, or rather about the nature of the strategy that could and would have been implemented had the political conditions in Europe been optimal. At least one fact is clear: the American strategy was based on the assumption that Europe would be bankrupt, both economically and politically, at the time of the peace,[21] and that the role of the United States as supreme arbiter would be thus guaranteed. But the situation by the time of the Armistice was quite different. From the American point of view, it was a premature peace; the European countries were not exhausted to such an extent that their political influence had been destroyed, and the American war effort was not yet at the height that guaranteed the possibility of a dictated peace. In other words, when the peace conference opened, the Americans were in a disadvantageous bargaining position; moreover, the European political situation also worked against the American program. Although the revolutionary ferment—and consequently also the popularity of the Wilsonian program—had reached a height in 1917, the tide had turned in late 1918, and, at least in all Allied countries as well as in the United States, there was a conservative/reactionary trend.[22]

What, then, was the American strategy? If we are to trust the few references in the House Diary and the policy that we can deduce from the letters of Baker and Colcord to House, Wilson's approach was something like this: at the end of the war, the United States would be dominant economically, militarily, and politically. All European countries would be completely exhausted, and the United States thus would be able to dictate the peace on its own terms, that is, along the lines of the Fourteen Points and related statements. Moreover, this exhaustion would have caused a leftward trend in European politics. The conservative/nationalistic governments of both the Allies and the Central Powers would be replaced by liberal/socialist-social democratic governments, and they would implement the Wilsonian peace program. Naturally, Wilson considered this situation ideal. But if it did not materialize, what then?

This scenario did not materialize; the German peace offer, from the American point of view, was premature, although Wilson, for various reasons, did not feel that he could reject it. Furthermore, Wilson was keenly aware that "too much success or security on the part of the Allies will make a genuine Peace Settlement exceedingly difficult, if not impossible." But Colonel House, in the Pre-Armistice negotiations, was not able to secure this program.[23] There are many indications that Wilson was in a quandary about what to do in the period between October 1918 and January 1919. He was confronted with totally unforeseen circumstances. This quandary explains his inept appeal to the American public on the eve of the November elections and his vacillation and uncertainty toward the organization and proceedings of the peace conference.

The result was a clash between conflicting interests, not only between the different countries involved, but also between competing political factions inside the countries concerned. The outcome, the Versailles Treaty, is one of the most disputed documents in recent history, but that is not the subject of this paper. Instead my problem concerns whether there are any indications that Wilson, despite the "objective" political conditions, held on to his political strategy. I think there are; and my thesis is that, if we want to understand the more intricate elements of Wilsonian foreign policy, we have to analyze his Italian policy immediately before and during the peace conference. For the Italian situation, at least as it was presented to Wilson, provided the ideal conditions which the Wilsonian strategy had anticipated.

On October 26, 1918, Baker analyzed the Italian situation for Frank L. Polk, Counselor of the State Department, and, of course also for Colonel House and Wilson. In this report, Baker stated, first, that if "there is one thing this war has done in Europe more than another, it is to awaken labor to a new sense of power." This observation, in Baker's opinion, was especially true of Italy. As he pointed out: "In England and France the radical and labor groups are not anti-war, . . . The actual pacifist elements are relatively small, but there is among the under-classes a great amount of unrest and war-weariness, sharpened by a profound distrust of the governments. But in Italy the whole labor and socialist group is not only intensely anti-government but is far more war weary than either the French or the British, and more or less permeated with a peace-at-any-price spirit which has been counteracted by the other forces of the nation only with the greatest difficulty." He thought that the situation was dangerous and probably uncontrollable, at least if the war lasted much longer. Baker also pointed out that in Italy, as in England and France, the socialist and radical groups were not only not decreasing in numbers and in power "(though you may have had reports to the contrary)," but were increasing, and the whole drift of political opinion in the nation seemed to be toward the left. He further corroborated the strength of the Italian Socialists. "The only leader in the world to day who in any way touches or inspires these masses in England, France and Italy," he stressed, "is Mr. Wilson, and if he wins in his program, it will be by virtue of their support, if he fails it will be by virtue of their loss of confidence." In all three countries, Baker had "found the radical leaders standing, so far as foreign policy was concerned . . . practically upon the program laid by Mr. Wilson." Their only questions were: "Does he really mean it?" "Can he count on his following to put it through?"[24]

Baker's judgment was that the Italian Socialists had been the most violent of any European political group in their antiwar views, but he also realized that the logic of events had modified their views. "Yet they still stand strongly for the 'International' and express the deepest sympathy for the Russian Bolsheviks. But there is no doubt that they are accepting Mr. Wilson's leadership in international affairs in this crisis. Of course he has the solid support of all the Reformist Socialists and indeed of all the true liberals of Italy. The difference, therefore, arises not upon the program, but upon the methods of achieving it." This distinction, in Baker's view, was one of the main problems facing Wilsonian diplomacy. Furthermore, Wilson would never be able to unite the governments of Europe, but he could unite the peoples, for they, in Baker's opinion, were all in substantial agreement with his program. In the following pages he then gave a more detailed analysis of the Italian socialist movement and its leaders and again stressed Wilson's influence.

Baker's report suggests not only some of the key elements in the Wilsonian strategy, but also demonstrates some of its inherent difficulties. The European followers of Wilson were not in power; even if they had been, they would have approached peacemaking differently. Baker later elaborated on this theme after the experiences of the peace conference,[25] but it is important to note that, at this early moment, he clearly pointed to the weakest spot in the Wilsonian strategy. Wilson had powerful opponents, not only on the right, but also on the left; his was a true middle position, such as is always difficult to hold in times of crisis. To the left of Wilson stood the Bolsheviks, who had a foreign policy program even more radical than Wilson's and a revolutionary domestic program which Wilson could not condone. Colonel House seems to have been willing to recognize the Bolshevik regime and believed that the new rulers of Russia would be democratic in due time. The young radicals who surrounded him not only were willing but eager to recognize the Soviet regime because

they believed—together with many European radicals and socialists—
that it would demonstrate the sincerity and goodwill of the western
democracies. Wilson himself was more reluctant. We do not know
why, but he certainly had a keen eye on American labor, which, as has
been said, had no sympathy whatsoever for the Bolsheviks. The fact
that Gompers supported this policy was even more damaging and
went directly against Wilson's own interests among European labor.[26]

Wilson's Italian policy is significant because Wilson himself chose to
make the Dalmatian problem a touchstone for his principles, and
because he wanted to use it as a testing ground for the various elements in his original peace strategy. His stance was not anti-Italian, at
least not at the beginning. He gave his consent to the Brenner frontier
at a very early moment in his conversations with the Italians, and,
although he was not willing to accept the Treaty of London line for
the Adriatic, he was willing to assign to Italy three key points in this
region—Pula, Vis, and Valona—as a recognition of Italy's strategic
needs. But the Italians wanted *both* the Treaty of London line *and*
Fiume (Rijeka), and thereby propelled themselves into a head-on collision with American principles.[27] It seems reasonable to infer that
Wilson willingly accepted this confrontation not the least because he
knew, through Baker's reports, of his popularity in Italy especially
among the Italian Socialists, but also among the Italian people as a
whole. He was also not blind to the fact that Italy was not a great
power. At any rate, the Dalmatian question was extremely well suited
as a test of principles, since the United States was the foremost spokesman of self-determination and, at the same time, *not* a signatory to the
Treaty of London.

En route to Europe aboard the *George Washington*, Wilson was en-
grossed by the Adriatic problem. Upon his arrival in Paris, he had
conferences with Prime Minister Vittorio Orlando and Foreign Minister Sidney Sonnino without reaching any understanding, and then
he went to Italy. On December 27, immediately before Wilson's arrival in Italy, Leonida Bissolati, the Reformist Socialist and one of
the President's strongest supporters in Italy, resigned from the government over the Adriatic question. He thought that Italy should
abandon the Treaty of London, and the aim of his resignation was
probably to provoke a "public debate over Sonnino's policy and to
carry on his fight against it from the outside." Bissolati probably also
wished to draw Wilson's attention to the fact that the Italian political

situation offered other possibilities than cooperation with Orlando. It
was, therefore, very natural that Bissolati wanted to meet Wilson
when the President came to Rome. What is important is that Wilson
not only accepted the invitation but even took the initiative for ar-
ranging a meeting and thereby directly intervened in the domestic
affairs of Italy.[28]

The Wilson-Bissolati meeting took place on January 4, and the two
leaders freely exchanged views and discovered a high degree of una-
nimity. The interview culminated with the following remark by Bissolati: "We are waiting for the word from you, to solve these problems.
This program, which I have indicated to you, with which Italy could
be freed from all Imperialism, would render her a stronger ally of
yours, Mr. President, in the struggle which you may have to maintain
against the excessive pretensions of French and English nationalism,
and therefore better able to aid you in your attempt to found the
League of Nations."[29]

In fact, this remark was a direct offer from Bissolati to Wilson:
support me, support "the other Italy," and you will have insured an
important ally in the implementation of the American program. This
conversation would have been remarkable in any circumstances, but,
seen in the perspective of what later took place, it assumes a new
significance. We do not know if Wilson was already contemplating a
more direct intervention in Italian domestic politics, but, later on,
when the crisis reached its climax, he seized upon the means that
Bissolati had recommended and appealed to the Italian people over
the head of the government in power.

For various reasons, the Wilson-Bissolati conversation had no immediate consequences,[30] and, for the time being, Wilson tried other
means, all of them showing a certain highhandedness toward the
Italians. In his approach to Italy, the American President carried out
the same policy that he had hoped to follow at the peace conference
had a more favorable political situation existed. Because of Baker's
reports on Wilson's overwhelming popularity in Italy, which probably
gave him an exaggerated idea of his possibilities of gaining support
among the Italian population, Wilson apparently decided, from the
beginning, to demonstrate his policy in Italy. He was also certainly
encouraged by the fact that a stern attitude toward Italy would be safe
or even popular in the United States. The conflict was also one of
principle: "Nowhere else did the new theories of international policy

championed by President Wilson come so definitely to an issue with the elements of pre-war and war-time diplomacy," James T. Shotwell has rightly remarked. In this exertion of the "new diplomacy," Wilson had, furthermore, the enthusiastic backing of his territorial experts.

This is not the place to go into a detailed discussion of the intricate and protracted Italo-American negotiations at the peace conference— negotiations which at the time seemed to split the entire American delegation into two competing factions which were for or against Italy. A few points, though, are worth remembering. The heart of the conflict lay over the port of Fiume, which the Italians chose to claim, even though it was expressly assigned to Yugoslavia by the Treaty of London. The American territorial experts could in no way accept this solution: it was both contrary to the principle of self-determination and also gave Italy control of the sole important port in the Adriatic (outside Trïeste), and thus the possibility of strangling the economy of the new Yugoslavian state. Wilson followed his experts a long way, although he was willing to find a "free-city" solution for Fiume along the lines of the Danzig settlement. But the Italians would not budge.

As we have seen, Wilson flirted openly with the Italian opposition in the interview with Bissolati in January 1919. By the beginning of February, Wilson actually took the initiative to get the Yugoslavs to ask him to mediate the conflict—on *their* terms.[31] Just before he left Paris in the middle of February 1919, Wilson was frustrated and, prodded by Herbert Hoover and Norman Davis, in fact had contemplated using his powerful economic weapon to restrain the Italians, but, for the time being, he refrained.[32] After Wilson's return to Paris in the middle of March 1919, a series of hectic and complicated negotiations ensued among all levels of the American and Italian delegations. At times, at least, the Italians played such a complicated diplomatic game that most observers felt repelled. In any event, neither the American nor the Italian government was willing to make the essential concessions. When the deadlock seemed an established fact, Wilson, on April 19, decided on direct economic sanctions.[33]

The ultimate weapon in Wilson's strategy, however, was the public appeal over the heads of any and all governments to set forth the liberal peace program as he conceived it. This approach was a vital element in his wartime strategy, and it also played a powerful role in Wilson's attitude toward the peace conference before the war had ended. It is clear from Baker's diary during the peace conference that he, too, felt the same way and actually kept urging Wilson to apply this, supposedly powerful, weapon against the devious tactics of the European governments. But others among Wilson's counselors advised this strategy, among them the economic adviser and trusted friend, Vance C. McCormick. And from Washington, Tumulty had long since recommended: "Only a bold stroke by the President will save Europe and perhaps the world."[34] While the policy which these advisers contemplated was a common appeal to *all* the peoples of Europe, Wilson directed his appeal to Italy.

When Wilson published his appeal to the Italian people on April 23, 1919, the vital compromises with the French and British governments had been made and the Germans had been invited to Versailles. During the serious crisis in the negotiations with the French—and, to a lesser degree with the British—in the first two weeks of April, Wilson was tempted to make a public statement, but in the end had chosen the less dangerous gesture of summoning the *George Washington* to Brest.[35] Breaking the alliance seemed too great a responsibility at that time. Now, however, with a treaty with Germany at least in sight, the whole situation had changed. If Wilson still wanted to prove that his principles meant anything at all, if he still wanted to assert himself as the leader of progress and liberal ideas throughout the world, this moment was his last chance. Moreover, in this policy he had the tacit approval of Lloyd George and Clemenceau.

Wilson's Italian manifesto has been described as "a capital error in judgement."[36] This evaluation is undoubtedly true insofar as its effect in Italy is concerned. If Wilson thought that his declaration of principles would arouse a public pressure which would cause the fall of the Orlando government, or at least increase its willingness to cooperate, he was completely mistaken. The reaction outside Italy, on the other hand, was far more positive, and the American response, in particular, was extremely favorable. "In both Britain and France the political as well as the trade union arms of the labor movement formally and publicly endorsed the President's appeal, calling on their premiers to return to the straight and lofty path of the Fourteen Points," and in the United States the President's stand on Fiume had "the support of practically every shade of unbiased American opinion." The press, the people at large, and, not least of all, Congress were behind him; even Republican Senators Hiram W. Johnson, Reed Smoot, and Albert B. Cummins closed ranks. As Tumulty cabled triumphantly: "This is your supreme hour, and I have never been so proud of you."[37] The American reaction indeed was so favorable that one is tempted to speculate whether the United States, rather than Italy, was the real aim of the appeal.

One is, therefore, tempted to conclude that, when the ultimate sanction in Woodrow Wilson's peace strategy was finally invoked, domestic policy was his main concern.

NOTES

1. For a more complete treatment and for the following argument, see my "Nyere Synspunkter på Woodrow Wilson's Udenrigspolitik," *Historisk Tidsskrift*, IV (Copenhagen, 1969), 107–38; partly reprinted in Inga Floto,*Colonel House in Paris* (Aarhaus, Denmark, 1973; 2d edn., Princeton, N. J., 1981), Appendix I.

2. (Ph.D. dissertation, University of Wisconsin, 1970.) The quotation is from Arno J. Mayer, *Political Origins of the New Diplomacy* (New Haven, Conn., 1959), p. 344.

3. Cf. n. 1, and Floto, *Colonel House in Paris*, pp. 252–57.

4. Arno J. Mayer, *Politics and Diplomacy of Peacemaking: Containment and Counterrevolution at Versailles, 1918–1919* (New York, 1969), pp. 167–77; Floto, *Colonel House in Paris*, pp. 32–33.

5. Floto, *Colonel House in Paris, passim.* On House and The Inquiry, see Lawrence Gelfand, *The Inquiry: American Preparations for Peace* (New Haven, Conn., 1963).

6. On this, see Floto, *Colonel House in Paris*; Christopher Lasch, *The American Liberals and the Russian Revolution* (New York, 1962); Mayer, *Politics and Diplomacy of Peacemaking*; Lawrence W. Martin, *Peace without Victory* (New Haven, Conn., 1958); John Reinertson, "Colonel House, Woodrow Wilson, and European Socialism."

7. For the problems concerning the diary, see Floto, *Colonel House in Paris*, pp. 11–24.

8. *Ibid., passim.* The quotation is from Victor S. Mamatey, *The United States and East Central Europe* (Princeton, N. J., 1957), pp. 81–85.

9. N. Gordon Levin, Jr., *Woodrow Wilson and World Politics: America's Response to War and Revolution* (New York, 1968), p. 66.

10. On these problems, see Mayer's two books, and Reinertson, "Colonel House, Woodrow Wilson, and European Socialism," especially his treatment of the relationship between the Gompers group and the House organization.

11. This at least was the criticism of many liberals such as Lincoln Colcord, R. S. Baker, and others.

12. The Diary of Edward M. House, Feb. 24, 1918, in the Papers of Edward M. House, Yale University Library; hereinafter cited as the House Diary and House Papers.

13. *Ibid.*, June 28, July 28, and Nov. 4, 1918; Floto, *Colonel House in Paris*, pp. 33–34.

14. Handwritten draft of letter No. 21 (Baker to Polk, Sept. 12, 1918), originally dated Sept. 3, 1918, in the Papers of Ray Stannard Baker, Library of Congress; hereinafter cited as the Baker Papers.

15. Baker to Polk, Aug. 10, 1918, *ibid.*

16. Baker to House, Nov. 1, 1918, *ibid.*

17. Floto, *Colonel House in Paris*, p. 34.

18. On the Bern Conference, see Mayer, *Politics and Diplomacy of Peacemaking*, pp. 373–409, and Reinertson, "Colonel House, Woodrow Wilson, and European Socialism," chap. 13; Floto, *Colonel House in Paris*, pp. 106–108.

19. Lincoln Colcord's extremely important correspondence is in the custody of his son, Brooks Colcord, Portsmouth, Maine, who kindly opened his house to me. The papers have been used by Christopher Lasch in his *American Liberals and the Russian Revolution* and especially by Reinertson. They will be hereinafter cited as the Colcord Papers.

20. Colcord to House, March 8, 1919, Colcord Papers.

21. WW to House, July 21, 1917, in Ray Stannard Baker, *Woodrow Wilson: Life and Letters*, 8 vols. (Garden City, N. Y., 1927–39), VII, 180–81. See also WW to House, Sept. 2, 1917, *ibid.*, p. 254.

22. On this, see especially Mayer, *Politics and Diplomacy of Peacemaking*.

23. On the Pre-Armistice negotiations, see Klaus Schwabe, *Deutsche Revolution und Wilson-Frieden* (Düsseldorf, 1971), chap. 2; and Floto, *Colonel House in Paris*, chap. 1. The quotation is from WW to House, Oct. 28, 1918, in Baker, *Wilson: Life and Letters*, VII, 523.

24. Baker to Polk, Oct. 26, 1918, Baker Papers.

25. Baker notebook, Baker Papers.

26. On American labor and the European socialists, see Mayer's two books, and Reinertson, "Colonel House, Woodrow Wilson, and European Socialism."

27. The following discussion of American-Italian relations at the peace conference is based on my analysis in *Colonel House in Paris*, chap. 5. Rene Albrecht-Carrié, *Italy at the Paris Peace Conference* (New York, 1938) is still the fundamental account in one of the principal languages. Ivo J. Lederer, *Yugoslavia at the Paris Peace Conference: A Study in Frontiermaking* (New Haven, Conn., 1963), and Dragan R. Živojinović, *America, Italy and the Birth of Yugoslavia, 1917–1919* (Boulder, Colo., 1972), have, however, added to our knowledge of the diplomatic game, while Mayer's *Politics and Diplomacy of Peacemaking* illuminates important facets of Italian domestic policy. Nevertheless, an up-to-date analysis of the Italian problem, based on French, British, American, and especially *Italian* sources, is still sorely needed.

28. Floto, *Colonel House in Paris*, pp. 90–92.

29. The quotation is from "Digest of the President's Conference with On. Bissolati," in T. N. Page to WW, Jan. 7, 1919, the Papers of Woodrow Wilson, Library of Congress; hereinafter cited as the Wilson Papers.

30. Floto, *Colonel House in Paris*, pp. 92–93.

31. *Ibid.*, pp. 100–101; Lederer, *Yugoslavia at the Paris Peace Conference*, pp. 146–55.

32. Floto, *Colonel House in Paris*, p. 219; Norman H. Davis to WW, Feb. 12, 1919; Hoover to WW, Feb. 12, 1919, Wilson Papers; Hoover to Bliss, Feb. 19, 1919, the Papers of Tasker H. Bliss, Library of Congress; Davis and Strauss to Rathbone, Feb. 13, 1919, House Papers; WW to Carter Glass, Feb. 19, 1919, Wilson Papers.

33. Floto, *Colonel House in Paris*, p. 230; WW to Norman H. Davis, April 19, 1919; Davis to WW, April 18, 23, and 29, 1919; WW to Henry M. Robinson (Shipping Board), April 28, 1919; WW to Glass, April 30, 1919, Wilson Papers; David H. Miller, *The Drafting of the Covenant*, 2 vols. (New York, 1928), I, 300–301.

34. Baker notebook, March 31 and April 2, 1919, Baker Papers; Tumulty to Grayson, April 5, 1919, Wilson Papers; Floto, *Colonel House in Paris*, p. 203.

35. Wilson's manifesto is published in Albrecht-Carrié, *Italy at the Paris Peace Conference*, Doc. 42, pp. 488–500. For the crisis of the conference in the beginning of April 1919, see Floto, *Colonel House in Paris*, chap. 4.

36. Albrecht-Carrié, *Italy at the Paris Peace Conference*, p. 144. On the reaction in Italy, see *ibid.*, pp. 144–49, and Mayer, *Politics and Diplomacy of Peacemaking*, pp. 701–12.

37. Mayer, *Politics and Diplomacy of Peacemaking*, p. 712; Current Intelligence Division, American Section, Weekly Review dated April 27, 1919, the Papers of William C. Bullitt, Yale University Library; Tumulty to WW, April 24, 1919, Wilson Papers.

Chapter Five

WOODROW WILSON AND

WORLD ORDER

KURT WIMER

In a discussion of "Woodrow Wilson and World Order," it is tempting to concentrate on Wilson's contribution to an international organization during the later phases of the war and the establishment of the League of Nations at the Paris Peace Conference. A treatment thus conceived is likely to cover familiar ground. The record of Wilson's contribution to the establishment of the League has been told—and well told—by many scholars, above all, the dean of the Wilson scholars, Professor Arthur S. Link.[1] Rather than repeat what has already been established, this study will concentrate on Wilson's blueprint for a new order at the time when he made his fundamental decision. Wilson made up his mind about basic aspects of his new order shortly after the outbreak of the war; he formed the important elements of his subsequent policy early during the period of neutrality. The President determined to make a war such as the one that had broken out in Europe impossible in the future. To be sure, Wilson adjusted his tactics to the realities of the situation and admitted that, in the war-torn world, he had to be "very careful to suit my action to the developments."[2] But his decisions during the autumn of 1914 were basic and firm and found expression in domestic policies as well as in relations with belligerents and neutrals.

A brief discussion of some of Wilson's personal characteristics and method of making decisions is helpful for an understanding of his design for a new order. Before he made a decision on a crucial issue, Wilson was eager to get all available evidence on the subject. He weighed carefully those factors which affected the problem and usually arrived at a decision after reflection. Occasionally, considerable time would elapse before he reached a conclusion. Reflection permitted him to gain perspective and enabled him to make a rational rather than an emotional decision. Emotionally, Wilson was predisposed toward the Allies. But he wanted to make sure that his judgment would be governed by America's interest, the permanent needs of humanity, and the true interests of the belligerents, rather than by sympathies with one side or the other. As Wilson explained, "The first thought is apt to proceed from impulse, is apt to proceed from prejudice, from predilection, from some transient sympathy, but we cannot afford to sympathize with anybody." He strove to achieve what he called his "sober second thought."[3] Ray Stannard Baker characterized Wilson's mind as "scientific." The President himself used this term in connection with the peace which he wanted to help establish at the end of the war. He wanted a "scientific peace," which, to him, was synonymous with "peace without victory." Significantly, Wilson still advocated a scientific peace after the war: "A statement that I once made that this should be a 'peace without victory' I believe holds as strongly today in principle as it ever did."[4]

Wilson adhered to core concepts. His League plan was a case in point. Many observers have noted that his design deviated from major League proposals advocated in the United States and elsewhere.[5] Wilson based his new order on the power of moral force which "principle and the spiritual obligation—the spirit of right and fairness" would sustain. As he put it: "The mistress of the modern world is opinion: the standard of opinion is the moral judgment of mankind."[6] Wilson was impatient by nature and eager to carry out his plans as soon as possible. Still, if the situation demanded it, he would wait, often with great impatience, until preconditions for the execution of his plan existed. "I never have had any patience with 'ifs' and conjectural cases. My mind insists always upon waiting until something actually does happen and then discussing what is to be done about that."[7] When circumstances indicated, he would compromise on matters which he considered subordinate to his main purpose; however, he could be counted on to adhere to his fundamental principles. In connection with his contemplated Pan-American Pact, Wilson was "quite willing to entertain and discuss any modification . . . provided we can be assured of the acceptance of the principle."[8]

Wilson made great efforts to win support for his projects but was willing to employ daring methods to overcome opposition. In general, he tried to convince through persuasion and education, and he often used informal diplomacy. In the belief that people could be influenced through reason, he appealed to the common interest as well as to enlightened self-interest. If he could not gain the necessary support in this fashion, he was apt to use pressure, including public pressure and confrontation. If these measures failed to assure the desired result, Wilson was capable of going over the heads of opponents to their constituencies. He did not engage in this practice lightly. He used it only as a last resort, after he had become convinced that other means had failed or were unsuitable. Since the struggle over the League of Nations involved a confrontation with the Senate, it is well to recall that, in principle, Wilson condemned this procedure. His clear preference was for the President to "establish intimate relations of confidence with the Senate on his own initiative, not carrying his plans to completion and then laying them in final form before the Senate to be accepted or rejected." He considered a cooperative approach with the Senate to be in "the true spirit of the Constitution."[9] Interestingly, he sought senatorial approval for his Pan-American Pact early during the negotiations but persisted in his course despite indications of a negative response.[10]

Another characteristic of President Wilson was his penchant for secrecy—especially his resolve not to divulge his project for a new order prematurely. Wilson's peace policy early during the war remained largely unrecognized because the secretive President failed to communicate fully with his advisers. Wilson deliberately kept his innermost thoughts regarding peace plans from the highest ranking members of the cabinet, and, to a lesser degree, from Colonel House.[11] House, Wilson's closest adviser, was convinced that he was intimately acquainted with the President's thoughts and intentions. The Colonel even had the impression of a complete identity of views.[12] There is no doubt that House had ready access to Wilson and an ample opportunity to get to know Wilson's mind. Still, there were differences of opinion between the two men which included the all-important issue of peace and the way it was to be brought about.[13] Perhaps their teamwork was at its best when House was in personal touch with the President. In any event, claims that House initiated many of Wilson's peace policies are extremely dubious. The view that, "in this area, the policies of House were the policies of the United States" is difficult to reconcile with the patterns of Wilson's presidential leadership.[14]

Even as a young scholar, Wilson conceived the general principles for organized international life to be based on the American model of a federated democracy. He envisaged "a wide union" of states "with tolerated divisions of prerogative." Governments would join together "for the pursuit of common purposes, in honorary equality and honorable subordination."[15] Democratically governed countries would constitute the foundation for the union of world states. Wilson anticipated that the United States would lead the nations in steady progress toward democracy because the United States had the best form of self-government. In cooperation with England, which had previously given Europe an inspiring example of self-government, the United States could readily promote "that concert of nations which is the best security for the peace of the world."[16] Two years later Wilson wrote: "The day of our isolation is past." Looking forward to this development, he appealed: "We need not fear the expanding scene. It was plain destiny that we should come to this."[17] Wilson intended his internationalism as a counterforce to imperialism. Professor Hidesaburo Kusama recently put it another way: "Wilson, too, was an imperialist, but he was a 'moral imperialist,' interested in expanding American influence abroad not by force but by humanity and teaching the way of self-government."[18]

Before the war, Wilson's references to an international organization remained general. His vision for Americans was to be "instruments of humanity" whose concerns should be with "the true and lasting comfort and happiness of men everywhere."[19] At Mobile, Alabama, the new President spoke on behalf of "human rights" and "national integrity." He pledged that the United States would "never again seek one additional foot of territory by conquest."[20] Wilson continued to look to the spread of democracy as the surest safeguard of peace. He was concerned about embedding peace firmly in the popular mind and speculated that it would come when it was as popular as war: "Then we will hang up the symbols of peace in our households and say, 'Our son served humanity.' "[21] When the war started in Europe, Wilson's mind was on peace, but he had not yet worked out a comprehensive formula for its restoration and preservation.[22]

Within two weeks after the outbreak of the European war, Wilson devised a far-reaching program for a new international order. He examined the conditions which brought Europe to her present predicament and concluded that relations among nations had to be put on a different basis if a similar catastrophe was to be avoided in the future. The task was staggering. But Wilson never hesitated to pursue a cause which he recognized as his duty: "We must face the situation in the confidence that Providence has deeper plans."[23] Determined to meet the challenge, he sought ways of curbing imperialistic national ambitions and rivalries. In particular, he deliberated on ways of organizing nations to prevent future wars. During the first month of the war he had several conversations with members of his family and close friends about the need for a new postwar order. His brother-in-law, Stockton Axson, recalled in great detail the first of these conversations which took place in "early" August 1914. Wilson told Axson that "the great settlement of the world would not be by arms but by the negotiations which would follow" the fighting. Wilson then identified four principles which in the future should govern the relations of nations:

1. There must never again be a foot of ground acquired by conquest.
2. It must be recognized in fact that the small nations are on an equality of rights with the great nations.
3. Ammunition must be manufactured by governments and not by private individuals.
4. There must be some sort of an association of nations wherein all shall guarantee the territorial integrity of each.

Wilson explained each point. His comments on the last principle revealed his full vision for his contemplated new order.

> It was absolutely essential that there should be a union of the governments of the world—all combined to protect the integrity of each. . . . Any country which should attempt violations on any other country would thereby automatically bring on war. . . . Modern conditions had brought the world into such a close neighborhood that never again would it be possible for the world at large to regard a quarrel between two nations as a particular and private quarrel. . . . An attack in any quarter was an attack on the equilibrium of the world. . . . The safety of the world demanded

such a combination of the force of the nations as would maintain peace throughout all the world.[24]

Some two years later Wilson recalled his conversations in August 1914 with Dr. Axson and reaffirmed his commitment to the guiding principles which he had then enunciated. He considered their realization necessary "for the preservation of world peace."

In the autumn of 1914, Wilson considered strict neutrality as the most promising policy for the United States to bring about a stable postwar world. There was then a consensus among the American people in favor of neutrality. Wilson shared this opinion, but his reasons transcended the commonly accepted views. For Wilson, neutrality was not merely America's traditional policy nor "the petty desire to keep out of trouble." He explained: "I am interested in neutrality because there is something so much greater to do than fight." The United States would uphold the processes of peace and safeguard the advances which mankind had made through the law of nations. To Wilson, neutrality imposed restraints which included the subordination of personal feelings to the well-being of humanity in the service of peace: "The test of friendship is not now sympathy with the one side or the other, but getting ready to help both sides when the struggle is over."[25] He sought even-handed treatment of all belligerents and hoped that the United States would serve as an example to the world in her "effort at perfect impartiality."[26] In the war-torn world, the application of this standard presented difficulties, and Wilson attempted to apply neutral policies as rigorously as circumstances permitted. This is not to say that he considered neutrality in itself an adequate policy for the United States. Neutrality was "negative." It merely constituted a foundation on which he hoped to build a positive program for permanent peace.[27]

From the beginning of the war, Wilson wanted to become a catalyst for a fair settlement with good prospects for permanency. The United States encouraged the belligerents to find a suitable settlement which could be made lasting through an exchange of pledges. In his appeal of August 18, 1914, Wilson urged the American people to hold themselves "ready to play a part of impartial mediation," and, on December 8, 1914, he told Congress of his "dearest present hope" to find "the opportunity to counsel and obtain peace in the world and reconciliation and a healing settlement."[28] Wilson wanted the war to end in "deadlock" so that peace without victory could become the basis for a lasting peace. He condemned the imperial aspirations of both sides and favored a settlement that would not deviate drastically from the *status quo ante bellum*. Above all, he wanted a just peace. No other had a chance to last or deserved to endure. Should one group of nations succeed in "enforcing its will upon others," the resulting unjust peace would "be sure to invite further calamities."[29] He feared that the belligerents might not agree to the kind of settlement that he had in mind as long as they perceived a chance for total victory. The challenge to his diplomacy, therefore, was to induce the belligerents to conclude a peace of accommodation.

The national interest of the United States reinforced Wilson's conclusion. From this point of view, too, Wilson had misgivings over the prospect of victory by either side. While an Allied victory would not "hurt greatly the interests of the United States," he was uneasy lest peace on Allied terms might lead to Russian domination of Europe as well as to other undesirable consequences.[30] His apprehension over the implications of a possible German victory was also marked. Contrary to a widely held view, he did not consider such an eventuality as an immediate threat to the security of the United States. However, he feared that this outcome might jeopardize democratic institutions and necessitate American preoccupation with military affairs. Peace based on stalemate would avoid these dangers. Accordingly, America's national interest coincided with the needs of humanity for a negotiated peace which would make a new order possible.

Wilson pursued policies designed to bring about a peace settlement which could be made lasting through a league of peace. He was aware that conditions in Europe did not permit public advocacy or even discussion of his plans for world peace: "I must refrain from comment . . . in matters touching peace just now until the moment comes when I can act."[31] He adjusted his peace diplomacy to developments and was careful to carry his program only to "the first practicable step."[32] After his initial formal mediatorial overtures proved fruitless, Wilson turned to informal diplomatic exchanges with the countries at war. These efforts acquainted the major belligerents with Wilson's basic ideas for world peace during the first months of the war. In turn, Wilson became aware early of the fundamental attitudes and responses of the warring nations. He was, therefore, in a position to plan his subsequent strategy and tactics on the basis of information rather than surmise.

Wilson and the German leaders learned of each other's plans for peace through Austria. House, in early October 1914, communicated the essential features of Wilson's peace program to the Austrian Ambassador, Constantin Dumba, who promptly passed on the proposals to his government. The Austrian government authorized Dumba to tell House that the proposals were "worthy of consideration," provided that the German Ambassador agreed.[33] Ambassador Johann Heinrich von Bernstorff objected. His instructions were to refrain from taking steps toward rapprochement and to let the Allies declare their conditions of peace first.[34] In these circumstances, Dumba was to limit his comments to appreciative remarks about his government's interest in Wilson's plan. Dumba went further and revealed to House that Austria would have cooperated with the President had it not been for German objections. House so informed Wilson, who thus became aware—some three months after the outbreak of the war—of the negative German reaction to his peace proposals.[35]

The Austrian government sent Wilson's peace proposals to German Chancellor Theobald von Bethmann Hollweg with the request for common action. Bethmann Hollweg, in reply, clarified Germany's reactions. He speculated that American mediation "promised little practical success," largely because America's aim of Anglo-German reconciliation would be most difficult to achieve.[36] Germany also objected to the manner in which Wilson sought peace through an international congress. The Chancellor, a *"Realpolitiker,"* considered Wilson's "world-redeeming tendencies for peace" irrelevant if not harmful. Wilson would raise questions of disarmament, mediation, world peace, and a host of other irksome issues: "The more utopian they are the more they would increase difficulties of practical negotiations."[37] Thus Wilson's call for permanent peace, which the President hoped would facilitate the way to immediate peace, had an adverse effect on German leaders.

The Imperial Chancellor also reacted negatively to Wilson's specific proposals. These proposals were:

I. No considerable or decisive territorial cessions which would lead to new desires for revenge by damaging permanently national interest or self esteem.

II. Mutual guarantee of territorial integrity of all Powers (large and small).

III. Guarantees against prevailing militarism; by this is meant general partial disarmament on land and sea. The state to take over all arsenals, weapons' factories and dockyards so that the egotistical interests of private industry can be eliminated. An international commission to control the execution of the agreed partial disarmament so that the ratio of forces in relation to water and to land cannot be changed secretly by a Power in its favor.

The Wilsonian proposals also contained a suggestion that "guarantees had to be created so that peace would be ensured for at least fifty years."[38]

Bethmann Hollweg's comment on Wilson's first point was somewhat noncommittal. Depending on "the fortunes of war," he speculated about the possibility of some German territorial gains. (Interestingly, Foreign Secretary Gottlieb von Jagow's initial draft considered point number one as "by and large acceptable.") The Chancellor regarded the President's second point as "an empty formula" and ruled out his third point as unrealizable. Bethmann Hollweg doubted the usefulness of "all" of Wilson's proposals because they were permeated by an "impractical delirium for peace." Still, he considered it poor diplomacy to reject the American proposal "in principle." He suggested instead to give an impression of "sympathetic acceptance" without "touching closely on the specific points."[39] To insure common action, the Chancellor permitted his Austrian counterpart to read a draft letter of Under-Secretary Arthur Zimmermann to Colonel House. It stressed Germany's sincere appreciation of America's offers and her desire for restoration of peace. However, Germany was involved in a war forced upon her by her enemies which made "it impossible" for her "to take the first step towards making peace." Requests for overtures should come from the other side. In short, a diplomatically worded rejection.[40]

Wilson, some two months after the outbreak of the war, advocated significant peace ideas to the British which were incorporated later in the Covenant of the League of Nations. In mid-September, the President thought it wise to establish informal contacts with British leaders. He asked Colonel House, his chief emissary for informal diplomacy, to seek clarification of the minimum terms on which the British would conclude peace. House promptly confirmed that England would negotiate on the basis of what later became known as the two-point program: "The surmise that all England wants is a permanent guaranty of peace, by disarmament and other effective measures, and a proper indemnity for Belgium, is quite right."[41] Wilson was convinced that Britain's allies would follow—or could be made to follow—her lead. Wilson's major objective, therefore, was to induce England to negotiate with Germany without trying to crush her. House's approach at that time was based on concepts of balance of power. "If the war continues either Germany or Russia becomes supreme in Europe. Both alternatives are fatal to balance of power. It would be better to begin negotiations before the balance is upset." At the same time he cautioned the British not to reject or disregard German offers for negotiations lest "England incurs the danger of losing sympathy here [in the United States]."[42] There was no reply aside from the British Ambassador's repeated expressions of disinclination for negotiations with Germany. Early in October, Wilson asked House to get in touch with the British Foreign Secretary, Sir Edward Grey, and to point out to him in clear language the danger of postponing peace negotiations. The Colonel's letter included the following Wilson-inspired provisions: Manufacture of arms by governments only with arrangements for inspection "by representatives of all nations" and removal of "all sources of national irritation" to prevent "a sore spot" from growing into "a malignant disease." Most important, Wilson asked for a guarantee for the inviolability of territorial possessions: "When the war is ended and the necessary territorial alignments made, it seems to me, the best guaranty of peace could be brought by every nation in Europe guaranteeing the territorial integrity of every other nation."[43]

Backed by their allies, the British responded that they wanted no immediate American initiative for peace. Should Wilson ignore this advice, he might jeopardize his chance for mediation later. Wilson waited for developments—to be sure it was a "watchful waiting." Meanwhile, he counted on British leaders to give him "a hint" when his mediation would be welcome. Sir Cecil Spring Rice, British Ambassador to the United States, was hopeful that this time would arrive, but he was not now prepared to say just when.[44] Late in November, Henry van Dyke, American Minister to Holland, returned to the United States from Europe. He told Wilson that Allied statesmen recognized the "eager desire" of the United States to bring the war to an early conclusion but counseled against further American initiatives "at this time."[45] Van Dyke also transmitted to Wilson "a personal, unofficial message" from Grey about Britain's attitude toward American participation in a postwar peace: "The presence and influence of America in the council of peace after the war will be most welcome to us provided we can be assured of two things: First, that America stands for the restoration of all that Germany has seized in Belgium and France. Second, that America will enter and support, by force if necessary, a league of nations pledged to resist and punish any war begun without previous submission of the cause to international investigation and judgment."[46] While this message contained no hope for early peace negotiations, it encouraged Wilson in the belief that Britain—in contrast to Germany—would welcome American participation in the peace settlement following the war.

In November and early December 1914, Wilson sought wider backing for his peace plan. The results of the off-year elections of November 3 "distressed" him. He feared that people abroad, "where alone I care for personal prestige just now," would raise questions "whether I could really be accepted as the spokesman of the United States." His concern led him to review his plans and reexamine "all the means available for carrying them out."[47] Hitherto, Wilson had considered it "very desirable that a single nation should act" as mediator. He anticipated that the United States would be that nation and speculated that "when the time comes we shall receive an intimation that our intermediation would be acceptable."[48] After the election this policy seemed inadequate. Even if the belligerents should ask for Wilson's intermediation—a big if—he might not be able to make the interests of humanity prevail. Wilson concluded that he needed broader and more effective backing, and he hoped to find that support by organizing the neutrals for peace. With the help of the neutrals, he would be in a commanding position at a conference of all nations which he contemplated calling at the proper time. At this conference the belligerents would have to deal with him, not only as the President of the United States, but also as the spokesman of the other neutrals. Backed by such a combination, he could exert great moral pressure on the nations at war. If moral pressure should be insufficient, the same combination could institute an economic boycott against the belligerents which refused to attend a conference or failed to accept provisions which the interests of the world demanded.[49] To test the possibility of realizing his plans, Wilson asked House in mid-December to get in touch informally with the ambassadors in Washington of the major Latin American countries. He also asked the Colonel to go to Europe to lay the "indispensable groundwork" for peace.[50] In an effort to initiate peace negotiations, House would try to induce the leaders of the belligerent countries to accept reasonable terms that could be guaranteed. He would also inform them of Wilson's plan to call a conference of all nations and explain to them its need and purpose. House wrote in his diary on December 20, 1914: "He [Wilson] said he needed me on two Continents."

Wilson's Latin American policies should be seen in the context of his quest for permanent peace. By forming a "model" league of nations in the western hemisphere, he would demonstrate to the belligerents the value of a security organization. He explained to House that the significance of his contemplated Pan-American Pact would transcend the western hemisphere. Countries outside the Americas might join it at the end of the war and thereby "enlarge it to a world organization."[51] Wilson insisted that the Pan-American League be based on the central pledge of a "mutual guarantee of political independence" and "mutual guarantees of territorial integrity." These provisions became part of the first article of his draft of a Pan-American Pact which he submitted on February 1, 1915, to Argentina, Brazil, and Chile. The draft treaty also provided for settlement of disputes, governmental control of munitions, and delay of hostilities.[52] When Chile hesitated to accept central obligations, Wilson thought of concluding the treaty without her: "It would not be wise to let some enter upon other terms than the rest. I think the understanding should be the same for all who come in, otherwise some very confused responsibilities might arise."[53] In May, Wilson told the Pan-American Financial Conference that he wanted the Americas to show the world "the way to peace, to permanent peace."[54] This guiding purpose revealed the direction of Wilson's peace policies both immediately and in the long run. In the context of his plans for a peace conference, Wilson looked at Latin America as the nucleus around which the neutrals might unite in favor of terms which would make permanent peace possible. Later, although the Pan-American Pact could not be consummated, Wilson used the central idea of this abortive pact as the guiding principle of the Covenant of the League of Nations: "The whole family of nations will have to guarantee to each nation that no nation shall violate its political independence or its territorial integrity. That is the basis, the only conceivable basis, for the future peace of the world, and I must admit that I was ambitious to have the states of the two continents of America show the way to the rest of the world as to how to make a basis of peace."[55]

To facilitate a just peace at the earliest possible moment, Wilson considered it advantageous to have two conferences. He expected the countries at war to settle their territorial and other immediate differences in a conference of belligerents, or, as Wilson called it, "the first convention." The United States, the other neutrals, and the belligerents would meet in a "second convention," which would consider "questions growing out of the war."[56] Wilson planned to convene this convention, preside over it, and guide its proceedings. While the belligerents negotiated at the first convention, the second convention could deliberate about revision of international law, principles of future civilized warfare, rights of neutrals, etc. House in Europe expressed only limited expectations of a second convention,[57] but Wilson hoped that it would play a crucial role in the making of the peace. The second convention could exert a significant influence on the belligerents by inducing them to accept reasonable terms in anticipation of guarantees which it could arrange if the belligerents concluded a guaranteeable peace. There was thus a subtle interrelation between the two conventions. Only a fair peace could lead to a league of nations with guarantees for stable borders, but the prospect for guarantees (to be worked out by the second convention) might induce the belligerents to accept more moderate terms and make a fair peace possible. House summarized Wilson's position when he told Spring Rice: "His [Wilson's] point of view is that he will have nothing to do with the discussion of terms of peace, but *may be* with [the] question of a guarantee against a recurrence of what happened last year."[58]

House reported to Wilson from Europe that belligerents and neutrals enthusiastically accepted his plan for a second convention. During the early part of House's trip, Wilson was far from pleased with the Colonel's prolonged stay in England. House initially concentrated his efforts on the vain attempt to achieve an early peace based on Britain's "two-point program." Wilson's effusive praise of the Colonel's accomplishments was associated with the latter's glowing accounts of laying the groundwork for the second convention. House reported that German leaders received this plan cordially and that leading ministers assured him that "Germany will stand with us for a second convention."⁵⁹ According to House, support and cooperation from British leaders was even more far-reaching and extended to the "freedom of the seas" in which Wilson was vitally interested: "When peace is concluded such a measure [freedom of the seas] will be adopted. Grey speaks of it all the time and with growing fervor. His only reservation is that there shall be equal freedom of the land, which will doubtless also be brought about through the desire of all nations."⁶⁰ The Colonel disclosed Wilson's intentions for a second convention to American ambassadors stationed in European neutral countries and reported their favorable reaction.⁶¹ Wilson was pleased with these reports, but House's overly optimistic accounts may have made him too hopeful of what he could expect, especially from the belligerents.⁶² Wilson's impressions of British reactions to his peace plans remained relatively untested for a considerable period of time, but he soon had an opportunity to ascertain Germany's true intentions.

Following the sinking of the *Lusitania* on May 7, 1915, Germany sent Francis van Gheel Gildemeester, a Dutch subject, to the United States in an attempt to soften the impact of that incident. Wilson used the occasion to convey to Germany his overall aims for a peace of accommodation along the following lines:

1. The status quo in Europe
2. Freedom of the seas to such a far-reaching extent that it would amount to neutralization of the sea
3. Adjustments of colonial possessions.⁶³

Wilson let it be known that he wanted to expedite peace mediation by convening a conference of all nations. He expressed optimism about German cooperation in the belief that "the above mentioned conditions of peace would be so favorable to us [Germany] that we might accept them more readily than our enemies." At the same time, he let the Germans know that he had the power to secure the compliance of the Entente powers. If a belligerent country should fail to cooperate, "the neutral states should obligate themselves to cut off those belligerents which should refuse to attend the conference from importation of necessities of life, munitions, etc." This threat of an economic boycott was directed against England and her allies because, as Wilson pointed out, Germany was "cut off anyway from foreign commerce."⁶⁴ When the Germans failed to respond, they confirmed Wilson's apprehension that his peace proposals were unacceptable to them. Some five months later, Wilson still believed that Germany's peace plans excluded the United States: "I have expected all along that Germany would, when she thought that the time had come to talk of peace, try to exclude us from a part in the settlement of terms."[65] Since Germany would not cooperate with him, he drew closer to the Allies in his efforts to achieve the kind of peace that he thought the world needed.

In the House-Grey Memorandum of February 1916, Wilson went far to cooperate with the Allies to bring about the kind of peace he had in mind. England and France would invite Wilson to call a conference at a time they considered opportune. If Germany should refuse to attend or if she should insist on unreasonable terms at the conference the United States would "probably" join the Allies as a belligerent.[66] The offer remained within the framework of Wilson's overall goal for peace. He was ready to cooperate with either side which would let him call a conference on the basis of reasonable peace terms. To overcome opposition, he was prepared to exert effective pressure on belligerents who were unwilling to accept reasonable and guaranteeable terms. To be sure, Wilson's quasi-promise in the House-Grey Memorandum was more far-reaching than the corresponding pledge that he had held out to Germany in the Gildemeester probe. Just the same, Wilson considered an economic boycott as an effective means of compelling the Allies if they resisted a reasonable peace settlement.[67] In short, Wilson's basic commitment in the House-Grey Memorandum remained in line with his efforts to bring about a peace of accommodation which could be guaranteed by a league of nations.[68] Months later, Wilson realized that the British did not intend to ask him to call a conference so long as they perceived a chance for victory. He was disappointed and disillusioned.

Subsequently, Wilson relied on public pressure to induce the belligerents to move toward peace. On May 27, 1916, he advocated publicly a "universal association of nations" which was to provide for each nation "a virtual guarantee of territorial integrity and political independence." The United States was ready to become "a partner" in such an organization if the belligerents would conclude peace based on the following "fundamental" principles:

1. People have a right to determine their own sovereignty.
2. The rights of small states have to be respected in the same way as those of the large nations.
3. The world has a right to be free from wars of aggression.

Wilson insisted that the belligerents had to settle their own immediate concerns: "Our interest is only in peace and in its future guarantees."[69] Wilson disclosed his most comprehensive vision of peace in a speech to the Senate on January 22, 1917. He was now ready to "uncover realities" and declared publicly that "peace without victory" was his guiding policy for a lasting settlement: "Victory would mean peace forced upon the loser, a victor's terms imposed upon the vanquished. It would be accepted in humiliation, under duress, at an intolerable sacrifice, and would leave a sting, a resentment, a bitter memory upon which terms of peace would rest, not permanently, but only as upon quicksand. Only a peace between equals can last." Other indispensable principles for a sound peace included the equality of nations and the right of peoples to choose their own sovereignty. Wilson looked forward to United States participation in a League for Peace based on these principles. He was confident that a world league could provide effective security by becoming "the organized major force of mankind." It would make possible future disarmament on land and sea. Wilson characterized the principles on which the league would be based as "American principles, American policies," to which liberal forward-looking people everywhere would subscribe. "They are the principles of mankind and must prevail."[70]

After the severance of relations with Germany, Wilson considered calling a conference of neutrals to avoid American belligerency. He had thought all along that the neutrals could "affect the whole course and the ultimate results of the war."[71] Wilson soon realized that it was not possible to hold an "actual conference" and sought instead some other "cooperative action . . . upon which neutrals might at this time draw together in a League of Peace."[72] Encouraged by an overture from the Swiss Federal Council, Wilson drafted and revised a significant document which he called the "BASES OF PEACE." It contained four essential points: two mutual guarantees and two mutual agreements. Through the guarantees, he sought to insure "political independence" and "territorial integrity" for all nations. However, the United States would only guarantee "territorial arrangements" if their "conformity with the general principles of right and comity" would assure "their reasonableness and natural prospect of permanency." Through one of the mutual agreements, Wilson sought to rule out "economic warfare" in the postwar world. Wilson was disturbed by Allied designs of continuing economic warfare against Germany after the war as arranged for by the Paris Economic Conference of 1916. There was no place in his new order for combinations seeking "to throttle the industrial life of any nation." The other mutual agreement was designed to "limit armaments, whether on land or sea." Realization of this complex issue depended in large part on the participation of a sufficient number of nations in "these covenants" to constitute "the major force of mankind."[73]

In a "GENERAL NOTE" appended to the "BASES OF PEACE," Wilson explained his expectation of an evolutionary development of a full-fledged league. He questioned the wisdom of forming "at the outset any permanent tribunal or administrative agency." Instead he advocated "an office of correspondence through which all matters of information could be cleared up, correspondence translated by competent scholars, and mutual explanations and suggestions exchanged."[74] Wilson preferred the gradual emergence of an international organization. His main concern was that nations should accept a few core principles and exchange meaningful pledges. He was satisfied to let experience and history do the rest: "All that we can hope for is to agree upon definite things and rely on experience and subsequent exchanges of treaty agreement to develop and remove the practical difficulties."[75]

American participation in the war did not change Wilson's fundamental aims for peace. While he was certain henceforth of a seat at the peace table, his challenge remained to attain sufficient influence to secure the terms that he considered necessary for a just and permanent peace. He was optimistic about such a prospect at the end of the war even though he considered his influence limited at the outset: "England and France *have not the same views with regard to peace that we have* by any means. When the war is over we can force them to our way of thinking, because by that time they will, among other things, be financially in our hands; but we cannot force them now."[76] As the war progressed, he tried to lay the foundations for his peace plan in ways that were possible. Early in December 1917, he urged House, then in Paris at an inter-Allied conference, "to discuss terms of peace in a spirit conforming with my January address to the Senate."[77] At the conference, House tried to secure a statement regarding "general war aims, and the formation of an international association for the prevention of future wars."[78] The "Associated Powers" failed to endorse his resolution. In turn, the Colonel ruled out a resolution acceptable to the others and let it be known that "they might draw up a resolution to suit themselves," but "in no event would the United States sign it."[79] Subsequently, Wilson enunciated peace aims unilaterally. In his famous address to Congress of January 8, 1918, he outlined his essential peace program in fourteen points. His last point dealt with the formation of an association of nations to guarantee the political independence and territorial integrity of all states. He reiterated his principles in a message to Congress on February 11, 1918, and in an address at Mount Vernon on July 4, 1918. Finally, in a speech in New York City on September 27, 1918, he clarified his economic peace plan and asked that the league become an integral part of the peace settlement. In the armistice negotiations of October 1918, Wilson was able to make his program the basis of the peace negotiations.[80]

Wilson wanted the Covenant framed at the peace conference to consist of a limited number of core pledges to which nations had to agree. He discouraged the formulation of a constitution for a league even during the latter part of the war.[81] In his judgment, it was best to concentrate on central pledges:

> My own conviction . . . is that the administrative *constitution* of the League must *grow* and not be made; that we must *begin* with the solemn covenants, covering mutual guarantees of political independence and territorial integrity (if the final territorial agreements of the peace conference are fair and satisfactory and *ought* to be perpetuated), but that the method of carrying those mutual pledges out should be left to develop of itself, case by case.[82]

Wilson deplored the fact that proponents of a league usually started with rigid organizational structures: "They are talking about organization, but they have the cart before the horse. I do not myself feel that I could write out a plan of international organization, and I do not know who can."

Seemingly contrary to this tenet, Wilson, in the summer of 1918, asked House to draw up a detailed draft of a constitution of a league and even took issue with House's suggestions shortly afterward. Wilson obviously wanted to have a possible version in hand. For tactical reasons, Wilson considered it wise to "prepare some plan of organization for the proposed League" to "prevent being forestalled by others."[83] To keep the league machinery simple, Wilson, shortly before the peace conference, thought that it would be wise for the ambassadors assigned to some small neutral country (the Netherlands or Switzerland) initially to constitute the league. However, Wilson was not dogmatic about such an arrangement and did not press the issue. On the other hand, he conducted skillful summit diplomacy to make the League "the first work of the Peace Conference."[84] He succeeded in this endeavor.

The plenary session of the Preliminary Peace Conference of January 25, 1919, adopted a resolution to create a League of Nations "as an integral part of the general Treaty of Peace."[85] The conference also authorized the establishment of a commission to draw up a constitution. The commission, under Wilson's chairmanship, drew up the Covenant of the League of Nations in the beginning of February 1919. At Wilson's insistence, the following pledge was inserted: "The High Contracting Parties undertake to respect and preserve as against external aggression the territorial integrity and existing political independence of all States members of the League."[86] Wilson considered it the heart of the Covenant.

Wilson believed that nations would moderate their claims as a result of membership in a protective League with effective guarantees for their territorial integrity and political independence. He was disappointed when the leaders of the great powers failed to take the League seriously. On the other hand, realization of the significance that Wilson attached to the League played a great role during the negotiations. The British went along with Wilson's desire to draft the Covenant early in the conference because they hoped thereby to "ease other matters."[87] After the Covenant was drawn up, the great powers skillfully used the League issue to secure special concessions through "threats or insinuations that they would not subscribe to the League unless their demands were conceded."[88] Wilson disliked compromises of this kind, but made concessions for the sake of the League. In the end, he admitted that "many of the results" of the Peace Conference were "far from ideal." He counted on the League of Nations to rectify shortcomings in the future.[89]

Wilson based his new order on fundamental moral principles. But he was also a realist. He himself remarked that his basic policies would have been the same had he been a "sheer Machiavelli." In essence, he attempted "to work out a purely scientific proposition, 'What will stay put?'"[90] His formula for lasting peace was to have members of a postwar league of peace assume fundamental obligations provided the terms of the emerging settlement were guaranteeable. He conceived the fundamental principles for a new order shortly after the outbreak of the war and considered it his sacred mission to make them a reality in ways open during American neutrality, war, and peace. "It was a mission of peace, of sacrifice, of leading the nations into a new international community organized to achieve right ends."[91]

NOTES

1. See Arthur S. Link, "Woodrow Wilson and Peace Moves," *The Higher Realism of Woodrow Wilson* (Nashville, Tenn., 1971), pp. 99–109.
2. WW to James Bryce, Oct. 9, 1914, the Papers of Woodrow Wilson, Library of Congress; hereinafter cited as the Wilson Papers.
3. WW to the Daughters of the American Revolution, April 19, 1915, Wilson Papers. Wilson wrote to Edith Bolling Galt: "I have to keep a vigilant watch on my emotions." WW to Edith Bolling Galt, May 26, 1915, *ibid*. See also WW to E. B. Galt, June 9, 1915, *ibid*.
4. Wilson on his trip to Europe, Dec. 1918, the Charles L. Swem Collection, Princeton University Library. Two months after the war started, Wilson advocated "a peace without victory." Mary E. Hoyt, Memorandum of Oct. 1926, p. 21, the Papers of Ray Stannard Baker, Library of Congress; hereinafter cited as the Baker Papers. For Wilson's use of, and even preference for, the term "scientific peace" for "peace without victory" see Wilson's comments as cited in Arthur S. Link, *Wilson*, 5 vols. to date (Princeton, N. J., 1947–), v, 268; Baker characterized Wilson's mind as "scientific" in his notes of a conversation with the President on May 11, 1916. Notebooks, Baker Papers.
5. Warren F. Kuehl, *Seeking World Order* (Nashville, Tenn., 1969), p. 276. See also Calvin D. Davis, *The United States and the Second Hague Peace Conference* (Durham, N. C., 1975), chap. 19, and David S. Patterson, *Toward a Warless World* (Bloomington, Ind., 1976), pp. 254–55.
6. Wilson's "Outline of Welcoming Remarks" for address to American Bar Association, Oct. 19, 1914, Wilson Papers. For the influence of Wilson's Calvinistic background on his political thought, see Link, "Woodrow Wilson and His Presbyterian Inheritance," *Higher Realism*, pp. 3–20.
7. WW to E. B. Galt, Aug. 18, 1915, Wilson Papers.
8. WW to William Jennings Bryan, March 8, 1915, the Wilson-Bryan Cor-

respondence, the National Archives; hereinafter cited as the Wilson-Bryan Corr.

9. Woodrow Wilson, *Constitutional Government in the United States* (New York, 1908), pp. 139–40.

10. According to Chandler P. Anderson, the Senate Foreign Relations Committee "almost unanimously refused to sanction" the Pan-American Pact which Wilson submitted informally while Bryan was Secretary of State. The Diary of Chandler P. Anderson, March 10, 1919, Library of Congress.

11. For Wilson's reluctance to reveal his "whole mind" to William Jennings Bryan and Robert Lansing, see the Diary of Edward M. House, June 24, 1915, in the Papers of Edward M. House, Yale University Library; hereinafter cited as the House Diary and House Papers. The same entry also shows that Wilson was not quite in agreement with House's estimate of his own contribution: "The President tried to minimize what I had done." *Ibid.* In his diary, House mentioned from time to time that he had insufficient information about Wilson's plans. An early illustration is House's record of Dec. 3, 1914, *ibid.* Wilson considered House faithful, loyal, devoted, and wise. Above all, the President felt comfortable with him. Still, Wilson thought of House as a "counsellor" with limitations: "Intellectually he [House] is not a great man. His mind is not of the first class. He is a counsellor not a statesman." WW to E. B. Galt, Aug. 28, 1915, Wilson Papers.

12. House Diary, Jan. 25, 1915. The Colonel's exaggerated identification with Wilson is reflected in an entry in his diary of Sept. 28, 1914: "As far as I can see, his [Wilson's] thoughts and mine have run parallel for a long while, almost from youth."

13. House, in mid-December 1914, revealed a significant difference of opinion with Wilson in negotiations with England about peace. On his own authority, the Colonel, on December 11, withdrew a letter he had written a week earlier to Ambassador Walter H. Page which Wilson had approved. Index to House Diary, Dec. 11, 1914. House explained that he did not want to "unduly press" the British to consent to mediation. His diary also reveals that he did not favor Wilson's policy of "peace without victory." He wrote: "I feel they [the British] are determined to make a complete job of it while they are in it, and I also feel in my heart that it is best for Germany, best for Europe and best for the world, to have the issue settled now for all time to come." *Ibid.*, Dec. 14, 1914. After a mild rebuke from Wilson, House promptly fell in line with Wilson's policy. *Ibid.*, Dec. 16, 1914.

14. Ernest R. May, *The World War and American Isolation 1914–1917* (Cambridge, Mass., 1959), p. 78. Attributing to House exaggerated influence is understandable because the Diary of Colonel House has been the major source of our intimate knowledge of Wilson for a long time. Today, the extensive collection of documents and interpretations by the editors of *The Papers of Woodrow Wilson* provide many new insights. On House's relations to Wilson, see also Albert S. Burleson to R. S. Baker, April 28, 1927, and Carter Glass to R. S. Baker, March 27, 1926, Baker Papers.

15. Woodrow Wilson, "The Study of Administration," in Arthur S. Link,

David W. Hirst, John E. Little *et al.*, eds., *The Papers of Woodrow Wilson*, 37 vols. to date (Princeton, N. J., 1966–), vol. 5, p. 380; hereinafter cited as *PWW*.

16. *The Princeton University Bulletin*, Nov. 1900, p. 12. Significantly, at the time of the formation of the postwar league, Wilson cooperated most closely with the British.

17. *PWW*, vol. 12, pp. 226–27.

18. Hidesaburo Kusama, "Wilson's Ideals for a League of Nations" (unpublished MS., Aichi Prefectural University, Nagoya, Japan, 1972), pp. 7–8.

19. *PWW*, vol. 22, p. 353.

20. *Ibid.*, vol. 28, p. 451.

21. *Ibid.*, vol. 25, p. 130.

22. When war broke out, House had just returned from Europe where Wilson had sent him to explore through informal diplomacy the possibility of an understanding among the United States, England, France, and Germany on armaments and other matters. Charles Seymour, ed., *The Intimate Papers of Colonel House*, 4 vols. (Boston, 1926–28), I, 235–75, and Link, *Wilson*, II, 314–18. The war also abruptly ended a Wilson-approved initiative for a third peace conference at The Hague. WW to Bryan, Jan. 29, 1914, Wilson Papers.

23. WW to House, Aug. 3, 1914, House Papers.

24. WW to Axson, "early" Aug. 1914. Axson dictated his recollections of his discussion with the President on the *George Washington* on the way back from the Peace Conference. See Axson's "Sketches of the League of Nations Idea," which Professor Link made available to the author. While Axson did not claim to reproduce Wilson's exact words, he was certain that he recalled "with perfect clearness" the "heart of what he said" during the first of three conversations held in August 1914. During the second conversation, Dr. Cary T. Grayson, Wilson's personal physician, was present. Those present during the third conversation included, among others, Colonel House. *Ibid.*

25. Address at the Associated Press luncheon, April 20, 1915, *New York Times*, April 21, 1915.

26. WW to Bryan, Aug. 17, 1914, Wilson Papers. On the following day, Wilson appealed to the people: "We must be impartial in thought as well as in action, must put a curb upon our sentiments." Aug. 18, 1914, Wilson Papers.

27. "Neutrality is a negative word. It is a word that does not express what America ought to feel." Ray Stannard Baker and William E. Dodd, eds., *The Public Papers of Woodrow Wilson*, 6 vols. (New York, 1925–27), III, 378.

28. *Ibid.*, p. 225.

29. Memorandum of Herbert B. Brougham, Dec. 14, 1914, *PWW*, vol. 31, pp. 458–59.

30. *Ibid.*, p. 143. For Wilson's attitude regarding the Allies and Germany, see Spring Rice to Grey, Sept. 3, 1914 (following the Ambassador's interview with Wilson on September 1) and Dec. 3, 1914, the Papers of Sir Edward Grey, F.O. 800, vol. 84, Public Record Office; hereinafter cited as Grey Papers. See also WW to House, Aug. 25, 1914, Wilson Papers.

31. WW to John Martin, Oct. 2, 1914, Wilson Papers.

32. WW to Richard H. Dabney, Jan. 4, 1915, Wilson Papers. As early as

October 9, 1914, the President wrote: "I shall be very careful to suit my action to the developments." WW to Bryce, *ibid*. Wilson explained the reason for the secrecy of his peace plan as follows: "My feeling is that I ought at present to express no opinion about any comprehensive plan of world peace. Such an expression of opinion on my part just now would, I think, be more irritating to the belligerent powers than helpful to the cause of practical and immediate peace." WW to Raleigh C. Minor, Jan. 5, 1915, *ibid*. For the same reason, he refrained from advocacy of "some particular measure of international organization just at this juncture." It would be "a harness" which the belligerents were "not yet in a humor to wear." WW to Theodore Marburg, Feb. 3, 1915, *ibid*.

33. House and Dumba had a conference on October 6, 1914. House to WW, Oct. 6, 1914, House Papers. On the following day, Dumba sent a comprehensive report of Wilson's plan for peace to his government. He indicated that the proposals emanated from Wilson and that House had had similar talks with the German and British Ambassadors. A copy of Dumba's report is found in G.H.Q., No. 21, Vol. 1, attached to Leopold Berchtold to Bethmann Hollweg, Nov. 10, 1914, Papers of the German Foreign Office, Bonn; hereinafter cited as the German Foreign Office Papers. For Austria's instructions to Dumba, see the telegram of the Austrian government to Dumba, Oct. 31, 1914, Austrian State Archives, Vienna; hereinafter cited as Austrian State Archives. The original Austrian draft instructions were composed by Berchtold himself and used the word "acceptable" for Wilson's proposals. *Ibid*.

34. Dumba to Berchtold (via Rome), Nov. 7, 1914, Austrian State Archives. Bernstorff's instructions from Berlin were of Sept. 12, 1914, G.H.Q., No. 21, Vol. 1, German Foreign Office Papers.

35. House to WW, Nov. 11, 1914, Wilson Papers. See also House Diary, Dec. 3, 1914.

36. Bethmann Hollweg to Berchtold, Nov. 23, 1914, W.K., No. 2, Vol. 1, German Foreign Office Papers. In the final version of this reply, the Chancellor eliminated a significant paragraph for diplomatic reasons. This paragraph characterized England as "our most stubborn enemy" with whom only a "foul peace" could be achieved which would mean "continuation of a latent state of war for years to come." *Ibid*.

37. *Ibid*. Germany opposed a general conference because of unfavorable voting prospects: "Two big powers against three." The neutrals might tip the balance further against Germany. *Ibid*.

38. G.H.Q., No. 21, Vol. 1, German Foreign Office Papers (my translation). Dumba's communication to Berchtold of October 7, 1914, was attached to the letter of Berchtold to Bethmann Hollweg of November 10, 1914. *Ibid*.

39. *Ibid*. (my translations).

40. *Ibid*. The letter of Zimmermann to House of December 3, 1914, was in answer to a letter from House of September 5, 1914. Zimmermann "purposely delayed" a reply. Zimmermann to Jagow, Nov. 17, 1914, W.K., No. 2, Geh. Vol. 1, *ibid*. House received Zimmermann's answer on December 26 (House Diary, Dec. 27, 1914) and sent it to Wilson on the next day. Wilson Papers.

41. House to WW, Sept. 20, 1914, Wilson Papers. See also E. Grey to Oscar S. Straus, Sept. 26, 1914, the Papers of Oscar S. Straus, Library of Congress. Straus sent this letter to Wilson at the President's request. WW to Straus, Oct. 10, 1914, Wilson Papers.

42. Spring Rice to Grey, Sept. 20, 1914, Grey Papers. Spring Rice, in a cover sentence, explained that he transmitted House's views *verbatim*. *Ibid*. House, on September 22, sent an almost identical version of this telegram to Wilson. He failed to mention that he was the author of the message. Instead of "balance of power," House used the term "equilibrium." Wilson Papers. For Bernstorff's offers to negotiate, see Reinhard R. Doerries, *Washington-Berlin 1908/1917* (Düsseldorf, 1975), pp. 106 ff.

43. House to Walter H. Page, Oct. 3, 1914, for transmission to Grey, House Papers. At Wilson's insistence, the guarantee of territorial integrity was later included in the Covenant of the League of Nations as Article 10. The other suggestions mentioned above are reflected in Articles 8 and 11 of the Covenant.

44. House to WW, Oct. 8, 1914, Wilson Papers. The British considered an American peace move an "unfriendly act." Link, *Wilson*, III, 206. The French were against American "mediation in any form." Bertie to Grey, Nov. 10, 1914, Diary of Francis Bertie, Public Record Office, F.O. 800/181.

45. *New York Times*, Dec. 3, 1914. Van Dyke had a luncheon meeting with Wilson on December 2, 1914. *Ibid*.

46. Henry van Dyke, *Fighting for Peace* (New York, 1917), p. 242.

47. WW to Nancy S. Toy, Nov. 9, 1914, Wilson Papers. House noted in his diary that Wilson was "distressed" about the result of the elections. He deplored his "loss of prestige . . . in Europe." House Diary, Nov. 4, 1914.

48. WW to Bryan, Oct. 8, 1914, Wilson Papers. Wilson favored a single mediator because "the difficulties and complications would be many and the outcome much more doubtful if there were several mediators."

49. Ambassador Henry Morgenthau knew of Wilson's fall-back plan to use economic weapons against the European belligerents if other means failed. Ambassador J. M. Pallavicini to Berchtold, Oct. 8, 1914, Austrian State Archives. See n. 67, *infra*. Wilson and House made numerous references in late November and early December to Wilson's expanding foreign policy. See House Diary, Nov. 25, 1914; House to WW, Nov. 30, 1914, Wilson Papers; and WW to House, Dec. 2, 1914, House Papers.

50. WW to House, April 1, 1915, House Papers. Wilson's plan for a conference of all nations emerges from a careful study of volumes 31–34 of *The Papers of Woodrow Wilson*. Wilson called it the "second convention." See nn. 56 and 57, *infra*.

51. House to Breckinridge Long, Nov. 20, 1921, referring to the events of "winter of 1915," Diary of Breckinridge Long, in the Papers of Breckinridge Long, Library of Congress. Wilson also told the Colonel that such a pact would be "wise" for "our own relations with the other American States." WW to House, Dec. 2, 1914, House Papers.

52. Draft Pan-American treaty, Jan. 29, 1915, *PWW*, vol. 32, pp. 159–60.

For Wilson's initial two-point draft see the House Diary, Dec. 16, 1914. Wilson anticipated that the main elements of the draft treaty would be included later in the "final European settlement." WW to Lansing, Aug. 5, 1915, Baker Papers.

53. WW to Bryan, March 8, 1915, Wilson-Bryan Corr. Wilson's later attitude toward United States participation in the League of Nations was in line with this position.

54. Address, May 24, 1915, Baker and Dodd, eds., *The Public Papers of Woodrow Wilson*, III, 334.

55. Address to Mexican editors, June 7, 1918, *ibid.*, v, 227. For Wilson's thought of making the Latin-American countries the nucleus of the neutrals in his contemplated peace conference, see Bernstorff to Bethmann Hollweg, May 29, 1915, André Scherer and Jacques Grunewald, eds., *L'Allemagne et les Problèmes de la Paix*, 2 vols. (Paris, 1962), I, 108; hereinafter cited as *L'Allemagne et la Paix*.

56. WW to Bryan, Dec. 17, 1914, the Papers of William Jennings Bryan, Library of Congress. This letter gives a full description of Wilson's contemplated conference of all nations. Bernstorff, after a talk with House, reported to the German government that Wilson contemplated to convene a conference at The Hague. Bernstorff to German Foreign Office, Dec. 18, 1914, G.H.Q., No. 21, Vol. 1, German Foreign Office Papers. The German reaction was immediate and negative: "Count Bernstorff is being notified that we would like to conclude peace with our enemies directly avoiding a conference in the future as in the past" (my translation), Dec. 22, 1914, *ibid.*

57. In his discussions with Grey, House thus characterized the second convention: "It would merely be the assembling at the Hague and the adopting of rules governing the game." House to WW, Feb. 9, 1915, Wilson Papers. Wilson may not have revealed his full plan for the second convention to House. The Colonel asked him twice during his European trip to write to him more about the second convention. House to WW, March 15 and April 12, 1915, *ibid.*

58. Spring Rice to Grey, Jan. 14, 1915, Grey Papers (italics added). Wilson still believed in 1918 that "if nations knew they were in a protective league they would be willing to accept different boundaries and smaller areas." The league would help to solve many problems and "smooth over insuperable difficulties." House Diary, Sept. 24, 1918. See also WW to Wiseman, Oct. 16, 1918, the Papers of Sir William Wiseman, Yale University Library, and House Diary, Dec. 14, 1918.

59. House to WW, March 23, 1915, Wilson Papers. A few days later, House reported that the idea of a second convention "has been cordially received" in Germany. House to WW, March 26, 1915, *ibid.*

60. House to WW, May 27, 1915, *ibid.*

61. The Colonel spoke to American envoys to Switzerland, Spain, and Italy about the second convention. He revealed to the latter, Thomas Nelson Page, "the whole program." House to WW, April 3, 1915, *ibid.*

62. The German records fail to confirm House's reports of Germany's

favorable reaction to suggestions of a second convention. For the reaction of British leaders to the freedom of the seas, see the Diary of Maurice Hankey, June 25, 1915, cited in Stephen Roskill, *Hankey: Man of Secrets* (London, 1973), p. 185.

63. Bernstorff to Bethmann Hollweg, May 29, 1915 (my translation), in Scherer and Grunewald, eds., *L'Allemagne et la Paix*, p. 108. See also telegram of Arvid Taube to Jagow, June 3, 1915, cited in Karl E. Birnbaum, *Peace Moves and U-Boat Warfare* (Stockholm, 1958), pp. 343–44.

64. Bernstorff to Bethmann Hollweg, May 29, 1915 (my translation), in Scherer and Grunewald, eds., *L'Allemagne et la Paix*, p. 108. The difficulties which Birnbaum and other German authors have experienced in attributing this communication to Wilson will disappear when we realize that Wilson's peace effort had been at the center of the American peace program on a continuing basis since the autumn of 1914. See, particularly, Bernstorff to Bethmann Hollweg, May 29, 1915, n. 1, *PWW*, vol. 33, pp. 280–82.

65. WW to Lansing, Oct. 31, 1915, the Papers of Robert Lansing, Princeton University Library; hereinafter cited as the Lansing Papers, Princeton.

66. Arthur S. Link, *Wilson*, IV, 132–38. See also George W. Egerton, *Great Britain and the Creation of the League of Nations* (Chapel Hill, N. C., 1978), chap. 2, and John Milton Cooper, Jr., "The British Response to the House-Grey Memorandum," *Journal of American History*, LIX (March 1973), 958–71.

67. Morgenthau said that, if the British refused to go along with moderate peace terms, Wilson contemplated effective means to overcome their obstruction. Wilson, Morgenthau said (my translation), "intends to prohibit export of grain and foodstuffs from the United States to Europe to exert thereby strong pressure especially on England which could be hit hard through the drying up of food imports." Pallavicini to Berchtold, Oct. 8, 1914, Austrian State Archives. In June 1915, House confirmed England's vulnerability when he speculated that an Allied victory might "not come at all if their American supplies were for any reason shut off." House to WW, June 16, 1915, Wilson Papers.

68. According to House, Wilson "would throw the weight of the United States on the side of those wanting a just settlement—a settlement which would make another such war impossible." House Diary, Feb. 14, 1916.

69. Baker and Dodd, eds., *The Public Papers of Woodrow Wilson*, IV, 184–88. Edward H. Buehrig characterized Wilson's offer of United States cooperation to suppress future aggression as an "inducement to the belligerents to agree to 'peace without victory.'" Edward H. Buehrig, "Woodrow Wilson and Collective Security," in Buehrig, *Wilson's Foreign Policy in Perspective* (Bloomington, Ind., 1957), p. 48.

70. Baker and Dodd, eds., *The Public Papers of Woodrow Wilson*, IV, 407–14.

71. WW to E. B. Galt, Aug. 22, 1915, Wilson Papers. As late as February 2, 1917, Wilson still believed that the neutrals should "unite" and that the United States "might coordinate the neutral forces." Wilson thought of making this attempt publicly, but the cabinet convinced him otherwise. Franklin K. Lane to George W. Lane, Feb. 9, 1917, Anne W. Lane and Louise H. Wall,

eds., *The Letters of Franklin K. Lane* (Boston, 1922), p. 234. See also the Diary of Robert Lansing, Feb. 4, 1917, the Papers of Robert Lansing, Library of Congress.

72. Wilson's notes relating to his "reply to the suggestions of the Swiss Federal Council," undated, but composed in early February 1917, Wilson Papers.

73. "BASES of PEACE," enclosed with Lansing to WW, Feb. 8, 1917, *ibid.* At Wilson's request, Lansing reviewed the President's original draft of the "BASES of PEACE" on February 7, 1917. Lansing's three-page memorandum was enclosed in the letter just cited. Wilson sent his revised draft of the "BASES of PEACE" to Lansing on February 9, 1917. WW to Lansing, Feb. 9, 1917, Records of the Department of State, National Archives, 763.72/3261½. Wilson used the term "economic warfare" in his first draft as the third point of his "BASES." Lansing evaluated the contemplated Allied postwar trade discrimination in Lansing to WW, Feb. 7, 1917, Wilson Papers.

74. Wilson's "BASES of PEACE" is of special interest because it appears to be the only extant document for a league of peace which Wilson himself drafted. It consists of four points and three explanatory notes typed on Wilson's typewriter covering approximately two pages. A third page contains Wilson's "GENERAL NOTE" to the "BASES of PEACE."

75. WW to Lansing, Feb. 9, 1917, cited in n. 73.

76. WW to House, July 21, 1917, House Papers.

77. WW to House, Dec. 1, 1917, *ibid.*

78. House Diary, Nov. 21, 1917.

79. *Ibid.*, Dec. 1, 1917. For details, see David F. Trask, *The United States in the Supreme War Council* (Middletown, Conn., 1961), p. 34, and Sterling J. Kernek, *Distractions of Peace during War* (Philadelphia, 1975), pp. 67–68.

80. A comprehensive account of Wilson's policy immediately after the war is found in Arthur Walworth, *America's Moment: 1918* (New York, 1977). For a less favorable interpretation of House's diplomacy see Inga Floto, *Colonel House in Paris* (Princeton, N. J., 1981). The basic study for American preparation for peace under Colonel House remains Lawrence E. Gelfand, *The Inquiry* (New Haven, Conn., 1963). For Wilson's peace policies in relation to Germany, see Klaus Schwabe, *Deutsche Revolution und Wilson-Frieden* (Düsseldorf, 1971). For recent studies of Wilsonian policy in relation to England see Egerton, *Great Britain and the Creation of the League of Nations*.

81. Wilson rejected as "folly" the elaborate league schemes of League to Enforce Peace "butters-in" and others. "We must head them off one way or another." WW to House, March 20, 1918, House Papers. Many supporters of a league found Wilson's league stand puzzling. William Howard Taft even thought that Wilson had "changed his mind" about supporting a league. Taft to Charles F. Scott, April 19, 1924, the Papers of William Howard Taft, Library of Congress.

82. WW to House, March 22, 1918, House Papers. For similar expressions, see WW to J. S. Strachey, April 5, 1918: "I have all along been of the opinion that it would be impossible to effect an elaborate and active organization." Baker Papers. See also House Diary, Aug. 15, 1918.

83. WW to Oscar T. Crosby, July 6, 1918, and House to Crosby, Nov. 1918,

Baker Papers. Wilson was then concerned with premature publication of the British Phillimore report, or a plan for a league of nations. For the Phillimore report and British attitudes toward Wilson and a league, see Wilton B. Fowler, *British-American Relations, 1917–1918* (Princeton, N. J., 1969), chap. 8, and Egerton, *Great Britain and the Creation of the League of Nations*, chap. 4. House's draft is entitled "Suggestions for a Covenant of a League of Nations." It has a preamble and twenty-three articles. House to WW, July 16, 1918, the Papers of Ray Stannard Baker, Princeton University Library.

84. Sir William Wiseman to A. J. Balfour, Dec. 15, 1918, the Papers of Arthur J. Balfour, British Museum. In the same report Wiseman wrote: "He [Wilson] has a very open mind as to the form of the League, its scope and the machinery by which it should be operated." Lord Derby, the British Ambassador to France, reported that Wilson advocated "a sort of general Parliament of Ambassadors" at which "every nation great or small shall have one vote." Derby to Balfour, Dec. 22, 1918, *ibid*. See also WW to Members of the American Delegation, Dec. 9, 1918, the Papers of William C. Bullitt, Yale University Library. For Wilson's summit diplomacy involving the League see my "Wilson and Eisenhower: Two Experiences in Summit Diplomacy," *Contemporary Review*, CXCIX (June 1961), 284–95. Wilson attended the Paris Peace Conference in person largely because he felt that he was personally needed to "head the Commission." He told Vance McCormick that "House won't do." McCormick to R. S. Baker, July 15, 1928, Baker Papers.

85. The text of the resolution is in *Papers Relating to the Foreign Relations of the United States 1919: The Paris Peace Conference*, 13 vols. (Washington, 1942–47), III, 201.

86. *Ibid*., p. 324.

87. Lloyd George to Imperial War Cabinet, Dec. 30, 1918, Minutes of Imperial War Cabinet, p. 47, the Papers of Sir George Foster, Public Archives of Canada. With British help, Wilson was able to overcome French opposition to making the Covenant the first item on the agenda of the conference. In general, realization of what the League meant to Wilson made opponents more conciliatory. According to Lansing, France and Italy permitted Wilson to "go ahead with the League of Nations in the hope that he will not oppose their claims." Polk to Lansing, Jan. 25, 1919, Lansing Papers, Princeton.

88. Lansing to W. C. Stebbins, May 1919, Lansing Papers, Princeton.

89. WW to George D. Herron, April 27, 1919, Wilson Papers. On July 5, 1919, Wilson discussed with his advisers on the *George Washington* the policy to be adopted in the United States toward imperfections of the Versailles Treaty. They agreed that the imperfections should not be publicly aired. The Diary of Thomas W. Lamont, July 5, 1919, the Papers of Thomas W. Lamont, Baker Library, Harvard University. Wilson was "of course" much more enthusiastic about the Covenant than about the rest of the treaty. Wiseman to House, July 19, 1919, House Papers.

90. Confidential remarks of WW to foreign correspondents, April 8, 1918, the Papers of Joseph P. Tumulty, Library of Congress.

91. Link, *Higher Realism*, p. 135.

Chapter Six

WOODROW WILSON AND

COLLECTIVE SECURITY

HERBERT G. NICHOLAS

There are in the history of political ideas certain terms which owe their wide employment, not to their effectiveness in clarifying an issue, but rather to their success in embracing its inherent contradictions, evoking a seeming coherence while in fact preserving the elements of contrariety that have invested it with its peculiar intractability. In the history of the United States, "popular sovereignty" was such a term; in the history of the western world between the wars, "collective security" was another. It is, incidentally, interesting to note that the term was slow in gaining acceptance; the earliest usage recorded by the *Oxford English Dictionary* is in 1934, appropriately by Winston Churchill.[1] Yet if the verbal coinage, with its fusion of the ideas of joint action and mutual protection, had to wait until the 1930s, the concept was an indispensable part of western thinking about international relations from at least 1918 onward. In promoting the concept to this central position in the arguments of diplomats, politicians, journalists, and, eventually, voters, no one was more potent than Woodrow Wilson. He may not have fathered it, but, once he adopted it, he made it strikingly his own.

In exploring the fascinating history of Wilson's relationship with this concept, it is necessary to make the historian's effort of recreating the intellectual climate in which this relationship developed. As it happens, it all fell within my lifetime, yet it belongs to a world which has as nearly vanished as the Middle Ages. In this context, the phrase "prewar" means "pre-1914," when the international system, or lack of system, was one totally dominated by the sovereign state, which might indeed delegate sovereignty downwards to subdivisions, federal components, colonies, or dependencies, but which knew virtually nothing of delegation upwards or outwards. The alliances or ententes which were a feature of the European power struggle, although they might seem to subsequent analysts as unbreakable bonds of collective insecurity dragging their component states inexorably into mutual conflict, were conceived by their authors and directors as putting no limitations on national sovereignty save those of an exclusively moral or prudential variety. Moreover, if this was true for Europe, it was even truer for the United States, where even the concept of alliance was touched with the Founding Fathers' primal curse, and where the self-consciousness of the sovereign state was sanctified by the awareness that the United States was what its inhabitants had come to, Europe was what they had left behind. To preserve this unfettered liberty of national self-determination, free from the constraints and commitments of an older, sullied continent, was the primary obligation of every American President, diplomat, soldier, or sailor. It was this tradition, this national cornerstone, that Wilson was inviting the United States to reject. Small wonder that he was not immediately successful.

What led Wilson to embark on such a perilous undertaking in the first place? Leaving on one side considerations of what might be called his personal or private motivation, let us consider the objective factors which destroyed the pre-1914 international system of sovereignties and presented even the United States with a set of novel, distasteful, and ineluctable choices which no President, however un-Wilsonian, could indefinitely ignore.

At the heart of all the other factors forcing change was the changed nature of war. The classical state-system, for all its superficially Hobbesian assumption of a strife of all against all, in fact rested on a nineteenth-century confidence in the mutuality of interests, especially of economic interests, and in the normality of peace and the exceptionality of war. Moreover, war was not only an interruption and an abnormality; it was even, when it erupted, still limited and controlled—limited by its technology and controlled by certain transnational codes of morality and convenience. There were exceptions, of course: the Thirty Years War had been one such, but that was long ago. Not since Napoleon had there been a serious risk of interstate conflict getting, as it were, out of hand. It was thus perfectly possible in 1914 to conceive of war as something that one could contract out of, especially if one enjoyed the territorial advantages of remoteness and the defensive asset of a two-ocean navy. In 1914, neutrality seemed not merely the best, but the only course for the United States. (Remember that, for a brief period, it had seemed a perfectly feasible course even to Sir Edward Grey.)

However, the war of 1914, once launched, soon showed itself to be very different from all its predecessors. It was neither limited nor controlled, and it swiftly passed beyond its European breeding ground to make itself felt around the world. In a small degree, this was due to new technology, as represented by the submarine. However, it was due much more to the new totalitarianism of modern war itself—its mobilization, not merely of larger military forces, but also of entire populations, and its subordination of every element of a nation's life (including the whole range of what had once been considered private concerns, from prayer to money-making) to the achievement of a single aim—victory. Thus the "rules" of war went out of the window. Wilson's limited success in preserving them on the high seas lasted as long as it did merely because, in order to wage total war, each side wanted something which only the United States could give—economic assistance. Total war meant economic war. The United States, diplomatically and militarily neutral, tried to maintain the old pre-1914 distinction between business as usual and belligerency as something carried on by governments against each other. But in fact the sophisticated distinctions between contraband and noncontraband, between "absolute" contraband and "conditional" contraband, etc., rapidly disintegrated under the pressures of the war machine. In a conflict so pervasive, small powers could not hope to resist being sucked in, willy-nilly, as adjuncts to one side or the other, and large powers were left with only one choice: either to insist upon their "rights" at the high risk of having to go to war in order to protect them, or to contract out of the world of international dealings, including of course economic and financial dealings, altogether. This was the choice that, quite apart from any diplomatic maneuvering aimed at shaping the peace or determining the nature of a postwar settlement, increasingly dominated Wilson's diplomacy with every year that the war dragged on.

It is true that the full and formal recognition of this novel state of affairs (as, e.g., in Article xi of the League Covenant: "Any war or threat of war . . . is hereby declared a matter of concern to the whole League.") had to wait until later, but it is not true, as Sir Alfred Zimmern, for example, implies, that this was a unique perception of Senator Elihu Root in 1918.[2] It is fully implied in Woodrow Wilson's thinking at least as early as his speech at Omaha on October 5, 1916: "What disturbs the life of the whole world is the concern of the whole world, and it is our duty to lend the full force of this nation, moral and physical, to a league of nations which shall see to it that no one disturbs the peace of the world without submitting his case first to the opinion of mankind." In fact, no percipient observer can fail to be aware that this conviction increasingly dominated Wilsonian diplomacy from early 1915 onward.

Indeed, to say that modern war anywhere is a matter of concern to everyone is to state nothing more or less than what was obvious and irrefutable, even in 1916. Whether Wilson was wise to present this incontestable axiom in the wrapping of a moral issue, as he tended to do whenever moving the United States toward an acceptance of war with the Central Powers, is something that can here be left on one side. But one has to admit that, even after Wilson has been driven to a recognition of its cruciality for American foreign policy, old habits and formulae still persisted in his thinking. This is perfectly reflected in the continuing prominence that he accorded to the idea of the freedom of the seas. Thus he wrote to House on May 16, 1916, in the muddied wake of the House-Grey Memorandum: "If we move for peace it is upon these lines: 1. Such a settlement . . . as the belligerents may be able to agree upon. . . . 2. A universal alliance to maintain freedom of the seas and to prevent any war begun either a) contrary to treaty covenants or b) without warning and full inquiry—a virtual guarantee of territorial integrity and political independence."[3] The conjunction and virtual equation of the two ideas—the new League and the old claim to an unlimited freedom of the seas—still persisted. Freedom of the Seas was Point Two of the Fourteen Points, of which the establishment of a League of Nations was the fourteenth. Sir William Wiseman was quick to detect the link between the two objectives in Wilson's thinking about the peace settlement. In a memorandum dated October 20, 1918, Wiseman noted: "The second condition, referring to the Freedom of the Seas, would mean nothing without the League of Nations. If it meant anything, it would be a declaration that the laws of war and of peace should be the same at sea, except as they may be varied by international action—the only expression of which we have at present is international law. Clearly, the clause can be taken only in connection with a League of Nations."[4]

But Wiseman also perceived that a League of Nations, while it made freedom of the seas obligatory, would also make it, as an object of a special crusade, superfluous:

> If there should be instituted a valid and operative League of Nations, freedom of the seas would appear to be a logical and proper corollary. No war could under the postulated conditions come to exist except between the League as a whole and some non-assenting State, or some recalcitrant member. In that event . . . the seas would be closed to the vessels of the non-assenting State or recalcitrant member, and all trade with such nation by all other States would be prevented by the same power. This result would infallibly follow upon the creation of a League of Nations—for a League which did not concern itself with maritime matters would hardly be worth having.[5]

However, up to the very moment of Wilson's arrival in Paris it seemed as if he still rated the freedom of the seas as highly as ever, and as if its wartime idolization would make it a focus of controversy at the peace conference.[6] In fact, it was not. As Wilson himself explains it, the logic of collective security eliminated it from the agenda:

> One of the principles I went to Paris most insisting on was the freedom of the seas. Now the freedom of the seas means the definition of the right of neutrals to use the seas when other nations are at war, but under the League of Nations there are no neutrals, and therefore what I have called the practical joke on myself was that by the very thing that I was advocating it became unnecessary to define freedom of the seas. All nations . . . being comrades and partners in a common cause, we all have an equal right to use the seas.[7]

The other habit that persisted, or, if you prefer, the other old spirit that had to be exorcised, was the historic aversion of new-world America to the alliance system alleged to be a hallmark of old-world power politics. It is this system which, time and time again, in Wilson's analysis, is contrasted with the kind of diplomacy that peace requires.

"Henceforth alliance must not be set up against alliance, understanding against understanding."[8] "I am proposing that all nations henceforth avoid entangling alliances which would draw them into competitions of power, catch them in a net of intrigue and selfish rivalry, and disturb their own affairs with influences intruded from without."[9] "We still read Washington's immortal warning[10] against 'entangling alliances' with full comprehension and an answering purpose."[11] Eventually, the stigma attaching to the alliance concept was, of course, given quasiofficial recognition by Wilson's insistence that American belligerency did not make the United States an "Ally" in the war against the Central Powers, but only an "Associated Power." By contrast, the new organization which was to be the cornerstone of the new diplomatic order was called a "league" or a system of "mutual guarantees" or a set of "covenants" or a "society of nations"—anything but an alliance, however unentangling. What exactly was it that made this new association so clearly and significantly a nonalliance?

Let us go back to our starting point—the ineluctable fact that war anywhere spreads everywhere. The validity of this assumption had been demonstrated by April 1917 when the United States was forced into the war on the side of the Allies. *De facto*, whatever Wilson might call it, an Allied-American alliance came into being. Yet Wilson in one sense was right to avoid the label, inasmuch as victory for such an alliance would not of itself do anything to settle this major problem of involuntary involvement in the ineluctable war. To continue the alliance into the peace would merely guarantee, on the most optimistic assumption, that henceforth the United States would be on the more powerful side in any future conflict. It would not prevent the outbreak of such a conflict. Nor would it turn the ineluctable into the avoidable; indeed, it would do the reverse, unless the United States reneged on its commitments to its allies.

So, in line with the logic of this argument, a United States which has gone into "the war to end wars" must look forward to a postwar relationship which transcends the partnership of the fighting years. It must envisage today's enemy turning into tomorrow's League of Nations member. That this presented a tactical problem, Wilson was fully aware. The earlier objective of "peace without victory," enunciated in the great speech of January 22, 1917, was undoubtedly in part prompted and initially sustained by the realization that, ultimately, any league would have to include Germany, and that an Allied victory could only postpone the date when victor and vanquished would sit at the same board together. Wiseman reported Wilson as saying as late as October 16, 1918, that "Germany ought to be present when the League of Nations is constituted."[12] But Wilson knew better than to press for this at Paris, and, indeed, the issue presented no serious problem then or immediately afterward, although there was in fact a surprisingly diffused acceptance by all present, including the French, that the League would in the relatively near future approach universal membership.

No, the difficulty presented by Germany and other ex-enemy states was not purely tactical. There was a more fundamental problem of membership, which hardly surfaced at Paris, and which concerned the nature of the League itself. Wilson's thinking, from the beginning, undoubtedly rested on an assumption of universal membership. "There must be an association of nations, *all* bound together for the protection of the integrity of *each*."[13] "A universal alliance" was Wilson's phrase for it when he wrote to House on May 16, 1916.[14] "An universal association of the nations" he called it in the speech to the League to Enforce Peace on May 27, 1916.[15] "The nations of the world must unite in joint guarantees," he said in the speech accepting renomination on September 2, 1916.[16] "An organization of peace which shall make it certain that the combined power of free nations will check *every* invasion of right . . . a tribunal of opinion to which *all* must submit" is the language employed in the address of July 4, 1918.[17]

Yet beneath this surface assumption of universality one can detect certain shadings. In the draft peace message to the belligerents of November 27, 1916, a slightly different impression is conveyed: "A league united and powerful enough in force to guarantee the peace of the world against further breach by injustice or aggression."[18] The fourteenth point spoke only of "a general association of nations," which could mean either universality or something less. The speech to Congress on February 11, 1918, regarding the German and Austrian replies to the Fourteen Points Address referred to "covenants which must be backed by the united force of all the nations that love justice and are willing to maintain it at any cost."[19] In these passages there is a recurrent note of selectivity, of some states (those which "love justice," etc.) having a greater responsibility and power than the rest. There is even (to anticipate our argument) a suggestion of an *alliance.* Some of this, of course, is to be explained by the belligerent context of these remarks; they relate, not to a plan made *in vacuo,* but to an organization being shaped with the specific objective of preventing a recurrence of present hostilities. But they are pointers to a more fundamental problem.

In a league of all nations, formed because all are affected when an outbreak of war touches any, there will necessarily be "bad" states as well as "good," however we define those terms. If the league is to retain its truly universal, nonpartial, impartial nature it must arrive at its decisions, as in fact Article xv of the Covenant provided, by "the agreement of all the members." In that event, how can it preserve the peace of the world when the threat to that peace comes (as it did in 1931 over Manchuria and in 1936 over Abyssinia) from one of its own members? Wilson never squarely faced this issue. (A lot of the other League champions evaded it too.) There is an interesting exchange in the third meeting of the Commission of the League.[20] Wilson had proposed that "only self-governing states shall be admitted to membership." (This survived as Article 1 § 2 of the Covenant: "Any self-governing State . . . may become a member.") Three schools of thought can be detected in the ensuing debate:

1. That of the pragmatists, who used something very much like the criterion for recognition of a state in international law. They interpreted self-governing as broadly meaning "not governed by anyone else."

2. That of the French, who would apply a "good behavior" test for membership. "There should be no doubt left of the character of the new member. That member should be without reproach" (Léon Bourgeois).

3. That of Wilson, who said that the Germany of 1914 had really been an absolute monarchy, that the war had been fought for democracy, and that the Covenant ought somewhere to recognize the principle of democracy, and that, although Bourgeois' "moral test" was "of course right," it was too hard to define, while a self-governing state, even if also hard to define, could always be recognized when one saw it.

The three views can be translated into three views of the League's function. The pragmatists saw it as a conference organization, with some vague and unpredictable potentialities of growth. The French, as represented by Bourgeois, saw it as a continuation of the wartime alliance, with the "immoral" states being those which would seek to upset the settlement and who, consequently, would be excluded. Wilson saw it as an agency through which the liberal aspirations of humanity would revolutionize the character and conduct of international affairs—would in fact realize the new world envisaged in the League to Enforce Peace speech, in which "nations must in the future be governed by the same high code of honor that we demand of individuals."

One can, I think, fairly descry, through these and other utterances, the Wilsonian model of world society. It is one which is analogous to that of eighteenth-century atomic theory, with the world conceived as a molecule and its component atomic elements being nation-states. These states are in varying degrees of development, but all aspire under the impulse of self-determination to a condition in which each represents a "nation" (which often, but not necessarily, e.g., the United States, constitutes a racial or linguistic entity). The characteristic of this nation is that it is freely self-determined under conditions of classic democratic theory—free elections, civil rights, responsible government, etc. A nation so organized is, in Wilson's view, almost by definition nonaggressive, law-abiding, and a responsible and moral member of the world society—exactly as a free, uncoerced, uncorrupted individual is the atomic unit out of which is built the nation-state. There is, consequently, such a natural harmony of behavior between these properly constituted nation-states that serious conflicts, such as lead to war, are inconceivable between them. Phrase after phrase of Wilsonian oratory opens a window on this Newtonianly ordered cluster of national atoms—they enjoy guaranteed "territorial integrity and political independence," they are a "family of nations," they are able to mobilize "the might of mankind in the common interest of civilization," they will inhabit "a new day" in which they "will avoid entanglements and clear the air of the world for common understandings and the maintenance of common rights."[21]

"Instruction," said Edward Gibbon in one of those flashes of cynicism which all teachers know, "is seldom efficacious save on the rare occasions when it is superfluous." It is tempting to criticize Wilson's world model on similar grounds—that, in an international community composed of such internally democratic and externally pacific entities such as he posits, there would be no need for a League of

Nations to constrain or to protect. Contemplating the gap between the Hobbesian world of sovereign states, which between 1914 and 1919 had just been revealed in all its uncontrolled savagery, and the ideal image of the "new diplomacy," embodied in the League, it is easy to blame Wilson's vision for its lack of realism and irrelevance to the pressing needs of the hour. Yet before doing so, we should remember that, if there is to be any progress away from a world of anarchic and grasping sovereignties, there must be some model in the statesman's mind of the alternative organization of world affairs by which he can be guided as he tries to lead his own and other societies out of a state of total parochial selfishness.

Aristotle, after he had asked himself the question, How do men acquire virtue, or develop a good character, concluded that it was by no other method than by doing good acts: "By doing the acts that we do in our transactions with other men we become just or unjust."[22] What is true for individuals is no less valid for societies. The simple dilemma,

> If all states are good, the League is superfluous
> If all states are not good, the League is unworkable,

whatever its merits as logic, can thus be seen to be false to the known facts of life. There is not, as Wilson was a good deal too fond of imagining, some overnight conversion, some switch from an old to a new kind of diplomacy, and the acquisition by states of a good or just character as a precondition and guarantee of good behavior and just institutions. (Wilson, similarly, was all too prone to believe that the League, once established, would, by its virtuous potential, make up for and magically correct any injustices in the treaty settlement itself.) But Wilson was right in erecting the League and the new diplomacy associated with it as a model of the international society at which men of good will should be aiming. And, in fact, in his less messianic moods, he was very well aware of this and of the process of international evolution that it implied. In March 1917, he told the French Ambassador that he had no illusions about the League of Nations to be formed and realized that it would have to begin with an entente and with the obligation to submit international disputes to a conference of countries not directly involved. Perhaps that could create, little by little, precedents which would break the habit of recourse to war. It would be an experience to try.[23] According to Isaiah Bowman, in talking about the League to the members of The Inquiry en route to Paris, Wilson "particularly emphasized the importance of relying on experience to guide subsequent action."[24] Wilson was not averse to speaking of the League as something which would grow. His celebrated comment after the reading of the text of the Covenant to the plenary session of the peace conference on February 14, 1919, was: "A living thing is born."[25]

It is, however, one thing to accept Wilson's League as an ameliorative institution with universal membership, in which the morally developed states bring their less developed fellows along by example and censure and by the diplomatic equivalents of smiles and frowns. It is another thing to accept this and another thing to rely on it as an agency which would, as Wilson told the same session of February 14, 1919, "secure the peace of the world." The touchstone here is the question of force. Would this new substitute for the old alliance diplomacy be able, in the last resort, to enforce its will? Would it in fact be a League to Enforce Peace?

Wilson was in no sense a pacifist. The person who urged "force, force to the uttermost" was perfectly capable of envisaging and employing all the force at his command, once he had satisfied himself that the end required the means. He did, however, have a sensitive repugnance to (rather than, like Theodore Roosevelt, a positive relish for) physical force and, what was more important, a keen awareness of the brutalizing and intoxicating effects which resort to force can produce in the generation of mass emotions. ("It is a fearful thing to lead this great peaceful people into war" was the utterance not of a war-monger, nor yet of a pacifist, but of a leader with a rare perception of what modern war does to those who wage it.)

It is hardly surprising, therefore, if the line of Wilson's thinking about force and the League, insofar as we can trace it through his recorded utterances, is not entirely simple and straight. From the beginning, if we can trust Axson's reports of his conversations with Wilson in August 1914, Wilson envisaged that any nation which broke its "bond" with the world association would "bring upon herself war, that is to say punishment, automatically." Yet his League to Enforce Peace speech is silent on this issue, and his speech accepting renomination some three months later is none too explicit: "Whatever is done to disturb the whole world's life must be tested in the court of the whole world's opinion before it is attempted."[26] Yet there is an increasing disposition to spell out the full implications of the indivisibility of war. In the election campaign, speaking at Omaha and Cincinnati, Wilson pledged the "full force of this nation, moral and physical, to a league of nations."[27] His draft of the peace message to the belligerents of November 27 speaks of "a league of nations . . . united and powerful enough in force to guarantee the peace of the world against further breach by injustice or aggression,"[28] and his address to the Senate on January 22, 1917, which followed on the failure of his peace initiative, was emphatic on this theme: "It will be absolutely necessary that a force be created as a guarantee of the permanency of the settlement so much greater than the force of any nation now engaged or any alliance hitherto formed or projected that no nation, no probable combination of nations could face or withstand it. If the peace presently to be made is to endure, it must be a peace made secure by the organized major force of mankind."[29] A similar note is struck in the report to Congress on the replies of the Central Powers to the Allies' request for peace aims (February 11, 1918): "Covenants must now be entered into which will render such things impossible for the future, and these covenants must be backed by the united force of the nations that love justice and are willing to maintain it at any cost."[30] Wilson used very similar language in June to strengthen the first House draft of the Covenant—the first occasion on which the question of sanctions came up for explicit decision. Where House had envisaged merely a "blockade" and a closure of "the frontiers" of the offending "power to commerce and intercourse with the world," Wilson added "and to use any force that may be necessary."[31] Of the Phillimore Plan for a league, which declined to entertain seriously any idea of sanctions, Wilson told Wiseman that it "had no teeth"; by contrast the League he had in mind "must be virile."[32]

Virility, however, is a matter of degree. "I think," said Wiseman, "the President looks to economic pressure to supply the main force which might be used to support the League. He feels there must be force, but recognises the practical difficulties."[33] That Wilson's mind was moving in this direction is implied by his remarks to The Inquiry team on board the *George Washington* in December: "In cases involving discipline [an odd term to use] there was the alternative to war, namely, the boycott; trade, including postal and cable facilities, could be denied a state that had been guilty of wrong-doing."[34]

It is not necessary to trace the evolution of Wilson's thought at Paris on this issue. He was, of course, as were the British, wholly opposed to the French plan for a League with an international army and general staff. That would have made of the League simply a permanent military alliance of the victors. But Wilson was prepared initially to take the view that any power which broke its covenants "thereby *ipso facto* [became] at war with all the members of the League," and so, exposed to a range of possible sanctions which at least envisaged the Council's employment of "effective military or naval force." But when Miller pointed out[35] that this, as far as the United States was concerned, would cut across Congress's monopoly of the warmaking power, the clause was amended to the significantly weaker version embodied eventually in Article xvi: "shall *ipso facto* be deemed to have committed an act of war against all other Members of the League." From then on, the Commission was well set on the road which ended up by making economic sanctions obligatory and military sanctions merely recommendatory. Indeed, even in respect of economic sanctions, the Commission left such wide loopholes as to make them, when tried, totally ineffective.

There is no record of serious debate at Paris about the implications of sanctions. This is in large part because the debate on the totally unrealistic French plan preempted the agenda, but also because no other national delegation, certainly not the British, was prepared to face up to the real challenge that the sanctions issue presented, to work out its full implications, and to relate them to the level of international development which the western world had reached by 1919. (We should not think too hardly of them for this. There was hardly any more realistic thought devoted to this subject at San Francisco in 1945.) Instead, energies were expended on seeing to it that while lip-service was paid to sanctions, loopholes should be created large enough to allow states desirous of evading their obligations to do so. Still less, of course, did the battle for ratification fought in the Senate and across the United States provide for a cool and intellectually unflinching examination of what was involved in making the League an agency for maintaining and enforcing peace. Wilson came out of his arguments and encounters with his senatorial opponents much better than many subsequent critics have given him credit for. If he was not always unambiguous, his opponents were seldom clear; if he was too often disposed to lose himself in a rhetorical *altitudo*, they were even more often determined to combine clap-trap with narrow-mindedness. But in the melée, careful elucidation of what the League involved and what was its likely *modus operandi* became hopelessly overlaid with extravagances and irrelevances.

Intellectually, the issue in essence was brutally simple. There could be a universal League which would endeavor by every agency and device of publicity and persuasion to lower the international temperature, to bring third-party disinterestedness to bear on partisan conflicts, to provide machinery for peaceful change and conciliation, and so to reduce the risks of war and to promote peaceful relations between states. Alternatively there could be an alliance which would embrace "good" states the world over, however "goodness" was to be defined, which would regard an attack on one as an attack on all and would present a firm front against the pretensions and aggressions of the "bad" states, and, with reasonable luck, would have a sufficient preponderance of power on its side to deter the "bad" from wars which they could not win. What could not be obtained in 1919, even if the United States had been willing to make every sacrifice of tradition and constitutional shibboleth to secure it, was a League which combined universality with collective security. The alliance which would constitute no "entanglement" because it would be a "concert of power"[36] was, to this degree, bound to be shown up as a rhetorical device for squaring the circle.

But before we denounce Wilson for not eating his own rhetoric and for not ruthlessly settling for one or the other horn of this intellectual dilemma, there are two sets of considerations which ought to be borne in mind. The first is that, out of the many shifting shades of emphasis and rhetoric in Wilson's exposition of the League idea, it does on balance seem fairly certain that, of the two alternatives listed above, it was the first that commanded his predominant assent—both before Paris, as we have seen, and afterward. There are the recurrent themes of the superiority of the "moral" element in history and of the power of public opinion which point to a belief that the success of the new organization would derive from its peace-inducing processes rather than its force-wielding potentialities. Wilson never seriously envisaged even economic sanctions; most of the time he speaks of a "boycott," which, almost like a social ostracism, would bring the offender to his senses. Repeatedly, in fact, he envisages the League's quasi-parliamentary processes—investigation, conciliation, debate, etc., together with the enforced "nine months' delay," on which he lays great stress—as sufficient to dissuade any would-be aggressor from carrying out his threats.

So much for Wilson's own expectations, which we may deride or accept a vicarious responsibility for, as we wish. But beyond them lies a further set of considerations. What, with the experience of the League and the United Nations now behind us, would we have wished him to do? Settle for a mere alliance, such as a world of exhausted victors and disarmed vanquished scarcely required? Surely not. Settle for a merely deliberative forum, a kind of nonlegal world court? Again the answer must surely be no. The Covenant was not wrong to envisage sanctions more powerful than words, despite all the obvious difficulties and risks in applying them. *Of course* any movement from verbal censure to any kind of positive action was full of hazards and ambiguities, intellectual and practical. But once it is accepted that "what disturbs the whole world is the concern of the whole world," there is no logical stopping place short of world government. But to say this is not to make nonsense of the Wilsonian design. The world does not wait for logical stopping places. Between chaos and world government, there are many practical stopping places, and they will all, in varying degrees, involve a blend of peaceful persuasion by an embryonic world public opinion and a show (and perhaps use of) force by a less-than-universal collective-security grouping. They will all be untidy intellectually (and perhaps practically); they will all involve hazards of spreading war as well as always be repugnant to intellectuals with tidy minds and a passion for peace. Wilson was such an intellectual and at times wriggled and equivocated under these harsh necessities. But in relation to this central, crucial issue of his time, he came nearer to transcending his personal and national limitations than any other statesman who had the responsibility of shaping the settlement of 1919.

NOTES

1. "The great principle of collective security is the only principle that will induce Honorable Gentlemen opposite to make any preparation for the defence of this island."
2. Sir Alfred E. Zimmern, *The League of Nations and the Rule of Law, 1918–1935* (London, 1936), pp. 229 ff.
3. Arthur S. Link, *Wilson*, 5 vols. to date (Princeton, N. J., 1947–), v, 41.

4. Wilton B. Fowler, *British-American Relations, 1917–1918* (Princeton, N. J., 1969), p. 293.

5. *Ibid.*, p. 294.

6. It was still present as a "further suggestion of additional articles" in Wilson's first Paris Draft of January 10, 1919, printed in David H. Miller, *The Drafting of the Covenant*, 2 vols. (London, 1928), II, 92.

7. Speech at San Diego, Sept. 19, 1919, Ray Stannard Baker and William E. Dodd, eds., *The Public Papers of Woodrow Wilson*, 6 vols. (New York, 1925–27), VI, 294.

8. League to Enforce Peace speech, May 26, 1916, in *Proceedings of First Annual National Assemblage of League to Enforce Peace* (New York, 1916), p. 161.

9. Address to the Senate, Jan. 22, 1917, in Baker and Dodd, eds., *The Public Papers of Woodrow Wilson*, IV, 414.

10. The phrase was, of course, Jefferson's. Did Wilson's erroneous attribution reflect a subconscious determination to maximize the odium attaching to the idea by attributing such criticism to the Father of the Republic?

11. Address opening the campaign for the fourth Liberty Loan, Sept. 27, 1918, Baker and Dodd, eds., *The Public Papers of Woodrow Wilson*, V, 238.

12. Fowler, *British-American Relations*, pp. 289–90.

13. Conversations with his brother-in-law, Stockton Axson, in August 1914, in Ray Stannard Baker, *Woodrow Wilson: Life and Letters*, 8 vols. (Garden City, N. Y., 1927–39), V, 74.

14. Link, *Wilson*, V, 21.

15. *Proceedings of League to Enforce Peace*, p. 161.

16. Baker and Dodd, eds., *The Public Papers of Woodrow Wilson*, IV, 287.

17. *Ibid.*, VI, 234.

18. Baker, *Wilson: Life and Letters*, I, 386.

19. Baker and Dodd, eds., *The Public Papers of Woodrow Wilson*, V, 181.

20. Miller, *The Drafting of the Covenant*, I, 164 ff.

21. Address opening campaign for fourth Liberty Loan, Sept. 27, 1918, in Baker and Dodd, eds., *The Public Papers of Woodrow Wilson*, V, 258.

22. *Nicomachean Ethics*, Book II, 2.

23. Link, *Wilson*, V, 268.

24. Miller, *The Drafting of the Covenant*, I, 42.

25. *Ibid.*, II, 563.

26. Baker and Dodd, eds., *The Public Papers of Woodrow Wilson*, IV, 287–88.

27. Link, *Wilson*, V, 107, 149.

28. Baker, *Wilson: Life and Letters*, VI, 386.

29. Baker and Dodd, eds., *The Public Papers of Woodrow Wilson*, IV, 409.

30. *Ibid.*, V, 181.

31. See Baker, *Woodrow Wilson and World Settlement*, 3 vols. (Garden City, N.Y., 1922), I, 223.

32. Fowler, *British-American Relations*, p. 278.

33. *Ibid.*

34. Miller, *The Drafting of the Covenant*, I, 42–43.

35. *Ibid.*, p. 80.

36. Address to the Senate, Jan. 22, 1917, quoted in Link, *Wilson*, V, 267–68.

Chapter Seven

REFLECTIONS ON WILSON

AND THE PROBLEMS OF

WORLD PEACE

WHITTLE JOHNSTON

Of the many observations one might make on contemporary efforts (including those in the present volume) to understand Woodrow Wilson's foreign policies, two would seem of particular importance. The first is that those policies were of enormous significance; the second is that we do not yet have a determinative interpretation of them.

We may suggest their importance through a simple analogy. The attempt to understand international events during Wilson's two administrations may be looked upon as an effort, still largely uncompleted, to put together a gigantic picture puzzle. Wilson's foreign policies constitute many pieces to be fitted into the puzzle. Because they make up such a very large part of the puzzle, and touch so many other pieces at so many other points, we cannot understand the design of those other pieces—to say nothing of such design as the puzzle as a whole may have—until the Wilsonian pieces are fitted into place. Nor can we understand the meaning of our own time until we gain a clearer understanding of Wilson's time, given the continuing impact of the problems that he faced then upon those that we face now. To state but the most obvious of these questions: What is to be the role of the United States in the world? What should be its response to Communist Russia? What contribution can international organization make to the furtherance of world order? The continuity is equally strong at a rather more abstract level where we confront, as Wilson did, the vast snarl of problems clustered about the terms revolution, war, peace. The effort to understand Wilson's policies in these years is a task in historiography of the very first order.

While much light has been cast on many specifics of Wilson's foreign policy, and while flashes of insight have, from time to time, thrown a glow over a wider terrain, there does not yet exist a consensus on the *meaning* of Wilson's foreign policies as a whole, much less on their *merit*. One at times has the feeling that history may have put Wilson under double jeopardy: first, for his failure to achieve what he sought; second, for the inability of others to grasp the greatness of his effort or the complexity of his failure. Understanding of Wilson's foreign policies has often proved elusive because they involve the interaction of a statesman of exceptional brilliance with events of extraordinary complexity. To be sure, one never fits all the "pieces" into "place" in any major historical problem. Our historic existence does not present itself to us in such tidy patterns. But, on this side of perfection, matters of degree remain important. Not all historical problems are of equal weight or density; many involve less formidable men facing less demanding challenges. In such instances, the risks of "explanation" through distorted simplification decline. For Wilson's foreign policies, they remain high.

For purposes of illustration let a single celebrated instance suffice. In George Kennan's view: "As hostilities ran their course, hatreds congealed, one's own propaganda came to be believed, moderate people were shouted down and brought into disrepute, and war aims hardened and became more extreme all around." He later adds:

> A line of thought grew up, *under Wilson's leadership*, which provided both rationale and objective for our part in fighting the war to a bitter end. . . . This theory gave us justification both for continuing the war to its bitter and terrible end . . . and at the same time for refusing to preoccupy ourselves with the practical problems and maladjustments to which the course of hostilities was leading. . . . Under this theory things advanced *with a deadly logic and precision* to a peace which was indeed "forced upon the loser, a victor's terms imposed upon the vanquished, accepted in humiliation, under duress."

Simplicity of diagnosis invites simplicity of prognosis. If Wilson can be condemned as a militant idealist pushing war *à outrance*, the corrective is plain: that we be men of moderation acting in accord with the restraint of classic realism. Kennan elaborates this course in his prescriptions for an alternative policy:

> You could have refrained from moralistic slogans, refrained from picturing your effort as a crusade, kept open your lines of negotiation to the enemy, declined to break up his empires and overthrow his political system, avoided commitments to the extremist war aims of your allies, retained your freedom of action, exploited your bargaining power flexibly with a view to bringing its full weight to bear at the crucial moments in order to achieve the termination of hostilities with a minimum prejudice to the future stability of the Continent.[1]

It would be hard to imagine a more grievous misreading, if one set about the task consciously, of Wilson's intentions or policies. War aims did *not* harden and become more extreme all around, in very good part because *Wilson* never abandoned the convictions which underlay his insistence on a "peace without victory" and gave strength to those who shared those sentiments in the other belligerent states. Nor did the line of thought "under Wilson's leadership" provide rationale for fighting the war to a bitter end. Wilson undertook repeated efforts, before the entry of the United States, to bring the war to a negotiated settlement and always feared that a war without limit would make impossible a durable settlement. By the time that the United States entered the war, Germany's controlling strategy was to seek a definitive victory over the Allies in the West, before American aid could make a major difference. The withdrawal of Russia from the war gave awesome added momentum to the German drive for total victory. Only after the failure of the Hindenburg offensive in the summer of 1918 did the possibilities of a negotiated settlement with Berlin open up, and Wilson took immediate advantage of the opportunity. Beyond this, the Armistice which he masterminded *was* negotiated, not dictated. The crucial shift in the direction of an imposed settlement was plainly not his intention nor mainly his doing.

Kennan's prescription for the alternate course which Wilson *should* have followed is, in the main, an accurate description of the course which Wilson *did* follow. He kept open his lines with the enemy. He retained hope for the preservation of the Austro-Hungarian Empire until the hour was very late, and he changed his view only after it was obvious that the Hapsburg Empire was breaking up for reasons beyond his control. Wilson did tireless battle with the extremism of Allied war aims, kept an eagle eye on America's freedom of action, and seized the earliest possible moment to terminate hostilities "with a minimum prejudice to the future stability of the Continent." Kennan's picture of Wilson as a ruthless war leader intoxicated by his own moral idealism stems from the erroneous equation of a temporary tactic with a constant design. Wilson's stress on force without stint or limit was a short-term emphasis made necessary, in his view, by the drastic change in the course of the war. He always kept it subordinate to a long-term strategy of moderation. Kennan's skeptical words about the positive utility of force might well have been Wilson's: "It is essential to recognize that the maiming and killing of men and the destruction of human shelters and other installations, however necessary it may be for other reasons, cannot in itself make a positive contribution to any democratic purpose."[2]

This conclusion may serve as our point of entry for consideration of Wilson's general relation to the problems of revolution, war, and peace. Our thesis may be simply stated: the foreign-policy world of Woodrow Wilson was not divided into three equal parts. The overarching concern of his policy was to achieve a durable peace. To find the clue to his statesmanship in these years, we must focus on Wilson the peacemaker—not on Wilson the war leader, nor on Wilson the revolutionary.

His was an order of priorities far different from, say, a Theodore Roosevelt, for whom the use of force had about it, so often, an aura of exaltation and achievement. Wilson's patient persistent pursuit of peaceful paths for the resolution of disputes was an indelible mark of his statesmanship. One sees it, in the period of American neutrality, in the quest for a mediated end of the war; later, in the exploration of every means to protect American rights against Germany short of a declaration of war; in the determination to stop the fighting as soon as the foe had met quite specific and limited conditions; in the persistent effort to find a peaceful resolution of the conflicts in Russia; in the resolute resistance to Allied pressures for military intervention in Russia and then, when it was reluctantly undertaken, insistence that the scale be small, the goal limited, the constraints strict, the termination swift.[3]

To be sure, Wilson did find that force, in one form or another, became necessary in each of these instances. But, in each, he made use of it as a reluctant last resort, with a heavy heart at the failure of civilized alternatives and with a sense of foreboding at what the costs would be. Surely one detects a pattern here—and in his conception of the League of Nations as well. The intrinsic difficulties in understanding Wilson's policies are formidable in their own right; we need not impose our own upon them. The question of whether Wilson did, or did not, favor the use of force as a sanction to uphold the rulings of the League of Nations is, it may be submitted, an artificial one.[4] His view of the role of force in the League was completely in character with him. The defining characteristic of the League of Nations lay in provisions for the peaceful settlement of international disputes. If these failed, there were provisions for the application of nonmilitary sanctions against the offenders. If these too should fail, there can be no doubt that Wilson viewed force as a last resort. But he saw in the persistence of questions on the workability of forcible sanctions an inability to grasp the larger architecture of the League. He was not a little impatient with the narrowness of these criticisms. For Wilson, the concept of the League of Nations was far richer than that of collective security.

The primacy that Wilson attached to peaceful processes does not make of him a pacifist who eschewed force under any and all conditions. There was a powerful combative streak in his nature, and he resolutely called his people to arms in defense of the right that was more precious than peace. His temperament brings to mind that of a two-fisted Quaker, stalwart in defense of any slight to his honor, but ever dutiful to the promptings of conscience that it is the peacemakers who are blessed in the eyes of the Lord. Again, we are caught in Wilson's complexities. In assessing the policies of simpler men, it is often a matter of either/or. For Wilson, we are better advised to assume it is both/and. There was indeed such a thing as being too proud to fight.

It is not our concern here to depict Wilson the war leader. Ample testimony makes clear how formidable was his role in this capacity. It is our contention that we can understand Wilson as war leader only if we work our way back from an understanding of Wilson as peacemaker. For Wilson, the meaning of the war was dependent on the nature of the peace that followed it. The achievement of a just peace was for him a form of Aristotelian final cause: it was this end that gave the motive power to his own effort and what he asked of his nation. The justification to be assigned the horrid sacrifices of the war was also largely dependent on the final verdict rendered upon it by the nature of the peace concluded at its end.

An appreciation of the primacy of peace among Wilson's priorities casts light on another of the indelible traits of his diplomacy—its unity. He constantly sought to relate part to whole in an integrated pattern. Wilson's major decisions in these years cannot be understood as a series of discrete encounters. He could not take comfort from the maxim, "You win some, you lose some," by which the workaday politician (or athlete) eases his adjustment to the exigencies of the competitive game and softens his frustrations at its unpredictable outcomes. If Wilson lost the *last* round, in a real sense he lost them *all*. Were he to fail in his effort to build a durable peace, no interim success in the conduct of the war or of diplomacy could offset this final shortfall. In that sense, it was foreordained that Wilson would make the supreme effort, in the autumn of 1919, to save the entire foundation of his policy and his belief. That gallant and crippling final tour spoke to the essential character of the man and his policies.

Emphasis on the primacy that Wilson attached to the achievement of a durable peace also casts a harsh light on the close of his presidency. The events of these final months have to them very jagged edges. Compelled to run the gauntlet among them, Wilson suffered grievous wounds. We diminish the meaning of these events if we blur their tragic dimensions. And Wilson's somber forebodings of what might be the consequences of failure were to be realized many times over.

What of Wilson's views on revolution? To label him "the conservative as liberal," as Richard Hofstadter did in his celebrated essay, poses as many problems as it resolves.[5] If Burke be taken as the embodiment of conservatism, then the description is clearly apt, given Burke's enormous impact on Wilson. But one of the most important insights that Wilson drew from Burke was the futility of equating conservatism with a stand-pat defense of the status quo. Wilson was always moving, always adapting, always learning, always growing. Beyond this, there were of course powerful elements of liberalism in Burke, nowhere more clearly revealed than in his great *Speech on Conciliation with the Colonies*. Hofstadter is inclined to start Wilson's career too far to the right and stop it too near the center. Although the characterization lacks the merit of literary grace, it would be more precise to classify Wilson as a conservative liberal who became, in the course of his career, a progressive liberal. The term "revolutionary" is one of such high abstraction that it commonly casts darkness rather than light on analysis. In that house of mirrors, let us be content to show which reflections obviously distort Wilson's features. We are certain to err if we put a preoccupation with "revolution," in anything remotely resembling the Marxist-Leninist sense of that term, at the center of Wilson's concerns. For Lenin, violent revolution was at the core of historical reality; war and peace could only be understood if seen in relation to it. Wilson held a wholly different view of the dynamics and outcome of the revolutionary process.

Perhaps the most complete articulation that Wilson gave of his views is in this passage from *Constitutional Government in the United States*:

> Government may be said to have passed, roughly speaking, through four stages and forms of development: a first stage in which the government was master, the people veritable subjects; a second in which the government, ceasing to be master by virtue of sheer force and unquestioned authority, remained master by virtue of its insight and sagacity, its readiness and fitness to lead; a third in which both sorts of mastery failed it and it found itself face to face with leaders of the people who were bent upon controlling it, a period of deep agitation and full of the signs of change; and a fourth in which the leaders of the people themselves became the government, and the development was complete.[6]

For Wilson, these "stages of political growth" pointed to a clear-cut outcome:

> But the end, whether it comes soon or late, is quite certain to be always the same. In one nation in one form, in another in another, but wherever conviction is awakened and serious purpose results from it, this at last happens: that the people's leaders will themselves take control of the government as they have done in England, in Switzerland, in America, in France, in Scandinavia, in Italy, and as they will yet do in every country whose polity fulfills the promise of modern time.[7]

The fulfillment of this promise would be in accord with the Anglo-American experience: "When the fourth and final stage of constitutional development is reached . . . one or other of two forms of government may result: the parliamentary English form or the American form."[8]

When governments are truly democratic the world over—when, that is, they give authentic voice to the will of their people—they will find their interests to be largely in harmony. It was not, in Wilson's view, the German or the Austrian or the Turkish peoples who had wanted war in 1914, but rather the autocratic governments of those empires acting largely against the popular will. However, the Great War made even clearer the existence of a latent global will—of which Wilson saw himself as a chief articulator—moving governments toward a generally democratic pattern. The attempt, through retarded governmental forms, to stay this process would enjoy but temporary success. The entrance of the United States into the war reinforced these tendencies. The workings of a vigorous League of Nations would further sustain them by supplanting strategic preoccupations with a community of power that would make it possible to draw state boundaries in accord with principles of justice, by aiding backward states through the stages of political development in the mandates provisions, and by expediting expression of the emergent legal community of mankind through the World Court.

Wilson hoped that, in the fourth stage of political development, even the violent orientation of Marxism-Leninism would be assimilated to the peaceful processes of constitutional democracy. However, when Lenin looked at Wilson's United States, he saw, not democracy, but capitalistic democracy, and insisted that the corruption of the first term destroyed any possible virtue in the second. For the "working people" of the world to realize the development toward which historic forces inevitably moved, it was necessary that they smash the oppressive state of capitalistic democracy and move to true "socialism." For Lenin, the First World War, rather than being a struggle by democratic peoples to further freedom against autocratic governments, was but an alignment of one gang of capitalistic oppressors against another. It could take on progressive meaning only if converted into a civil war by the international proletariat against capitalistic oppression.

What Wilson saw as the fulfillment of a progressive history, Lenin saw as the climactic stage in the degeneration of the old order and the prelude to its violent overthrow. What to Lenin was the inevitable course of progressive revolution, Wilson saw as a tyrannical deviation from the normal course of constitutional development. Wilson's point of rest was Lenin's point of attack. The precondition for the realization of the revolutionary vision of either was the neutralization of the revolutionary vision of the other.

Let us be on guard then against tendencies to assimilate Wilson's efforts to perspectives not his own. With an oversimplification which brevity necessitates, let us resist tendencies to see Wilson as either a "realist," in the meaning that Hans Morgenthau gave that term, or a "revolutionary" in any Marxist sense of that term. To picture him in either light—to make the violence of war or of revolution his primary interest—risks supplanting Wilson's priorities with those of the analyst. It is of course perfectly in order to ask if his policies would have been more effective if he had been more "realistic" or more "revolutionary," if he had given greater weight to this or that phase of the war, or this or that dimension of revolutionary upheaval. But let us hear these cases in their proper venue, as questions of "should have done" not "actually did do." We do not draw nearer to actuality by portraying Wilson as a bumbling realist or an incipient Marxist.

Wilson was largely an unassimilable force—always on guard against attempts to make himself the instrument of purposes not his own, quick to detect them, and even quicker to repudiate them. While it may be argued that he was not an original thinker in the philosophical sense, he was highly original in the combinations that he fashioned among existing ideas. In particular, he often brought a striking novelty to bear in his foreign policies. An aspect of the latter was the skill with which he moved from the formulation of foreign-policy goals in broad-gauged philosophical terms to the multiple nuances involved in the application of these goals to specific issues often of very narrow gauge. Wilson's brilliance is seen both in his articulation of abstract universals and in the range and virtuosity of his tactical ingenuity. Whatever be our judgment of Wilson the philosopher, surely we can make a strong case that he was among the most original statesmen in history, worthy of being understood in his own terms.

We are brought back then to our earlier thesis—that we will find the clue to Wilson's diplomacy in these years if we concentrate upon his efforts to achieve a durable peace and assess his policies toward war and revolution in light of his pursuit of this central goal. As one source of evidence to support this contention, we have previously cited the persistence of Wilson's efforts to find peaceful solutions to foreign-policy problems. We find another large body of evidence in Wilson's unbending determination to keep tight control of war aims and peace policy in his own hands. He showed a concern to guard his prerogatives here that he showed in no other policy area. This was the area of policy, par excellence, that could not be delegated. He defended his role in this domain against all challengers—within his own government, among the Allied states, and from revolutionary Russia.

From the abundant evidence that sustains this point, we may cite two familiar examples. First, the words to House on July 21, 1917, which Wilson emphasized to underline their importance: "England and France *have not the same views with regard to peace that we have* by any means. When the war is over we can force them to our way of thinking, because by that time they will, among other things, be financially in our hands; but we cannot force them now, and any attempt to speak for them or to speak our common mind would bring on disagreements which would inevitably come to the surface and rob the whole thing of effect."[9] Second, his response to House's proposal to win inter-Allied support for the following declaration at the conference of late November and early December 1917: "The Allies and the United States declare that they are not waging war for the purpose of aggression or indemnity. The sacrifices they are making are in order that militarism shall not continue to cast its shadow over the world and that nations shall have the right to lead their lives in the way that seems to them best for the development of their general welfare."[10] On December 1, Wilson wired to House: "The resolution you suggest is entirely in line with my thought and has my approval. You will realize how unfortunate it would be for the conference to discuss peace terms in a spirit antagonistic to my January address to the Senate."[11] In the event, agreement on a joint statement proved impossible, and each power went its own way. But the encounter was a revealing indication of Wilson's determination to preserve his freedom of action on the all-important issue of war aims.

An understanding of Wilson's peace policy is made difficult by its existence at many levels of generality. As has been noted, Wilson was ingenious, not only in the formulation of fundamental principles, but also in the tactical flexibility that he employed in their application. The consistency and continuity of his peace policy is to be sought, in the first instance, at the level of his fundamental principles and basic goals. To seek a comparable consistency at the level of their application to specific policy issues is to make demands on Wilson that no practicing statesman, however idealistic, can possibly honor. Aristotle's maxim provides a guide: "Look for precision in each class of things just so far as the nature of the subject admits."

Difficulties are compounded by the multiple interactions between Wilson's pursuit of certain basic goals and rapidly changing circumstances, both internal and external. The period from the entry of the United States into the war through the end of Wilson's second term was filled with massive changes and challenges in international and domestic politics. *All* had some bearing on the prospect whether Wilson could implement his principles in a comprehensive and consistent way. In the Fourteen Points Address, for example, Wilson made a major effort to relate his general principles to the specific terms of the coming settlement. Yet, by the time that the fighting had stopped, the course of events had already rendered certain of these specific provisions inapplicable. The abstractness of several of Wilson's formulations in the interval (e.g., the address at Mount Vernon on July 4, 1918), may be seen as an eloquent reaffirmation of universal principles. It may also signify a shrewd recognition by Wilson that, confronted with the indeterminate outcomes of rapidly changing situations, he dared not tie himself too tightly to specifics. A comparable complexity of interaction between the statesman of principle and the unpredictable dynamism of events is illustrated, many times over, in the course of the Paris Peace Conference.

Reinhold Niebuhr has noted:

> One might define a descending scale of relativity in the definition of moral and political principles. The moral principle may be more valid than the political principles which are derived from it. The political principles may have greater validity than the specific applications by which they are made relevant to a particular situation. And the specific applications may have a greater validity than the impulses and ambitions of the social hegemony of a given period which applies or pretends to apply them. But this descending scale of relativity never inhibits the bearers of power in a given period from claiming the sanctity of the pure principle for their power.[12]

Wilson himself was always the most sophisticated of Wilsonians. With the heavy pressures of his responsibilities, he well understood that his principles could not be applied with a perfect consistency to the myriad snarls of peacemaking. He knew that he had to act as a subtle man of principles rather than a simple man of principle. He had to seek outcomes that, on balance, seemed likely to further a durable settlement. Whatever the complex blend of several levels of generality in Wilson's policies, their tactical adaptation to changing developments could not fail to produce disillusionment among many of his followers or engender charges of hypocrisy against him. Wilson's disillusioned followers were several steps removed from his relentless encounters with recalcitrant challenges; they often saw in his quest for compromise the mark of betrayal and in his affirmation of continuity the confirmation of hypocrisy. But we cannot hold Wilson responsible for an attachment by his followers to his principles more intense than his own, except insofar as he had, through his zeal and eloquence, swayed them to belief in the possibilities of swift success beyond those that he himself entertained. In short, Wilson's own policies cannot be defined through either the hope or the despair of his followers.

A major task is thus set for us. What were Wilson's principles—at their different levels of generality—for a peaceful settlement? What were their major sources? Their paramount expressions? In what measure can the final settlement be said to embody them? What factors blocked their fuller application? Each of the papers in the present volume may be analyzed for the light it casts on one or another of the above questions. Or, for the sake of brevity, on two more general ones: What was Wilson's conception of a durable peace? What obstacles thwarted the fuller realization of his concept? As has been noted, each of the events in the foreign and domestic policies of the principal states had some bearing on the outcome. If we concentrate on the impact of some, to the exclusion of others, we shall not gain a clear picture of how each often affected the others, nor of the truly terrible complexities Wilson faced.

Arthur Link has reminded us that the foundations of Wilson's political thinking were the beliefs and values of the Christian tradition, and of Presbyterianism in particular. "Indeed, it is not too much to say that his Christian faith informed and influenced his every action and policy."[13] A second element of Wilson's thinking "with large implications for his foreign policy" was his belief in democracy. A third was his conviction that the American people had a special role to play in history which derived from the many dimensions of their uniqueness. These basic beliefs deeply influenced three aspects of Wilson's approach to foreign policy: his strong opposition to imperialism, his strong support for decolonization, and his strong abhorrence of war.

It may be suggested that another major source of Wilson's conception of the terms of a durable peace stemmed from his understanding of the causes of the Great War. He was steadily engaged in an assessment of the factors that had brought the war to pass, with an eye to their removal (or at least their mitigation) as a necessary condition to block war's recurrence. Thus Wilson's peace strategy was, in large measure, a systematic effort to prevent future conflict based on a realistic comprehension of the source of the current violence. His opposition to the annexation by one state of the territory of another, particularly when undertaken against the will of its inhabitants, may be seen as a generalization of his conviction that the annexation by Germany of Alsace-Lorraine in the Treaty of Frankfurt in 1871 was a major cause of the war. Wilson's adamant commitment to Article x of the League Covenant was also deeply rooted in the soil of reality, for had not the violation of the territorial integrity and political independence of Serbia and Belgium brought the calamity to pass and given to it worldwide dimensions? Nor was the great weight that he assigned to Paragraph 2 of Article xi the musing of an idle idealist: "It is also declared to be the friendly right of each Member of the League to bring to the attention of the Assembly or of the Council any circumstance whatever affecting international relations which threatens to disturb international peace or the good understanding between nations upon which peace depends." Had not another factor behind the war's coming been the failure of states to take common counsel in face of the Austro-Serbian crisis and to weigh the possibilities of peaceful resolution before issuing ultimata and drawing the sword? Finally, had not the reliance by states on the balance-of-power system, with priority assigned to the achievement of strategic frontiers, been the foundation of the entire structure of the old order? For peace to be durable, was it not essential to put the management of the security problem on a wholly new basis through the establishment of a community of power in the League, which only then would make possible convergence between political boundaries and principles of justice?

In most of the other specific proposals in his peace strategy, Wilson shows the same concern to understand—and then to counteract—the real causes of war. Wilson's principles of peace were fashioned from well-tempered steel forged from the rough ores of the old order in the fire of struggle.

If the Fourteen Points Address may be taken as Wilson's most famous attempt to spell out the implications of his general principles for the more specific terms of settlement, his great "Peace without Victory" address may be said to give us the richest public elaboration of his basic philosophy of the conditions of peace. If a recurrence of catastrophic war is to be avoided, a concert of power must be established to guarantee the permanence of the peace settlement—a force "so much greater than the force of any nation now engaged or any alliance hitherto formed or projected that no nation, no probable combination of nations could face or withstand it."[14] Unless the peoples of the new world are parties to the guarantee of this peace, such an overwhelming force cannot be created. But the peoples of the United States cannot be expected to guarantee a peace fashioned in accord with balance-of-power precepts: "The question upon which the whole future peace and policy of the world depends is this: Is the present war a struggle for a just and secure peace, or only for a new balance of power? If it be only a struggle for a new balance of power, who will guarantee, who can guarantee the stable equilibrium of the new arrangement? Only a tranquil Europe can be a stable Europe. There must be, not a balance of power, but a community of power; not organized rivalries, but an organized common peace." We have assurances that the belligerent states accept these points, but we must make clear to all their implications.

> They imply, first of all, that it must be a peace without victory. . . .
> Victory would mean peace forced upon the loser, a victor's terms
> imposed upon the vanquished. It would be accepted in humiliation,
> under duress, at an intolerable sacrifice, and would leave a sting, a
> resentment, a bitter memory upon which terms of peace would
> rest, not permanently, but only as upon quicksand. Only a peace
> between equals can last. Only a peace the very principle of which is
> equality and a common participation in a common benefit. The
> right state of mind, the right feeling between nations, is as neces-
> sary for a lasting peace as is the just settlement of vexed questions
> of territory or of racial and national allegiance.

This equality, of course, can only be of rights, not of population or of territory.

And there is a deeper thing involved than even equality of right among organized nations. No peace can last, or ought to last, which does not recognize and accept the principle that governments derive all their just powers from the consent of the governed, and that no right anywhere exists to hand peoples about from sovereignty to sovereignty as if they were property. . . . Henceforth inviolable security of life, of worship, and of industrial and social development should be guaranteed to all peoples who have lived hitherto under the power of governments devoted to a faith and purpose hostile to their own. . . . Any peace which does not recognize and accept this principle will inevitably be upset. It will not rest upon the affections or the convictions of mankind. . . . The world can be at peace only if its life is stable, and there can be no stability where the will is in rebellion, where there is not tranquillity of spirit and a sense of justice, of freedom, and of right.

There are many designs, of many different degrees of abstractness, interwoven in the complex tapestry of this address. At the most general level, Wilson is working, in simultaneous interdependence, with the two basic components of any durable peace: the organization of capabilities and the modification of intentions. States that have been at war with one another in the past may be expected to remain at peace in the future if they confront an alignment of forces that dooms such venture to failure from the outset, or if their purposes are so transformed that they see no need, and have no desire, to take up arms. Where both conditions obtain, i.e., a distribution of capabilities that makes the use of force seem futile and a harmony of intentions that makes it seem foolish, peace may be said to have a double guarantee. It was this double guarantee that Wilson sought.[15]

Wilson hammers out his basic points with syllogistic rigor: the peace cannot endure without America's support; Americans cannot support a peace that is not in accord with their principles; these principles are equality of right and the consent of the governed; therefore only a peace founded on such equality and such consent can endure. The interdependence of the two essential components of peace is stressed throughout: peace cannot be stable unless the balance of power is supplanted by a community of power, but a community of power is impossible unless the terms of settlement embody principles of justice and induce tranquility of spirit.

Although each component is intertwined with the other, Wilson's shift of emphasis in the development of the argument is revealing. In the earlier phases of the address, his main focus is on the organization of capabilities, and the issue of justice is cast largely in *instrumental* terms. That is, if the European statesmen expect Americans to help to maintain the settlement, they should, as a practical matter, bear in mind that certain principles are important to Americans. In the latter phases of the address, however, Wilson's tone shifts. The appeal to principle is no longer a tactical condition; it is a philosophical conviction. Unless the terms of peace be just and embody the two prime constituent elements of justice, freedom and equality, the peace settlement will rest only as upon quicksand. Wilson is here giving eloquent elaboration of Rousseau's profound insight: "The strongest is never strong enough to be always the master, unless he transforms strength into right, and obedience into duty."[16]

After Wilson's articulation of the basic moral principles upon which a durable peace must rest, and his deduction of the political principles which follow from these, Wilson descends to a lower level on the scale of relativity. He begins to spell out the specific policy recommendations that follow from these political principles. Here one sees, in preliminary sketch, proposals that are to appear, time and again, in different formulations and different combinations with other proposals in subsequent Wilsonian statements. For example: "So far as practicable . . . every great people . . . should be assured a direct outlet to the great highways of the sea"; "The freedom of the seas is the *sine qua non* of peace, equality, and cooperation"; "The question of armaments, whether on land or sea, is the most immediately and intensely practical question connected with the future fortunes of nations and of mankind."

From here Wilson's concern becomes even more specific. In effect, he asks, how can I, in the most expedient way, bring the American people to support these principles and policies? Here one sees a vivid illustration of Wilson's tactical ingenuity. He will make clear to the American people that these principles are in accord with, indeed, extensions of, the most cherished traditions of their foreign policy, not transgressions of them.

I am proposing, as it were, that the nations should with one
accord adopt the doctrine of President Monroe as the doctrine of
the world: that no nation should seek to extend its polity over any

other nation or people, but that every people should be left free
to determine its own polity, its own way of development, un-
hindered, unthreatened, unafraid, the little along with the great
and powerful.

I am proposing that all nations henceforth avoid entangling
alliances which would draw them into competitions of power. . . .
There is no entangling alliance in a concert of power. When all
unite to act in the same sense and with the same purpose all act in
the common interest and are free to live their own lives under
a common protection.

The address remains an unfinished tapestry. It still has many loose
ends that remain to be woven into it. But the major design stands
forth clearly, and the supporting designs are beginning to take shape.
We have examined it at some length because in it Wilson articulates,
with great lucidity, the basic philosophical components of his strategy
of peace, and also because it forces to our attention the several levels
of generality at which that strategy operates. As we move to consideration of the factors which frustrated any full realization of that strategy,
it is always necessary to remain aware of its complexity. Differentia-
tion is the precondition of meaningful evaluation. Out-of-hand con-
demnation—or exaltation—does not advance our understanding of
Wilson's policies or of the obstacles that often barred their realization.
There are many designs in the tapestry. Not all are of the same scale,
or symmetry, or durability.

It is no part of our present concern to try to disentangle the different levels of Wilson's strategy, much less to assess the measure of
success that he achieved at each. But let us keep in mind that Wilson is
working at all four of Niebuhr's levels simultaneously: What are the
moral principles that must underlie the peace? What political principles do we deduce from them? What are the implications of these
political principles in terms of specific foreign policies? How can one
guarantee that these policies will be implemented as formulated?

At the moral level, Wilson's strategy remains constant. He does not
waver in the conviction that a durable peace must be just, and that
justice signifies equality of right and preservation of basic liberties.
The same constancy is found, by and large, at the level of political
principles, for example, that the peace must be one without victory,
that governments derive their just powers from the consent of the
governed, that "no right anywhere exists to hand peoples about from

sovereignty to sovereignty." Difficulties of two sorts, however, arise when Wilson attempts to shape specific policies that accord with these political principles: ambiguity and contradiction. As an instance of the former: what is to be the unit and what the means through which the consent of the governed is to find expression? Does the principle point to national self-determination, does national self-determination mean national *sovereign* determination—that is, that each nationality is entitled to possession of its own sovereign state—or does it mean autonomy within the given state structure? Does the same policy apply to all nationalities, great and small? If to the former only, then what are the policy implications for the latter? As instances of contradictory implications, what policy does one follow when the lines of settlement in accord with national self-determination (however defined) diverge radically from those in accord with state security? Or when pursuit of peace without victory is in contradiction with a settlement that rests on the consent of the governed? Or where both the consent of the governed and the security of the state are at odds with the requirements of economic rationality? In the first set of problems, the needle on one's compass swings about erratically and points in no single direction; in the second, one's compass has several needles, and the direction of each is different.

While the account of Wilson's efforts to shape the policies of a durable peace abound with problems of both types, let us cite a specific example of each as indications of the generic difficulty. In his address to Congress on December 4, 1917, recommending a declaration of war against Austria-Hungary, Wilson stated: "We owe it, however, to ourselves to say that we do not wish in any way to impair or to re-arrange the Austro-Hungarian Empire. It is no affair of ours what they do with their own life, either industrially or politically."[17] The war aims and peace terms suggested by The Inquiry, in its report to Wilson in January 1918, include this policy recommendation:

> It follows that the more turbulent the subject nationalities become and the less the present Magyar-Austrian ascendancy sees itself threatened with absolute extinction, the more fervent will become the desire in Austria-Hungary to make itself a fit partner in a league of nations. *Our policy must therefore consist first in a stirring up of nationalist discontent, and then in refusing to accept the extreme logic of this discontent which would be the dismemberment of Austria-Hungary.* By threatening the present German-Magyar combina-

tion with nationalist uprisings on the one side, and by showing it a mode of safety on the other, its resistance would be reduced to a minimum, and the motive to an independence from Berlin in foreign affairs would be enormously accelerated.[18]

Wilson made use of this report in drafting the Fourteen Points Address, which he delivered before a joint session of Congress on January 8, 1918. Point Ten stated: "The peoples of Austria-Hungary, whose place among the nations we wish to see safeguarded and assured, should be accorded the freest opportunity of autonomous development."[19] By the following autumn, however, his policy had changed drastically, as is made clear from this new view of Point Ten:

> Since that sentence was written and uttered to the Congress of the United States the Government of the United States has recognized that a state of belligerency exists between the Czecho-Slovaks and the German and Austro-Hungarian Empires and the Czecho-Slovak National Council is a *de facto* belligerent government clothed with proper authority to direct the military and political affairs of the Czecho-Slovaks. It has also recognized in the fullest manner the justice of the nationalistic aspirations of the Jugo-Slavs for freedom.[20]

Over these ten months, Wilson had made a drastic policy shift from the interpretation of national self-determination as the freest possibility for autonomous development within a given state structure to national self-determination as national *sovereign* determination at the price of that traditional state structure. When one assesses the divergence between the situation that Wilson had originally expected to find at the end of the war and the one that he actually confronted, great weight must be assigned to this enormous transformation. Walter Lippmann, one of the authors of the January draft by The Inquiry, developed the significance of these changes in a book written while the Paris Peace Conference was still in session: "The peace which has actually to be initiated in Paris to-day is the result of the 1918 campaign. The Fourteen Points were written before that campaign was fought, and that campaign in its military, diplomatic, and social phases was the most penetrating conflict in modern history. Its conclusion was radical, and out of it nothing less could result than the necessity of creating a new framework for international society. The decision to fight that campaign meant that the world had burned its bridges. They were not burned in the Fourteen Points."[21]

As an illustration of the second type of problem, lines of settlement which were in accord with a state's conception of its security and strategic interests were often in conflict with lines in accord with national self-determination and the consent of the governed. While Marshal Foch, for example, could argue that a frontier along the Rhine was essential to France's future security, Wilson saw in such an egregious violation of self-determination the creation of an Alsace-Lorraine in reverse that would sow the seeds of future war. Wilson was fully aware of such problems and invested enormous energy in efforts to resolve them. He sought to undercut the intense preoccupation of European statesmen with strategic issues by putting forth an alternative proposal for the management of the security problem through the League of Nations. His procedural priorities at Paris reflected his philosophical priorities. He saw that, unless alternative arrangements were provided, traditional power considerations would override those of justice and make impossible a settlement in accord with Wilsonian principles. Once the League was included in the Treaty, however, possibilities for the just settlement of other issues would be opened up which would otherwise have been impossible.

The contradiction between these two perspectives constituted the most formidable policy problem that Wilson faced. It was, in the end, to prove insurmountable. His appeal to the League merely changed the form and forum of divergence; it did not end it. The French, for example, gave support to the League only to the degree that they saw it as an instrument for the continuation of France's traditional alliance policies, and they sought to interpret the Covenant to achieve the furtherance of this goal. Wilson, in contrast, saw the League as a radical departure from the pattern of historic alliances, and believed that it was only in these terms that he could hope to win support for it from his own people. A League that was strong enough for France, given her anxieties, would have been far too strong for the United States, given her reservations. Wilson's brilliant insight, of durable profundity at the level of political principle, could not be brought to life at the level of practical policy. Wilson was never able to fit this first essential piece in his structure of peace into place. Absence of the cornerstone gave the architecture of the League a very different aspect from that of his original design.

One destination to which consideration of the fourth level of generality—concern that policies will be implemented as formulated—brings us is to Wilson as administrator. Another great administrator, Herbert Hoover, has reminded us of this dimension of Wilson's ordeal. Hoover takes note of this dimension in his study on Wilson in order "to demonstrate the huge administrative burdens which Woodrow Wilson carried in Paris at the same time he was negotiating world peace." "They . . . indicate his administrative abilities," Hoover adds, "and, above all, his humane spirit. They . . . also show how the overwork required may have contributed to his final stroke."[22] We are brought, as a second destination, to the increasing importance that Wilson assigned to the League, as he explained to the Senate in his address presenting the treaty for its consideration. Even the skeptics at Paris had been won over to the support of the League: "The most practical of the conferees were at last the most ready to refer to the League of Nations the superintendence of all interests which did not admit of immediate determination, of all administrative problems which were to require a continuing oversight. What had seemed a counsel of perfection had come to seem a plain counsel of necessity. The League of Nations was the practical statesman's hope of success in many of the most difficult things he was attempting."[23] To be sure, this phase of Wilson's strategy has critics as well as champions, as this observation by George Kennan indicates: "We see, then, that in each case—in the Russian North as in Siberia—whatever merit may have resided in the President's decisions of July 1918 concerning America's course of action in those areas, was largely forefeited by the manner in which the decision was developed. In the one case, it was the diplomatic implementation that was faulty; in the other, the military."[24]

It proved difficult for Wilson to implement his complex strategy of peace in part because he was President "at a time when the structure of the executive branch was completely inadequate for its burdens."[25] In addition, "many of his subordinates, from secretaries of state down to division chiefs in the Department of State and ambassadors and ministers, were poorly trained for their positions or incompetent." Even at the top of his administration, Wilson encountered problems of loyalty, as in the case of Lansing and, to a varying degree, House. These difficulties were compounded by the inability of even Wilson's most intimate advisers—to say nothing of those of lower rank—to grasp the full structure of his grand design. In this sense, the problem of implementation was that there simply were not enough Wilsons to go around.

For all its importance, however, appreciation of these factors enables us to take but the first steps toward understanding the obstacles that thwarted the fuller realization of Wilson's strategy of peace. This may be seen if we keep in mind what are, in abstract formulation, the preconditions for any effective foreign policy: the forging of an intrasovereign and intersovereign consensus among diverse constituencies. Put in other words, the statesman who would be successful in his foreign policy has to achieve agreement on its terms among a wide diversity of internal groups and external sovereign authorities. Walter Lippmann, a close observer of this process, and of Wilson's role in it, delineates some of its dimensions in these comments on the Fourteen Points Address:

> The terms had to be such that the majority among the Allies would regard them as worth while. They had to meet the national aspirations of each people, and yet to limit those aspirations so that no one nation would regard itself as a catspaw for another. The terms had to satisfy official interests so as not to provoke official disunion, and yet they had to meet popular conceptions so as to prevent the spread of demoralization. They had, in short, to preserve and confirm Allied unity in case the war was to go on.

These were but the first needs to be met:

> They had also to be the terms of a possible peace, so that in case the German center and left were ripe for agitation, they would have a text with which to smite the governing class. The terms had, therefore, to push the Allied governors nearer to their people, drive the German governors away from their people, and establish a line of common understanding between the Allies, the nonofficial Germans, and the subject peoples of Austria-Hungary. The Fourteen Points were a daring attempt to raise a standard to which almost everyone might repair.[26]

To summarize and extend Lippmann's points: in order for Wilson to attain something like full success in the achievement of a durable peace, he had to approach consensus among five major constituencies, each diverse within itself: the American people, the Allies, the enemy powers, the defecting power (Russia), and the neutrals. While

100 percent support was, of course, neither essential nor expected, any substantial opposition would thwart realization of Wilson's strategy. After all, the destructiveness of the Great War itself had been the outgrowth of a military establishment speaking for a small minority which had placed itself in opposition to the vast majority of mankind.[27]

We may now rephrase the challenge that Wilson faced in foreign policy from the entry of the United States into the war until the end of his administration. Could he win substantial support for his peace strategy (at its four levels) among five major constituencies (each with major internal diversities) under rapidly changing strategic, diplomatic, political, and economic conditions? Wilson had to assess the changes in each of these constituencies with an eye to their effects upon achievement of the sort of peace that he sought. How did they retard, or how further, these prospects? What means did he have available, for each constituency, and for each type of problem, to encourage trends that advanced the prospects for a Wilsonian peace and to counter trends that worked against that prospect? Studies in this volume throw much light on these problems—for example, Professor Floto on Italy, Professor Unterberger on Russia, Professor Lundgreen-Nielsen on Poland, and Professor Wimer on the neutrals.

If the diplomatic precondition for the success of Wilson's strategy was that he win support from these five constituencies, the political precondition was the existence within each—or most—of groups that would support his policies. His challenge may, therefore, be put in somewhat more precise terms: what were the prospects that pro-Wilsonian groups would exercise power in each of these constituencies? What means were at his disposal to further the exercise of power by such groups? At first glance, one might conclude that the currents of history were flowing in a Wilsonian direction. It is of much value for Arno Mayer to remind us that states are complex entities and that on questions of war and peace they were by no means of one mind, especially after 1917.[28] There can be no doubt that the debate over the meaning of the war, and the terms of its possible settlement, took on a new range and complexity in 1917. While there had been occasional voices of divergence before that time, policy had been overwhelmingly cast in a traditionalist mold, both substantively and procedurally; that is to say, goals were largely defined in terms of state power and largely determined by executive prerogative. By 1917, a conjunc-

tion of massive pressures had shaken the foundations of traditionalism; it could no longer claim virtually uncontested sway. To cite but
the most obvious of these: the ghastly costs of what seemed an unend-
ing slaughter, the collapse of historic Russia followed by the lure of
new voices from the East, and the entrance of the United States under
the leadership of a President dedicated to the mobilization of worldwide progressive forces. Wilson moves to center stage as the plot is
undergoing extraordinary changes. Was not the moment made for
the man?

The drama of this encounter can be put in more familiar terms, of
course, when we recognize it as the struggle between the new diplomacy and the old. It is clear that Wilson challenged both the substantive and procedural foundations of traditionalism: he proposed a
settlement based on justice and a community of power which would
draw meaning and support from worldwide expressions of democratic opinion. We have noted above that it was impossible for Wilson
to carry out his principles with perfect consistency in each provision
of the peace settlement, and that this led some of his followers, in
disillusionment, to conclude he had thereby erased the distinction
between his diplomacy and that of the old world. From their stand-
point, the change was one of kind, not of degree. The struggle could
no longer be pictured as one between two sharply different approaches—one a rejection of the old and a promise of the new, the
other a restoration of the old with a grim prospect for more of the
same. Charles Seymour was later to put forward a sophisticated and
sympathetic variant of the same argument:

> Various historians, especially those writing from an American
> point of view, have presented the peace conference as though it
> were a clear-cut conflict between two sets of ideals, personified by
> Clemenceau on the one hand and Wilson on the other; a conflict
> between the evil of the old European diplomatic system and the
> virtue of the new world idealism. Such a picture is attractive to
> those who will not try to understand the complexities of historical
> truth. In reality the Peace Conference was not nearly so simple. It
> was not so much a duel as a general mêlée, in which the repre-
> sentatives of each nation struggled to secure endorsement for
> their particular methods of securing peace. . . .
> Inevitably each nation put forward a solution which was

colored by self-interest. This was, in a sense, just as true of the
United States as of France, Italy, or Great Britain. . . . Wilson's
idealism was in line with a healthy *Realpolitik*.[29]

However, while there was surely a narrowing of the difference between the old diplomacy and the new on some specific policy decisions, the differences between the two remained fundamentally
important. To obscure this, despite some elements of similarity, is to
miss the meaning of the whole Wilsonian effort. That program, in its
background, axioms, expectations, and application, was a profoundly
different approach to international politics from that of the ruling
continental statesmen.

Harold Nicolson begins his consideration of this issue with the rejection of one oversimplification: "The Conference has been represented, in particular by American propagandists of the type of
Mr. Ray Stannard Baker, as a conflict of the Powers of Light (represented by President Wilson) with the Powers of Darkness (represented by M. Clemenceau). Such a simplified dramatisation of the
issues is scarcely legitimate."[30] However, after contrasting Seymour's
sophisticated view to Baker's simple one, he grudgingly admits the
latter to be the more accurate: "I much prefer the processes of
thought adopted by Dr. Charles Seymour to the processes of emotion
indulged in by Mr. Stannard Baker. Yet I cannot but admit that of the
two it is Mr. Baker who more closely approximates to the truth. In
other words, the failure of the Conference of Paris to live up to its
own early ideals can only be understood if we start from the popular,
but not wholly inaccurate, assumption, that there did in fact exist a
conflict of principle."[31]

If a conflict of principles, and of the strategies derivative from
them, lay at the heart of these events, one must stand guard on two
fronts: against the tendency to see Wilson as an unacknowledged
practitioner of *Realpolitik* and against the temptation to see most European statesmen as converts to the new diplomacy. As has been
noted, there can be no doubt that there was a widening of the terms
of the debate over war aims by 1917 or that there was some growth in
the support for Wilsonian principles in several important states. The
critical question turns, not on the absolute growth of these trends, but
on their relative strength. Errors in policy projection rarely stem from
seeing things that are not *there*; they commonly stem from assigning

the wrong *weight* to what one sees, which in turn derives from the hopes that observers bring with them to what they see. Baker and Colcord (to follow Professor Floto's case study) saw trends that were real; they hoped that they would succeed; they projected their success. The rub comes with the recognition that many trends were "there" and, although some that were growing sustained Wilson's strategy, others, growing far more rapidly, subverted it.

An attempt to assess the weight to be assigned to factors that furthered the prospects for Wilson's new diplomacy as against those that thwarted such prospects compels us to face one of the most fundamental problems in international history: what are the domestic political consequences of international wars? The costs of war compel a society to justify its meaning to itself. In war's "moment of truth," the cohesion of a society is put into the crucible, to emerge strengthened, weakened, or destroyed. The outcome depends upon many factors, most notably the character of the belligerent society and the cost, course, and conclusion of the war. Quick and successful wars may sustain the justifications given them at the outset and strengthen the legitimacy of the belligerent society. Bismarck's wars of the 1860s and 1870s were of this character. The less solid the cohesion of the belligerent society, the less persuasive the war's justification, the more prolonged and costly its course, and the more humiliating its outcome, the more likely is its latent revolutionary potential to become actual, as one sees in China in the 1930s and 1940s. The First World War was prolonged, costly, for much of its duration indecisive, and, for many belligerents, humiliating in result. Its very course and cost challenged, in each of the European belligerents, the initial legitimization given for it and aroused revolutionary tendencies within them. In Russia and Austria-Hungary, these revolutionary tendencies played themselves out to the full, and the Great War became a Great Revolution. Other belligerents, for example, Germany, were also shaken by profound revolutionary pressures. But let us be cautious about overgeneralization. While the interconnection of war and revolution may be seen as the critical nexus of international history, the interaction of the two follows no determinate pattern. If Lenin and Wilson be taken (for the moment) as the two most powerful exponents of the new diplomacy, we should bear in mind that both were wide of the mark in their projections of the course of this interaction, in part because each gave to it a very different meaning.

In part these errors of projection stem from another source: the failure to appreciate the measure in which war also works, with massive power, to reinvigorate the most fundamental institutions of the state, i.e., those that have to do with the preservation and furtherance of its power in the relentless dynamics of the strategic-diplomatic struggle. We should not forget, as Professor Nicholas has reminded us, what war does to the modern state. There is a consensus that the effect of the war in its early years was to strengthen nationalistic and traditionalist forces; no one can deny the reality of the *Union Sacrée* or the *Burgfrieden*. Complexities began in 1917 when, as we have seen, there was a widening in the range of debate, and the unity of governmental policy was openly challenged. There is no disagreement on the point that, in absolute terms, there occurred an increase, within some segments of the belligerent populations, in support for the new diplomacy, in one or another of its formulations. Yet the critical question remains unanswered: what were the effects on foreign policy of this opening of the national dialogues, with a new intensity, of this introduction of novel elements into the debates? What, in particular, were the consequences for the achievement of a Wilsonian peace?

Groups truly supportive of Wilson's new diplomacy did not win control in any of the major belligerents. (We may, of course, ask under what conditions they *might* have come to win such authority in this or that state, as Professor Floto has done with regard to Italy. But this is a different question.) It is our thesis that we find an essential clue for their failure to win such authority when we direct our attention to the dynamics of the strategic-diplomatic struggle and the effects that this has upon the internal political and class alignments of states. The perspective should be one from the "outside in," so to speak, rather than from the "inside out." Needless to say, this is not a matter of either/or. The two perspectives are not mutually exclusive, although the matter of emphasis remains important. The strategic-diplomatic competition is like a vast ocean on which all ships of state must sail. We shall never understand the courses they take without scrupulous attentiveness to its currents.

The very focus on 1917, for example, as the year in which to highlight "the political origins of the new diplomacy" can be gravely misleading. While it is true that one sees an efflorescence of new perspectives, it is also true that one sees an enormous intensification of the old diplomacy. This *annus mirabilis* was, in truth, darkly ambiguous. It is bounded, at both its ends, by monumental transformations in the contours of the strategic-diplomatic struggle: the renewal of un-restricted submarine warfare by Germany in January and the con-clusion of an armistice on the eastern front in December. These transformations have no uniform political effect, as the Russian revo-lutions indicate. The March Revolution held the initial promise of double benefits to the western cause: in the hope that it would lead, strategically, to an invigoration of the Russian effort on the eastern front; diplomatically, to a clarification and strengthening of western war aims around the principles of democracy and the new diplomacy. The November Revolution dealt a devastating blow to both expecta-tions. Its strategic outcome was the termination of the eastern front; its diplomatic outcome, the dismissal of the proclaimed war aims of the western powers as meaningless hypocrisy and the reduction of both warring coalitions to the same level of degradation. Although these Russian developments no doubt led to some increase in political support in the belligerents for some aspects of the new diplomacy (as in the effects of the "Petrograd Formula"), one must weigh these against the increased political support for the old diplomacy conse-quent upon these drastic strategic transformations. The net result for the Allies was a sharp deterioration in their position, and this often led to intensified support for traditionalist policies because of a grow-ing sense of *anxiety*. For the Central Powers, the net outcome was a dramatic improvement in their strategic prospects, which often led to a strengthening of traditionalist forces through a growing awareness of *opportunity*. Although July 1917 was the month of the "new diplo-macy" of the Reichstag's "no annexations, no indemnities" resolution, it was also the month of the fall of Theobald von Bethmann Hollweg and the consolidation of power by Erich Ludendorff. After the defeat of Paul Painlevé in November in France, President Raymond Poincaré passed over Joseph Caillaux—advocate of a compromise peace—as his possible replacement and turned to Georges Clemenceau, whose one policy line was "*Je fais la guerre!*" To assess the political effects of these developments, it is, above all, necessary that we have an accurate understanding of the full political spectrum within each belligerent.[32]

If our primary focus in 1917 is on events in eastern Europe, we might initially concentrate on events in central Europe for 1918. As has been noted earlier, the disintegration of the Austro-Hungarian Empire by the end of the war confronted Wilson with situations very different from those that he had in mind when he proclaimed the Fourteen Points. The problems were far more formidable for a continental power such as France. The disintegration of Austria-Hungary removed a piece from the center of the European equilibrium that had been of critical importance from the very beginnings of the state system. Had the Austrian state remained in being, the possibilities of renewing the policies of Talleyrand or Kaunitz (i.e., of a tie between Paris and Vienna to counterbalance Berlin or St. Petersburg) would still have been open. Beyond this, French statesmen recognized from the first in the emergence of German Austria the possibilities of *der Anschluss*, which would even more gravely accelerate the relative growth of German power at the expense of French power. These anxieties were futher increased by the disappearance of the historic Russia, which imperiled a principle basic to French statecraft since at least the time of Francis I: utilization of the power east of the major power in central Europe to reduce the threat from that source to France. When we move ahead for a moment to 1919, these manifold fears are compounded, with the coming to power of Béla Kun in Hungary, and the possibilities of Communist domination in Austria and Germany. It now seemed that the severe blows already dealt the balance in eastern Europe would be combined with those in central Europe with the result that the whole traditional order of power in Europe would suffer irrevocable collapse. And, although events in Germany seemed, at the very end of the war, to take a turn in a Wilsonian direction, Professor Schwabe has shown us that the nationalistic reaction to the Versailles settlement was so strong it carried along the very groups on which Wilson had placed his primary reliance.[33] In these circumstances, it cannot occasion surprise to observe a convergence in power calculations based on the old diplomacy between a France that had passed through the valley of the shadow of death and a Poland that had been resurrected from the dead.

The divergence in policies that followed from the old diplomacy as against the new may be related to different assumptions about the character of the interdependence that exists among states, that is, about the international "system," in this simple meaning of that term. The distinction between the two should certainly not be seen as one between nationalism and internationalism. In many ways, the Allies had a far richer substantive understanding of the actual interworkings of the several states with one another and of the critical importance of the behavior of one upon the interests of the others than did Wilson. His internationalism, while far vaster in scope than theirs, was often much thinner in substance. One of the profound insights of traditional diplomacy had been this very awareness of the reality of interdependence—in time as well as in space—of the European states. From this perspective, the measure in which a settlement could be taken as legitimate was inseparable from its comprehensiveness. This instantly highlights a vast deficiency of the settlements in Paris: they left so much unsettled. To French statesmen, peace could not possibly be said to have been put on a stable foundation until the Russian role was defined with more clarity. One could not define the German role while countless loose ends remained untied in eastern Europe, for the adequacy of the peace with Germany depended on the clarity with which her role, on *all* her borders and in *all* her capacities, was defined. Interdependence in space was linked with interdependence in time. Since the German problem certainly could not be looked upon as "solved" from here to eternity and since the unrelenting struggle would surely persist, one had to give the most careful possible analysis of future power configurations. In French strategic thinking, remembrance of things past was intimately linked with apprehension of things to come. In the French determination to try to counteract what was seen as a deteriorating strategic position, there was a central preoccupation with what the future would hold. This awareness reinforced the French determination to maintain a presence in Russia and eastern Europe.

Wilson's efforts to win Italian support for his new diplomacy were also frustrated, in good measure, by the rich perversity of the European system. Another durable component of traditional diplomacy was the weight attached by states to their relative standing (which found primary expression in the principle of compensation in the classical balance of power). We find an illustration of this in Gaetano Salvemini's attack on Wilson's appeal to the Italian people over the heads of their leaders.[34] He argued that, unless sacrifices were imposed upon all, the legitimacy in the request that they be made by one was undercut. After France had already been accorded enormous gains in Alsace-Lorraine, the Rhineland, the Ruhr, and elsewhere, how was justice served when Italy was asked to show self-restraint? Salvemini's problem, within his frame of reference, was a real one. Given the nature of international politics, it was also insoluble. In the

absence of an international government that could impose such uni-
formity of self-restraint—or of any international legitimacy that could
give to it acceptability—and given the resultant primary dependence
by each state on its own resources in its own special situation, there
was no way that such sacrifices could be imposed upon all. Wilson's
appeal to justice could thus be turned upside down and dramatized as
an unjust burden imposed upon one.

For Wilson to succeed, it was necessary for him radically to redirect
the channels through which the turbulent currents of European statecraft surged. For him to fail, it was only necessary that these currents
continue to move in the deep beds which they had cut over many
centuries. To better appreciate the herculean task that Wilson had set
for himself, let us move from a consideration of clashes at the policy
level back up our ladder of abstraction and explore the divergence at
the level of political (and in some sense even moral) principle. Wilson's
"Peace without Victory" address was taken as a profound embodiment
of the philosophical foundations of the new diplomacy. Clemenceau's
Grandeur and Misery of Victory may be taken as a profound expression
of the philosophical foundations of the old diplomacy: "The developments of peace demand perhaps no less of systematic effort than the
conquests of war. Here indeed is the eternal problem of mankind,
since humanity is all concurrent activities, and since to live in society is
to be always in a perpetual state of confronting, with fleeting periods
of mutual agreement."[35] For Clemenceau confrontations are the
norm, periods of accommodation the exception. This leads him to a
Clausewitzian interpretation of the war: "The war, officially finished,
went on under new guises. . . . Clausewitz's saying, that war and
peace, springing from the same state of mind, are identical fundamental activities both aiming at the same end by different means,
begins to be current among the nations when they come to have an
inkling of the fact that there are states of stabilization more or less
enduring."[36] From this Clemenceau moves to express his skepticism
toward the role of moral formulas in international politics: "Countries
are different, interests are urgent, too often in conflict behind the veil
of literary manifestoes of impartiality, in which the most beautiful
formulas of universal equity have exhausted all the virtue and pith of
their ideology, without producing anything but fresh disorders more
or less skillfully disguised."[37] He closes by setting these political speculations in the larger framework of his philosophy of man and of
history:

> Our life throughout history, bandied about between battles and
> truces in the unending oscillation of all things, is at any moment
> but preparing for or stabilizing a new transient form of society for
> the momentary advantage of the strongest. . . . The idea of force
> is deeply rooted in man, as in the whole universe. . . . When the time
> came for negotiations . . . the problem was first and foremost to
> keep alive, before settling what we could, or what we wished
> to do with the life we had preserved.[38]

The nation must first live before it can debate if it will live justly.

The basic axiom of Wilson's strategy of peace was the conviction
that it is possible to fashion a settlement that will prove durable. From
this axiom, all his more specific policies flowed—for example, that a
major threat to the durability of peace is the aggressive action of
states, which renders a legitimate order impossible and creates deep
resentments from which subsequent conflicts are sure to arise. The
basic axiom of Clemenceau's strategy is the conviction that it is impossible to make a peace settlement that will rule out major wars in the
future. From this axiom, all his more specific policies flow, for example, that the first goal of the state should be to improve its relative
standing through the acquisition of any and all new assets of power,
particularly those that confer strategic advantage. It is the duty of the
statesman to put his people in the most advantageous possible position for the renewal of a struggle which is, in any case, inevitable.
Thus the two positions differ in their fundamental points of departure and in the most immediate policy implications that follow from
them. The one points toward the *restraint* of state ambition, the other
points toward the *realization* of state ambition.

It is hardly surprising to find that, from this starting point, Clemenceau viewed the League of Nations with cold skepticism. While Wilson
had said the Treaty would "take the Covenant under its wing, and the
world would be saved," Clemenceau found this view "a little short-
sighted—especially since no one dares even to raise the question of
putting executive power into the hands of our saviours." The League
was nothing more than an "epitome of the parliaments of all nations."
But how could it be otherwise, since "all executive power would be
denied it?" Its members could do nothing but talk, "when they ought
to decide and impose their decisions."[39] Clemenceau had a feeling of
deep bitterness toward the United States, in part because of the exag-

gerated expectations that it aroused over the League, in part because
it turned its back on European responsibilities:

> Your intervention in the war, which you came out of lightly, since
> it cost you but 56,000 human lives instead of 1,364,000 *killed*—to
> which must be added 740,000 men permanently disabled and
> 3,000,000 wounded—had appeared to you, nevertheless, as an
> excessive display of solidarity. And either by organizing a League
> of Nations, which was to furnish the solution to all the problems of
> international security by magic, or by simply withdrawing from the
> European schemes, you found yourself freed from all difficulties
> by means of a "separate peace."[40]

The old diplomacy, rooted in circumstances and beliefs radically at
odds with those of Wilson, penetrated French diplomacy in all its
aspects. When one seeks to capture the drama of Wilson's encounter
with it in imaginative terms, one is drawn toward the symbolism of
Greek mythology and the struggle between Hercules and Hydra, the
nine-headed serpent that grew two heads in the place of the one that
was cut off. Thwarted here, the old diplomacy always reemerged
there. Outmaneuvered by Wilson in the way in which the Armistice
was achieved, it sought to outmaneuver Wilson in the way in which
the Armistice was implemented. Ambitions denied in the West resur-
faced twice over in the East. Aspirations blocked in direct outlet were
manifested as diplomatic-military support for protégé states. Gains
denied territorial realization triumphed in functional form, as in the
reparations clauses. In his struggle with the old diplomacy, Wilson
faced an absolutely relentless opposition.

The First World War, by sharply increasing the sense of vulnerability of the historic states of Europe, greatly intensified their preoccupation with the improvement of their security position, and this
commonly gave added momentum to proponents of the old diplomacy. The fate of Britain's Liberal party, so close to Wilson in many of
its assumptions about international politics, is illustrative. Staunch
traditionalists such as Churchill, as well as articulate Liberals such as
Leonard Hobhouse, agreed that the course and outcome of the war
had invalidated many Liberal assumptions about international politics. The voters seemed to confirm these intimations at the polls, for,
once foreign policy issues were joined in the "khaki election," the
main emphasis in public opinion tended to be on the need for severe

terms for Germany to redress the precariousness of Britain's international position. The decline of the Liberal party that began in the war was not to be reversed; the interwar period was one of traditionalist dominance.

One finds here another clue to Wilson's inability to win substantial political support in the major European states for his new diplomacy—the ambiguous consequences that flowed from the implementation of the concept itself. Its two key components—justice and moderation in the *terms* of foreign policy and openness and democracy in the *processes* of foreign policy—were often contradictory, as many traditionalist critics noted. As the British instance showed, there was no automatic correspondence between the procedural and substantive aspects of the new diplomacy. On the contrary, the appeal to demos often produced outcomes far less moderate than those of cabinet diplomacy.

These considerations suggest a more complex conceptual ambiguity—that between the temporal and ethical connotations of the word "new." Proponents of the new diplomacy intertwine the two meanings: recent in time and in accord with moral norms. But not all that was new in the new diplomacy was in accord with Wilson's moral standards—particularly his sense of moderation; and not all that was old was in conflict with them. Many proponents of an older diplomacy wanted a peace without victory to preserve the historic states and states system of Europe. Many advocates of a knock-out blow were also supporting a form of "new diplomacy," but they had little in common with either Wilsonism or traditionalism. It is particularly misleading to group Wilson's policies and Lenin's under the heading of the "new diplomacy." Both were "new" only in the temporal sense, only in their opposition to what had gone before. In the ethical sense, Wilson's divergence from Lenin was far greater than his divergence from the old diplomacy.

We may gain a clearer insight into the profundity, and insolubility, of the moral dilemmas that Wilson faced if we borrow a few leaves from the notebooks of two continental philosophers, Arnold Wolfers and Friedrich Meinecke. Wolfers calls to our attention the difference (one which has existed over the centuries) between the outlook of the continentals on the role of morality in foreign policy, and that of the Anglo-Americans: "While the continentals were arguing about the dilemma of statesmen faced by the irreconcilable demands of necessity and morality, English and American thinkers in turn were engaged in a debate about the best way of applying accepted principles of morality to the field of foreign policy. . . .

"This was a philosophy of choice, then, which was bound to be ethical, over against a philosophy of necessity, in which forces beyond moral control were believed to prevail."[41] Wolfers traced the divergence in philosophical approach to this problem on the part of the Anglo-Americans to their geostrategic setting: "For the two 'island' countries, external attack or invasion were unlikely contingencies most of the time, so that self-preservation in a strict sense of the term rarely came to place restrictions on the leeway they enjoyed in respect to other policy objectives."[42]

Clemenceau's approach to the role of morality in foreign policy bears the heavy imprint of the continental perspective, Wilson's of the insular. The gulf was made all the wider by a further consideration: France's awareness that her relative power position was in decline and America's confidence that hers was on the rise. Wilson spoke for an insular state on the ascendant arc of its power, Clemenceau for a continental state on its declining arc.

Meinecke was preoccupied throughout his career with the problem of the clash between the statesman's obligation to uphold moral norms, on the one hand, and his commitment to safeguard the security of the state against threats from within and without, on the other hand. This clash had assumed a particularly harsh aspect in the era of Machiavelli, given the severity of the dangers that statesmen faced on both fronts in his time. By the time of Frederick the Great, the internal challenges to his Prussian kingdom had been largely surmounted. The external dimension of the dilemma continued to assert itself with relentless stringency, however, as these words of Frederick testify: "One sees oneself continually in danger of being betrayed by one's allies, forsaken by one's friends, brought low by envy and jealousy; and ultimately one finds oneself obliged to choose between the terrible alternatives of sacrificing one's people or one's word of honor."[43] Meinecke believed, however, that the course of nineteenth-century historical developments worked toward the mitigation of the external dimension of this problem. Statesmen should increasingly find it possible to reconcile service of their state's external interests with adherence to the moral law. The First World War smashed to the ground these optimistic elements in Meinecke's philosophy and led him to see the power drive as ubiquitous. For Meinecke, the dilemma of reason of state thrust itself forward with intensified exigency.

The contrast between the actions of the old autocracy of Germany and the new totalitarianism in Russia may serve as an illustration of the regression. Bethmann Hollweg's dismissal in 1914 of the guarantee of Belgium's neutrality as a "scrap of paper" was a brutal assertion of Germany's power, "justified" on the grounds of strategic necessity. For all its cynicism, however, it was still within the traditional universe of *raison d'état*. The words and deeds of the Communist rulers of Russia, however, bespoke a far more savage challenge. Lenin and his followers acknowledged no obligation to respect either the external or the *internal* security of any state, nor any normative principle which stood in the path of their furtherance of the "reason of revolution." The calculated violation of moral and legal norms was itself proclaimed by the Communist leaders to be a matter of principle. Statesmen now found it necessary to weigh their obligations to moral norms against the intensification of internal and external pressures on the survival of their states. War and revolution had hurled politics back toward the pitiless world of Machiavelli.

Had Meinecke's prewar projections proved correct, Wilson's efforts to transform the states system would have moved in accord with deeply-lying historical tendencies. As it was, he was confronted with nothing less than a massive breakdown of that system, which destroyed Meinecke's rather modest hopes, to say nothing of Wilson's own more optimistic ones. Elements of regression crowd in from many sides—in the breakdown of international law or of the classical balance of power; in the expansion of force and the emergence of the new tyrannies; in the destruction of economic rationality and the weakening of historic liberalism; and in the ruthlessness of the Third International, the ineffectuality of the Second, and the futility of the "Second and a Half."

International politics has always taken place within a state of nature—that is, in a setting with neither an agreed consensus on values nor a sovereign with a legitimate monopoly of force. In consequence, states have always found it necessary to place primary reliance on their own resources for the preservation of their autonomy. Over time, there have been important variations in the degree of moderation that has characterized international politics. At times, it has assumed the rather benign aspect of Locke's state of nature (as it did for much of the nineteenth century); at other times it has been shot through with the malign dimensions of Hobbes's state of war (as has been the case for much of the twentieth century). Wilson, a statesman of extraordinary political gifts, drew together the most creative strands of the insular tradition, reinforced by the realistic experiences of the nineteenth-century Lockean world, in his strategy of peace. It was a forbidding tragedy that he was called upon to try to implement this strategy in a world where the insights of insularity were being overwhelmed by the ruthlessness of *Realpolitik* and the harmonies of Locke by the violence of Hobbes.

Could it have been otherwise? Surely not through this or that change in the domestic political alignment of this or that state. To be sure, a growth in the authority in any major state of those who supported a Wilsonian world would not have been without importance. In politics, even marginal changes must be taken into account. But it is hard to see how such changes could have made enough difference to have made it possible to implement, in any comprehensive way, Wilson's strategy—unless one assumes that these changes took place, in some interconnected and cumulative fashion, in *all* of the principal powers. To make this assumption, however, is to neglect, not only the time required for change, but also the *timing* of the changes.[44] If one or two powers embraced the diplomacy of self-restraint while all the others adhered to the diplomacy of self-assertion, the very moderation of the former might well have heightened the aggressiveness of the latter. And to suppose that this transformation to moderation would come about universally and simultaneously is to assume that one is living in a world wholly different from that in which the European statesmen actually found themselves. It is to leave the world of fact for that of fancy.

The dilemma, systemic in nature, could only be mitigated by a systemic response. Another avenue offered more promise. Had Wilson been able to bring his own government and people to support, through the League of Nations, or treaties of guarantee, concrete security commitments, implemented with military dispositions in being, that fact would have begun to allay the anxieties of the Allies, most notably of the French, and significant creative possibilities would then have been opened up. As an instance, the French might then have been able to approach the question of reparations on the basis of economic rationality rather than of strategic anxiety. Short of such guarantees, it was inevitable that the French would politicize the reparations question, with all the tragic consequences that this would entail. The most important move that Wilson took in this direction was his signature, on the very day that he signed the Treaty of Versailles, of the Treaty on Assistance to France in the Event of Unprovoked Aggression by Germany. Senator Lodge's commentary on the subsequent fate of that treaty highlights, from another vantage point, the tragic incongruities of the situation in which Wilson found himself: "The Treaty was duly referred to the Committee on Foreign Relations. It was never taken up and never reported out. It would have been quite useless to do so, even if the Committee had favored it, for I do not think there was the slightest chance that the Senate would ever have voted to accept it. There was no desire on the part of the Senators of either Party at that stage to bind the United States irrevocably with agreements to go to war again under certain prescribed conditions."[45]

Walter Lippmann, in a famous indictment of Wilson's foreign policies in the First World War, characterized them as "legalistic and moralistic and idealistic."[46] Wilson's policies were indeed idealistic; this was a term he himself proudly used in their description. To call them moralistic is, however, already to lower an unfounded pejorative judgment upon them. Wilson sought, as have the greatest statesmen over the centuries, to further the prospects for a durable international order by strengthening the elements of justice in that order. His statesmanship was in the venerable tradition of Grotius, who closes his great work on *The Law of War and Peace* with an appeal to moral and religious principles: "For not only is every state sustained by good faith, as Cicero declares, but also the greater society of states. . . . Rightly the same Cicero says that 'It is an impious act to destroy the good faith which holds life together.' . . . And this good faith the supreme rulers of men ought so much the more earnestly than others to maintain as they violate it with greater impunity; if good faith shall be done away with, they will be like wild beasts, whose violence all men fear."[47] With these words of melancholy eloquence, Grotius attempted to counsel his contemporaries against the ruthless practice of power politics which characterized his own era. Wilson, with words of comparable eloquence, sought to give the same counsel to the men of his time. Lippmann's third characterization of Wilson, as "legalistic," is simply inaccurate. Wilson neither thought nor acted in "legalistic" categories. His enormous admiration for Burke ("the only entirely wise writer upon public affairs in the English language") rested squarely on Burke's ability to see beyond the narrow legal aspects of a question to its larger political implications.[48] For Wilson, this was always the precondition for effective statesmanship. To capture the spirit of Wilson's policies, it is necessary to reject Lippmann's careless trinity and refer to them, more simply, as idealistic and moral.

The clearest general insight that Wilson ever gave into the goals of his idealistic and moral policies was probably in this passage from a speech in 1912: "When I think over what we are engaged in doing in the field of politics, I conceive it this way. Men who are behind any interest always unite in organization, and the danger in every country is that these special interests will be the only things organized, and that the common interest will be unorganized against them. The business of government is to organize the common interest against the special interests."[49]

Wilson's was a normative theory that projected an estate taken to be good and attempted to organize understanding of the world and action in the world in order to achieve that good. In countless contexts, he defined his goal as the organization of the common interest: as President of Princeton on the eating clubs or the location of the graduate college; as Governor of New Jersey, in the regulation of utilities or the control of lobbies; as presidential candidate promising a "New Freedom" to America; as President of the United States confronted with problems of tariff or banking reform; as protector of American neutrality through upholding the moral law and undertaking efforts at a mediated settlement; as the greatest of the great men at the Paris Peace Conference trying to lay the foundations for a new world order.

Perceptive Burkean that he was, Wilson never believed that "world order" would emerge, perfected in design, from the mind of any man or the meeting of any statesmen. He well knew that it had to grow, step by step, process by process, over the long reaches of history. His own strategy of world order was fashioned, with penetrating realism, from powerful tendencies at work in the history of his own nation and his own time. Across his projected course, the turbulent events of war and revolution confronted *all* statesmen with dilemmas that outran the premises of insular statecraft and the moderation of the Lockean international system. They gave ominous accentuation to what Wilson knew was the heart of the problem: that in world politics the special interests are organized, but the common interest remains unorganized. Wilson's strategy of peace was an effort to organize the global common interest. It was the embodiment of a very great idea. As others have noted, it is the role of great ideas to make us feel small in the right way.

NOTES

1. George F. Kennan, *American Diplomacy, 1900–1950* (New York, 1951), p. 63, *et passim*. Emphasis added throughout. I will discuss Kennan's position, and that of a number of other leading critics of Wilson's foreign policy, in more detail in my forthcoming *Wilson, His Critics, and World Politics*.

2. Kennan, *American Diplomacy*, p. 88.

3. Professor Unterberger's contribution to the present volume gives lucid elaboration of the moderation of Wilson's Russian policies.

4. Inis L. Claude, Jr., has given the definitive analysis of Wilson's conception of collective security and the role of force in it in his *Power and International Relations* (New York, 1962), chaps. 4 and 5.

5. Richard Hofstadter, *The American Political Tradition* (New York, 1948), chap. 10.

6. Woodrow Wilson, *Constitutional Government in the United States* (New York, 1908), p. 28.

7. *Ibid.*, p. 38.

8. *Ibid.*, p. 40.

9. Ray Stannard Baker, *Woodrow Wilson: Life and Letters*, 8 vols. (Garden City, N. Y., 1927–39), VII, 180 (emphasis in the original).

10. *Ibid.*, p. 382.

11. *Ibid.*, p. 387. The January Address to which Wilson referred was his "Peace without Victory" Address.

12. *The Children of Light and the Children of Darkness* (New York, 1944), pp. 74, 75.

13. Arthur S. Link, *Woodrow Wilson: Revolution, War, and Peace* (Arlington Heights, Ill., 1979), chap. 1. For the material in this paragraph, I have relied heavily on Professor Link's first chapter which gives an excellent overview of the main sources and characteristics of Wilson's foreign policies.

14. Ray Stannard Baker and William E. Dodd, eds., *The Public Papers of Woodrow Wilson*, 6 vols. (New York, 1925–27), IV, 407–14. All subsequent citations of this address are drawn from this edition.

15. For a fuller discussion of these concepts and a general application of them to American diplomatic history, see Whittle Johnston, "Security and American Diplomacy," in *America's World Role in the '70s* (Englewood Cliffs, N. J., 1970) Abdul A. Said, ed.

16. J. J. Rousseau, *The Social Contract and Discourses* (New York, 1950), G. D. H. Cole, ed., p. 6.

17. Baker and Dodd, eds., *The Public Papers of Woodrow Wilson*, v, 132.

18. Ray Stannard Baker, *Woodrow Wilson and World Settlement*, 3 vols. (Garden City, N. Y., 1923), iii, 28 (emphasis in the original).

19. Baker and Dodd, eds., *The Public Papers of Woodrow Wilson*, v, 160.

20. *Ibid.*, p. 282.

21. Walter Lippmann, *The Political Scene: An Essay on the Victory of 1918* (New York, 1919), p. 15.

22. Herbert Hoover, *The Ordeal of Woodrow Wilson* (New York, 1958), p. 82. Hoover devotes chaps. 9, 10, and 11 to a consideration of Wilson's administrative problems at Paris.

23. Baker and Dodd, eds., *The Public Papers of Woodrow Wilson*, v, 546.

24. George F. Kennan, *The Decision to Intervene* (Princeton, N. J., 1968), p. 428.

25. Link, *Woodrow Wilson: Revolution, War, and Peace*, p. 15, *et passim*.

26. Walter Lippmann, *Public Opinion* (New York, 1965), p. 136.

27. Baker and Dodd, eds., *The Public Papers of Woodrow Wilson*, v, 95. Wilson states: "The object of this war is to deliver the free peoples of the world from the menace and the actual power of a vast military establishment . . . the enemy of four-fifths of the world."

28. Arno J. Mayer, *Political Origins of the New Diplomacy, 1917–1918* (New York, 1970).

29. Charles Seymour, ed., *The Intimate Papers of Colonel House*, 4 vols. (Boston, 1926–28), iv, 377.

30. Harold Nicolson, *Peacemaking 1919* (New York, 1965), p. 84.

31. *Ibid.*, pp. 87, 88.

32. Jean-Baptiste Duroselle has given us invaluable insights into French opinion in his essay in *Wilson's Diplomacy: An International Symposium* (Cambridge, Mass., 1973), Joseph Huthmacher and Warren Susman, eds.

33. Klaus Schwabe, *Deutsche Revolution und Wilson-Frieden* (Düsseldorf, 1971).

34. Arno J. Mayer, *Politics and Diplomacy of Peacemaking* (New York, 1969), p. 704.

35. Georges Clemenceau, *Grandeur and Misery of Victory* (New York, 1930), F. M. Atkinson, trans., pp. 181, 182.

36. *Ibid.*, pp. 182–84.

37. *Ibid.*, pp. 186–87.

38. *Ibid.*, pp. 187, 188, 189.

39. *Ibid.*, p. 179, *et passim*. Clemenceau gives his most extensive discussion of the League in chap. 10.

40. *Ibid.*, p. 175.

41. Arnold Wolfers and Laurence W. Martin, eds., *The Anglo-American Tradition in Foreign Affairs* (New Haven, Conn., 1956), pp. xx, xxi.

42. *Ibid.*, p. xxiii. As the margin of security provided by insularity declines, the pressures toward "continentalization" of the Anglo-American perspec-

tives mount. The weakness of the Liberal party and the strength of traditionalism speak to these effects in Britain after the First World War. America's margin of insularity, far wider than Britain's, proved in consequence more durable. But in the age of intercontinental nuclear missiles, the question is not so much if Wilson has ever gone to Paris as it is whether Clemenceau has not moved to Washington. I will examine this and related issues more fully in a forthcoming volume, *Wilson, the War, and the Balance of Power*.

43. Friedrich Meinecke, *Machiavellism, The Doctrine of Raison d'Etat and Its Place in Modern History* (New York, 1965), Douglas Scott, trans., p. 301. Richard Sterling has given a very useful overview of Meinecke's political thought in his *Ethics in a World of Power: The Political Ideas of Friedrich Meinecke* (Princeton, N. J., 1958).

44. For the applicability of these concepts to highlight the limitations of both socialist and liberal theories of international relations, see Kenneth Waltz, *Man, the State, and War* (New York, 1959), chaps. 4 and 5.

45. Henry Cabot Lodge, *The Senate and the League of Nations* (New York, 1925).

46. Walter Lippmann, *U.S. Foreign Policy: Shield of the Republic* (Boston, 1943), p. 37.

47. A convenient selection of key writings by Grotius may be found in *The Theory of International Relations* (New York, 1970), M. G. Forsyth, H. M. A. Keens-Soper, and P. Savigear, eds. The passage cited may be found on pp. 82–83.

48. The reference to Burke was made in an address on "The Meaning of a Liberal Education," given on January 9, 1909. Arthur S. Link, David W. Hirst, John E. Little *et al.*, eds., *The Papers of Woodrow Wilson*, 37 vols. to date (Princeton, N. J., 1966–   ), vol. 18, p. 594. See also WW to Ellen Louise Axson, Feb. 24, 1885, *ibid.*, vol. 4, p. 287: "Burke was a *very* much greater man than Cobden or Bright."

49. *Ibid.*, vol. 24, p. 204.

INDEX

Publication of Supplementary Volumes to *The Papers of Woodrow Wilson* is assisted from time to time by the Woodrow Wilson Foundation in order to encourage scholarly work about Woodrow Wilson and his time. All volumes have passed the review procedures of the publishers and the Editor and the Editorial Advisory Committee of *The Papers of Woodrow Wilson.* Inquiries about the Series should be addressed to The Editor, Papers of Woodrow Wilson, Firestone Library, Princeton University, Princeton, N.J. 08540.

Inga Floto, *Colonel House in Paris: A Study of American Policy at the Paris Peace Conference 1919* (Princeton University Press 1981)

Raymond B. Fosdick, *Letters on the League of Nations. From the Files of Raymond B. Fosdick* (Princeton University Press 1966)

Wilton B. Fowler, *British-American Relations, 1917–1918: The Role of Sir William Wiseman* (Princeton University Press 1969)

John M. Mulder, *Woodrow Wilson: The Years of Preparation* (Princeton University Press 1978)

George Egerton, *Great Britain and the Creation of the League of Nations* (University of North Carolina Press 1978)

Stephen L. Vaughn, *Holding Fast the Inner Lines: Democracy, Nationalism, and the Committee on Public Information* (University of North Carolina Press 1980)

Robert C. Hilderbrand, *Power and the People: Executive Management of Public Opinion in Foreign Affairs, 1897–1921* (University of North Carolina Press 1980)

Edwin A. Weinstein, *Woodrow Wilson: A Medical and Psychological Biography* (Princeton University Press 1981)